Escaping victimhood

DCAF

a centre for security,
development and
the rule of law

The Geneva Centre for the Democratic Control of Armed Forces (DCAF) is an international foundation whose mission is to assist the international community in pursuing good governance and reform of the security sector. DCAF develops and promotes norms and standards, conducts tailored policy research, identifies good practices and recommendations to promote democratic security sector governance, and provides in-country advisory support and practical assistance programmes.

DCAF PO Box 1360 CH-1211 Geneva 1 Switzerland
www.dcaf.ch

Escaping victimhood: Children, youth and post-conflict peacebuilding

Edited by Albrecht Schnabel and Anara Tabyshalieva

United Nations University Press

TOKYO • NEW YORK • PARIS

United Nations University Press
United Nations University, 53–70, Jingumae 5-chome,
Shibuya-ku, Tokyo 150-8925, Japan
Tel: +81-3-5467-1212 Fax: +81-3-3406-7345
E-mail: sales@unu.edu General enquiries: press@unu.edu
http://www.unu.edu

United Nations University Office at the United Nations, New York
2 United Nations Plaza, Room DC2-2062, New York, NY 10017, USA
Tel: +1-212-963-6387 Fax: +1-212-371-9454
E-mail: unuony@unu.edu

United Nations University Press is the publishing division of the United Nations University.

Cover design by Andrew Corbett
Cover photograph by Jeroen Oerlemans/Panos Pictures

ISBN 978-92-808-1211-4
e-ISBN 978-92-808-7180-7

Library of Congress Cataloging-in-Publication Data

Escaping victimhood : children, youth and post-conflict peacebuilding / edited by Albrecht Schnabel and Anara Tabyshalieva.
pages cm
Includes bibliographical references and index.
ISBN 978-9280812114 (pbk.) — ISBN 978-9280871807 (e-ISBN)
1. Children and peace. 2. Youth and peace. 3. Peace-building—Social aspects.
I. Schnabel, Albrecht, author, editor of compilation. II. Tabyshalieva, Anara, author, editor of compilation.
JZ5579.E74 2013
362.88083—dc23 2013037109

Endorsement

"This volume, focusing on children and youth in post-conflict situations, takes a very wide-angled view, including chapters on Europe, Asia, the Middle East and Africa. Taking a case study approach, the volume attempts to situate local conflicts and their effects on children and youth within an international peacebuilding and security context. The volume attempts to assert a sense of agency on the part of children and youth rather than perpetuating the idea of this group as a vulnerable population and victims of conflict."

Louise Vincent, Professor, Department of Political and International Studies, Rhodes University

Contents

List of figures and tables

List of contributors

Deborah Davis has a degree in political theory from the University of California, Berkeley. She has worked as a policy analyst and social development specialist at the World Bank for the past 20 years, with a recent focus on anti-corruption and governance, economic development and adaptation to climate change. Ms Davis has carried out field evaluations of community justice, democratization and gender empowerment projects in Indonesia, Rwanda and Afghanistan. She also edited the World Bank's policy research reports on financial integration, community-driven development and engendering development, and was a principle contributor to *Local and Community Driven Development: Moving to Scale in Theory and Practice* (World Bank e-book, 2010), which identifies the elements of successful local-level political change. Ms Davis's chapter on young mothers as peacebuilders in Macedonia appeared in this book's companion volume, *Defying Victimhood: Women and Post-Conflict Peacebuilding* (UNU Press, 2012). Before working in international development, Deborah Davis was an investigative reporter and author of a National Book Award-nominated biography of *Washington Post* publisher Katharine Graham, which analysed the power of the media in the United States during the Nixon era.

Azar Eskandarpour is a protection delegate at the International Committee of the Red Cross. She has a degree in political science from the University of British Colombia and a masters in international affairs from the Graduate Institute of International and Development Studies in Geneva. She has worked in research and analysis in the development and humanitarian fields with the

Canadian government and various UN agencies. Along with her contributions to various publications, she also co-published the issue brief "Strengthening Preventive Diplomacy: The Role of Private Actors" (Graduate Institute of International and Development Studies, 2011) while in a position at the Centre on Conflict, Development and Peacebuilding, Geneva. She specializes in conflict and security, international relations, human security, humanitarian action and resilience of civilian non-combatants in armed conflict. Her fieldwork includes missions to Sri Lanka, Bangladesh, Nepal and Afghanistan. She is currently based in Jammu and Kashmir, India.

Clare Feinstein is a senior-level professional in the field of children's rights with over 20 years of international experience. She specializes in child protection and care, and children's participation. She is currently the Africa representative for Save the Children's Child Protection Initiative and has previously worked for War Child Holland, the International Working Group on Child Labour, Amnesty International and as an international child rights consultant. Clare has a BA Hons from the University of Bradford, and an MA from the University of London. She has co-authored many publications on child protection, children's participation and peacebuilding.

Annette Giertsen has a degree in pedagogy from the University of Oslo. She worked as country representative for Save the Children Norway in Guatemala and Nicaragua for seven years, and since then as senior adviser on children's participation at Save the Children Norway's head office. During the past six years she has worked especially on children's and young people's participation in armed conflict, post-war situations and peacebuilding. This work has been scaled up to include more than 20,000 children and young people in close to 600 clubs and groups in more than 20 countries. Giertsen contributed to the International Peace Research Association conference publication for 2008, *Building Sustainable Futures – Enacting Peace and Development*, addressing rejuvenating conflict prevention by confronting the challenges of youth and conflict. For the past seven years she has also been working as a mediator in the Norwegian Mediation Service.

Valeria Izzi is an independent consultant and researcher. From 2003 to 2008 she served as a programme specialist with the UN Development Programme (Bureau for Crisis Prevention and Recovery) in New York. Her main area of interest is the political economy of international development aid, with particular focus on post-conflict African countries. Her latest research focuses on youth employment programmes and their potential contribution to peacebuilding processes. She holds an MSc from the School of Oriental and African Studies, University of London, and a doctorate from the Scuola Superiore di Studi Universitari e di Perfezionamento Sant'Anna, Pisa.

Kathleen Kostelny is a researcher, evaluator and programme adviser in the fields of early childhood development, child protection and children's psychosocial well-being. She has 25 years of experience working with international NGOs, UN agencies, and academic and government institutions. She has served as principal investigator for a number of research projects, including an outcome study of the effectiveness of child-centred spaces on young children's well-being in internally displaced persons camps in northern Uganda; the impact of chronic community violence on children's well-being in Chicago; an assessment of the impact of the Israeli military attacks and blockade on the education system in Gaza; and an ethnographic study of community-based child protection mechanisms in Kenya. She has helped develop community-based child protection programmes and conduct evaluations in emergency and post-conflict contexts, including in Afghanistan, Timor-Leste, Sierra Leone, Uganda, Kenya, India, Aceh and Sri Lanka, as well as in the United States during Hurricane Katrina.

Chetan Kumar works for the Bureau for Crisis Prevention and Recovery of the UN Development Programme, where he is head of the Conflict Prevention Group. He specializes in initiatives to build and apply national and local capacities for early warning and response, and the peaceful and inclusive management of transitions and conflict. He has directly assisted with initiatives in this regard in countries in Africa, the Asia-Pacific region, the Middle East and the Caribbean. He previously worked for the Office of the Special Representative of the UN Secretary-General for Children and Armed Conflict, and the International Peace Institute in New York. He is the author of *Building Peace in Haiti* (Lynne Rienner, 1998), and co-editor of *Peace-Building as Politics: Cultivating Peace in Fragile Societies* (Lynne Rienner, 2000) and *South Asia Approaches the Millennium: Re-examining National Security* (Westview, 1995). He holds a PhD in political science from the University of Illinois at Urbana-Champaign.

Henri Myrttinen is a senior researcher on gender in peacebuilding at International Alert in London. He has previously worked for numerous NGOs and research institutions, focusing mostly on Indonesia and Timor-Leste, but also working in sub-Saharan Africa and Central and Eastern Europe. He has taught at the Humboldt University and Free University in Berlin and the Willy Brandt School of Public Policy in Erfurt on issues of gender, peace and security and Southeast Asian regional studies. He has published extensively on issues of gender and conflict, and political developments in Indonesia and Timor-Leste. He holds a PhD in conflict resolution and peace studies from the University of KwaZulu-Natal, South Africa. His doctoral thesis focused on masculinities and violence in Timor-Leste gangs, militias and martial and ritual arts groups. His research interests include issues of masculinities, youth and sexual minorities in peacebuilding as well as intersectionalities between local understandings of gender and the supernatural.

David Nosworthy is a development and relief professional with experience in project management and coordination functions at both field and HQ levels. His area of special interest has been sustainable development, including promoting youth participation and rights-based programming. With extensive experience in facilitating learning and capacity building, he was editor of the first edition of training modules developed under the Action for the Rights of Children project, a UNHCR and Save the Children initiative. He is also author of a discussion paper, "Children's Security in Post-Conflict Peacebuilding", prepared as a contribution to the 10-Year Strategic Review of the Machel Study in 2007. As a fellow with the Geneva Centre for the Democratic Control of Armed Forces, he was editor of *Seen, But Not Heard: Placing Children and Youth on the Security Governance Agenda* (LIT, 2009). He has subsequently maintained his interest in youth and governance-related issues, and has contributed to this book in an independent capacity based on previous experience.

Claire O'Kane is a qualified social worker with a masters in applied social studies from Swansea University in Wales. She has more than 18 years of international experience in child rights, children's participation, citizenship, protection, care and peacebuilding work in development and emergency contexts including in Afghanistan, Bangladesh, Myanmar, Cambodia, India, Kyrgyzstan, Nepal, Pakistan, Sri Lanka, Tajikistan, the UK, Uganda, Viet Nam and West Central Africa. Claire worked with Save the Children for many years. From 2006 to 2008 she was one of the researchers for Save the Children Norway's global thematic evaluation on children's participation in armed conflict, post-conflict and peacebuilding that was undertaken in Bosnia and Herzegovina, Guatemala, Nepal and Uganda. She supported country teams and children's active participation in the process in Uganda and Nepal. Since early 2011 Claire has been working as an international child rights consultant. She continues efforts to support programming and advocacy concerning children's and young people's roles in peacebuilding and governance processes.

Vesselin Popovski is a senior academic programme officer and head of the Peace and Security section at the UNU Institute for Sustainability and Peace in Tokyo, Japan. In addition to undertaking research and postgraduate teaching in the fields of international relations, peace and security, international law, human rights, international criminal justice and governance, he has published numerous books and journal articles, including as co-editor of *Legality and Legitimacy in Global Affairs* (Oxford University Press, 2012) and *Norms of Protection: Responsibility to Protect and Protection of Civilians and Their Interaction* (UNU Press, 2012). He also initiated (with Andy Knight and Mojtaba Mahdavi) the project *Towards the Dignity of Difference* (Ashgate, 2012). He was previously a Bulgarian diplomat and then a NATO research fellow and lecturer at Exeter University, and has also taught at King's College London, Westminster University, Huron University and Russian State Humanitarian University.

Albrecht Schnabel is a senior fellow in the Research Division of the Geneva Centre for the Democratic Control of Armed Forces. He studied political science and international relations in Germany, the United States and Canada (where he received his PhD in 1995 from Queen's University). He has held teaching and research appointments at Queen's University, the American University in Bulgaria, Central European University, the United Nations University, Aoyama Gakuin University, swisspeace and the University of Bern. He currently serves as recurrent visiting lecturer for the annual security sector development course at the Asia-Pacific Center for Security Studies in Honolulu and the master of advanced studies in security policy and crisis management programme at the Swiss Federal Institute of Technology in Zurich. His publications have focused on ethnic conflict, refugees, human security, armed non-state actors, security sector reform, conflict prevention and management, peacekeeping and post-conflict peacebuilding. He co-edited, with Anara Tabyshalieva, this book's companion volume, *Defying Victimhood: Women and Post-Conflict Peacebuilding* (UNU Press, 2012). His experiences beyond academia include military service in the German armed forces, participation in OSCE election monitoring missions, training and teaching for the UN System Staff College and a term as president of the International Association of Peacekeeping Training Centres. In addition to a number of advisory and training activities on security sector governance and reform in the Southeast Asian and Asia-Pacific regions, he currently works on the role and impact of security sector reform in the contexts of development and peace processes, and on the urban dimension of security sector governance.

Anara Tabyshalieva is an assistant professor of history at Marshall University and a research fellow and former director of the Institute for Regional Studies in Bishkek, Kyrgyzstan. She has taught history, sociology and political science at several universities in Kyrgyzstan and the United States. Her publications have focused on politics, history, human security, development and gender issues. Among other works, she co-edited (with Madhavan K. Palat) *Towards the Contemporary Period: From the Mid-Nineteenth to the End of the Twentieth Century*, Vol. VI of the UNESCO History of Civilizations of Central Asia project (UNESCO, 2005) and wrote the report "Promoting Human Security: Ethical, Normative and Educational Frameworks in Central Asia" (UNESCO, 2006). She co-edited, with Albrecht Schnabel, this book's companion volume, *Defying Victimhood: Women and Post-Conflict Peacebuilding* (UNU Press, 2012). She has held visiting positions at the US Institute of Peace, Johns Hopkins University, the Centre for the Study of Islam and

Christian-Muslim Relations at the University of Birmingham and the United Nations University. Her areas of expertise include modern history, international relations, human security, social development, and women and children in post-conflict societies. She holds a master of international public policy from SAIS/Johns Hopkins University and MA and PhD degrees in history from the Kyrgyz National University.

Michael Wessells, PhD, is a professor at Columbia University in the Program on Forced Migration and Health. A long-time psychosocial and child protection practitioner, he is former co-chair of the IASC Task Force on Mental Health and Psychosocial Support in Emergency Settings. Recently he was co-focal point on mental health and psychosocial support for the revision of the Sphere humanitarian standards. He has conducted extensive research on the holistic impacts of war and political violence on children, and is author of *Child Soldiers: From Violence to Protection* (Harvard University Press, 2006). Currently he is lead researcher on inter-agency, multicountry research on community-driven interventions for strengthening linkages with government-led aspects of national child protection systems. He regularly advises UN agencies, governments and donors on issues of child protection and psychosocial support, including in communities and schools. Throughout Africa and Asia he helps to develop community-based, culturally grounded programmes that assist people affected by armed conflict and natural disasters.

Acknowledgements

This book has grown out of a research project on "The Roles of Women and Children in Post-Conflict Peacebuilding", initially conceived by the two editors of this volume in 2000 as a research activity of the Peace and Governance Programme of the United Nations University (UNU). At that time Albrecht Schnabel was a member of the programme, while Anara Tabyshalieva joined it for several months as a visiting research fellow from the Institute for Regional Studies in Kyrgyzstan. After securing project funds from the UNU and the Asian Women's Fund, the editors assembled a group of contributors and initial author workshops were held in Tokyo and New York to discuss the results of background research and first chapter drafts. Over time the project developed into two books, with a changing and growing number of contributors: *Escaping Victimhood: Children, Youth and Post-Conflict Peacebuilding*, and *Defying Victimhood: Women and Post-Conflict Peacebuilding*, which was published by UNUP in 2012 as the first of the two volumes that emanated from this project.

We could not have completed this book without the generous and dedicated support of a number of institutions and individuals, including adults, youth and children. We gratefully acknowledge financial support from the UNU, the Asian Women's Fund and the Geneva Centre for the Democratic Control of Armed Forces (DCAF). Albrecht furthermore thanks swisspeace and DCAF for providing institutional support for his work on this project. He wishes to acknowledge the Swiss National Centre of Competence in Research North-South: Research Partnerships for Mitigating

Syndromes of Global Change, co-funded by the Swiss National Science Foundation, and the Swiss Agency for Development and Cooperation and its Transversal Package Project Operationalising Human Security for Livelihood Protection (which he directed) for support in the preparation of this book. We thank Gustav Meibauer for research assistance, and Danail Hristov, Marc Krupanski and Raphaël Zaffran for editorial assistance and providing feedback on various drafts of the manuscript. We thank Yoshie Sawada at UNU's Institute for Sustainability and Peace for superbly and patiently managing the administrative part of the project. We are grateful to DCAF and LIT Publishers for allowing us to republish significantly revised and updated versions of two chapters (Chapters 2 and 6) which were originally written for David Nosworthy (ed.) *Seen, But Not Heard: Placing Children and Youth on the Security Governance Agenda* (LIT, 2009).

We thank UNU Press, particularly its editor Kae Sugawara and her predecessors Naomi Cowan and Robert Davis, for their continuous encouragement, support and patience during the preparation of this book. We thank Cherry Ekins for her excellent work in copyediting and proofreading the final manuscript, Clive Pyne for assembling a most useful index, Yoko Kojima and Adam Majoe for guiding and assisting us through the production process, and Marc Benger for skilfully organizing its dissemination. We greatly benefited from the very helpful and constructive comments of two anonymous peer reviewers in revising the initial draft manuscript. We owe a particular debt to many supporters and interview partners, including adults, youth and children, who work and live in post-conflict societies across the world and have generously shared their insights and knowledge with the contributors to this volume.

Finally, we are grateful to all contributors who have patiently and with great dedication remained committed to our joint research project. It is our hope that readers will be encouraged to support the creation of conditions for constructive and positive contributions of children and youth to the rebuilding of their societies.

Albrecht Schnabel
Anara Tabyshalieva
Geneva and Huntington/Bishkek
June 2013

List of abbreviations

ANSA	armed non-state actor
AP	additional protocol
CPA	child protection adviser
CPU	child protection unit
CRC	UN Convention on the Rights of the Child
CRIN	Child Rights Information Network
CSO	civil society organization
CZOP	children as zones of peace
DDR	disarmament, demobilization and reintegration
DRC	Democratic Republic of the Congo
ECOSOC	UN Economic and Social Commission
ECOWAS	Economic Community of West African States
Falintil	Armed Forces of the National Liberation of Timor-Leste
Fretilin	Revolutionary Front for an Independent Timor-Leste
GBV	gender-based violence
GUSCO	Gulu Support the Children Organisation (Uganda)
HRL	human rights law
ICC	International Criminal Court
ICL	international criminal law
ICTR	International Criminal Tribunal for Rwanda
ICTY	International Criminal Tribunal for the former Yugoslavia
IDP	internally displaced person
IHL	international humanitarian law
ILO	International Labour Organization
KORK	Kmanek Oan Rai Klaran (Wise Children of the Land) (East Timor)
LRA	Lord's Resistance Army

MAG	martial arts group
NGO	non-governmental organization
NRA	National Resistance Army (Uganda)
PBF	UN Peacebuilding Fund
PSHT	Persaudaraan Setia Hati Terate (East Timor)
RAG	ritual arts group
RUF	Revolutionary United Front (Sierra Leone)
SCIU	Save the Children in Uganda
SCSL	Special Court of Sierra Leone
TRC	Truth and Reconciliation Commission (Sierra Leone)
UN	United Nations
UNDP	UN Development Programme
UNESCO	UN Educational, Scientific and Cultural Organization
UNFPA	UN Fund for Population Activities
UNHCR	Office of the UN High Commissioner for Refugees
UNICEF	UN Children's Fund
UNPOL	UN Police
UNSCR	UN Security Council Resolution
UNTAET	UN Transitional Administration in East Timor
UPDF	Uganda People's Defence Force
WHO	World Health Organization

Part I

Introduction – Conceptualizing the roles of children and youth in post-conflict peacebuilding

1

Opportunities missed: Sidelining children and youth in post-conflict recovery and reform efforts

Albrecht Schnabel and Anara Tabyshalieva

Why do we need yet another text on the roles of children and youth in post-conflict peacebuilding? Over the past two decades the study of children and young people in post-conflict recovery has been marked by the publication of various books, reports and articles. Despite these noteworthy gains, important issues deserve further consideration. Many of these reports and projects tend to underestimate the dynamic roles of children and youth as peacebuilders in efforts to address security challenges. In addition, they do not differentiate between the diverse interests and needs that exist within various groups of children and young people. This volume discusses a range of responses from children and youth to challenges of post-conflict peacebuilding. The contributors consider the post-conflict moment as a window of opportunity for change that is not always capitalized on to assure the active participation and contribution of children and youth in rebuilding their societies. Moreover, the volume discusses the resilience and capacity of children and youth to address conflict management and post-war peacebuilding challenges; and the gaps that exist between knowledge and understanding, as well as the practice of empowering children and youth to allow them to escape the victimhood which they experience at least partly as a result of being excluded from a more active role in determining their own future in post-war society.

The book is based on the assumption that, in the aftermath of violent conflict, no society can afford to rebuild its future without the active participation of its young generation and consideration of their interests and

Escaping victimhood: Children, youth and post-conflict peacebuilding, Schnabel and Tabyshalieva (eds), United Nations University Press, 2013, ISBN 978-92-808-1211-4

needs. Yet, often trapped in a state of protracted victimhood, children and youth – and their needs and abilities – are at risk of being overlooked in the planning and implementation of post-conflict peacebuilding. More often than not, peacebuilding activities are designed and implemented without consideration for – let alone the participation and resulting empowerment of – children and youth. Children and young people constitute more than half the total population in most post-conflict countries, but they are frequently viewed as mere bystanders to peacebuilding efforts, disempowered and prevented from changing their fortunes in the midst of societies scarred by death, poverty and destruction. Their voices will continue to go unheard unless they can escape the chains of victimhood and their active agency in post-war recovery efforts is recognized, utilized and supported.

The findings of the book's companion volume (*Defying Victimhood: Women and Post-Conflict Peacebuilding*) highlight participatory roles of women and gender-specific aspects of peacebuilding.[1] The studies in this volume reveal that despite many parallels in the recovery process, the post-conflict risks for and roles of children are even more under-researched than those of women. It is becoming commonplace in international peacebuilding discourse to refer to women as active agents of change, but children and youth as a muted group are often relegated to a condition of victimhood.

The book is written with a broad multidisciplinary audience in mind. Readers who share concerns over the sidelining of children and youth in post-conflict peacebuilding will discover numerous contexts in which young people create the opportunities for self-help and strengthen their ownership of the peacebuilding process. We hope that scholars, practitioners, activists and students will find this book useful as they attempt to understand the roles of children and youth in post-conflict reconstruction.

Peacebuilding in the aftermath of armed violence

Peacebuilding efforts begin in the wake of violent conflict, even without prior political settlements and "in the absence of a peacekeeping operation or a formal peacemaking effort".[2] The UN's involvement in peacebuilding begins "once conflict – i.e. major, large-scale violence – has ended ... [although] ... some peacebuilding tasks can start even during conflict".[3] At that time, adversaries, state and non-state actors, civil society groups and representatives of the international donor community begin discussions about a future peacebuilding agenda. At such an early stage, all involved actors anticipate change and explore the needs, opportunities and requirements of the changes that will likely characterize their future society, although "this is where the international community has been weakest".[4]

In many cases, peacebuilding initiatives imply a myriad of activities, such as political and economic reconstruction; socio-economic recovery; disarmament, demobilization and reintegration (DDR) activities; repatriation of refugees and return of internally displaced persons (IDPs) to their homes; human rights monitoring and protection; creation of truth commissions; and community peace recovery and reconciliation. These activities respond to long-standing requirements for peace and stability. UN agencies and other international and regional organizations cooperate with national stakeholders to identify peacebuilding and state-building priorities and assist in developing and implementing activities to meet them.

Not only are children and youth often not involved in the planning and implementation of such activities, but they also do not figure prominently as recipients and beneficiaries of peacebuilding programmes. Local, national and international peacebuilding actors need to adopt child-sensitive approaches to integrate children and youth as proponents of post-conflict recovery. Although children and young people are quite visible as both victims and/or perpetrators in armed conflict, often a similarly active role is not granted to them when it comes to peacebuilding.

Real advances in promoting children's and youth's rights in post-conflict peacebuilding have been made over the last decades. But despite the advancement and empowerment of children and youth, many key problems remain. Children as victims and/or perpetrators of crimes face many challenges, such as a lack of physical security, exploitation and gender violence, as well as social and political marginalization. In most conflict-prone regions children and youth make up the majority of the population, but they are treated as a minority and denied their agency.

A window of opportunity for change?

The term "peacebuilding" was first coined by Norwegian peace researcher Johan Galtung in the 1970s.[5] Further developed by both academics and practitioners, it has evolved into a concept that covers "a multidimensional exercise and tasks ranging from the disarming of warring factions to the rebuilding of political, economic, judicial and civil society institutions".[6] In the 1990s UN Secretary-General Boutros Boutros-Ghali defined the term "as action to solidify peace and avoid relapse into conflict".[7] Later, in 2000, the Brahimi Report expanded "peacebuilding" as:

> activities undertaken on the far side of conflict to reassemble the foundations of peace and provide the tools for building on those foundations something that is more than just the absence of war. Thus, peace-building includes but is not limited to reintegrating former combatants into civilian society, strengthening the rule of law (for example, through training and restructuring of local police, and judicial and penal reform); improving respect for human rights through the monitoring, education and investigation of past and existing abuses; providing technical assistance for democratic development (including electoral assistance and support for free media); and promoting conflict resolution and reconciliation techniques.[8]

Progressively, the international community involved in peacebuilding discussions conceptualized the provision of security and development as mutually dependent processes inherent to post-conflict peacebuilding, along with the need to assure and consolidate national ownership of long-term, sustainable peacebuilding. Roger Mac Ginty, for instance, defines peacebuilding as "development-conscious peacemaking strategies attempt[ing] to bridge the gap between elite-level peace accords and the needs of all sectors of society".[9] According to this definition, peacebuilding is no longer limited only to those activities performed after the end of violent conflicts – without the adjective "post-conflict", peacebuilding encompasses a broad range of efforts to reform, but also to prevent, conditions that trigger and sustain violent conflict. Along those lines, the US Institute of Peace writes:

> Originally conceived in the context of post-conflict recovery efforts to promote reconciliation and reconstruction, the term peacebuilding has more recently taken on a broader meaning. It may include providing humanitarian relief, protecting human rights, ensuring security, establishing nonviolent modes of resolving conflicts, fostering reconciliation, providing trauma healing services, repatriating refugees and resettling internally displaced persons, supporting broad-based education, and aiding in economic reconstruction. As such, it also includes conflict prevention in the sense of preventing the recurrence of violence, as well as conflict management and post-conflict recovery. In a larger sense, peacebuilding involves a transformation toward more manageable, peaceful relationships and governance structures – the long-term process of addressing root causes and effects, reconciling differences, normalizing relations, and building institutions that can manage conflict without resorting to violence.[10]

Michelle Gawerc links peacebuilding with the provision of positive peace (another concept coined by Galtung), arguing that its objective "is to create a structure of peace that is based on justice, equity, and cooperation (i.e., positive peace), thereby addressing the underlying causes of violent conflict so that they become less likely in the future".[11] The UN's peacebuilding policy and practice reflect this broader understanding of peace, which has progressively expanded over the past decades. UN agencies strengthen peacebuilding and human security by means of standard-setting texts, technical assistance and capacity building.

Bar three countries (Somalia, South Sudan and the United States), all UN member states ratified the UN Convention on the Rights of the Child (CRC), adopted by the UN General Assembly in 1989. However, even though 193 countries have ratified the CRC, systematic violations of children's rights are common in practically all post-conflict societies. The CRC is the primary document that outlines the civil, political, economic, social, health and cultural rights of children. The greatest costs of post-conflict transition are the loss of educational opportunities, rampant child labour and the alienation of many children from the existing social fabric and society. Children encounter multiple challenges in post-conflict life; however, in practice discussions tend to focus mostly on DDR approaches to child soldiers. Gender issues in the aftermath of conflict are often ignored as well. Thus Nadine Puechguirbal notes that "gender-related work" might be considered "'later,' after 'real' issues, as defined by male managers, have been taken care of".[12]

The Graça Machel report (1996)[13] drew worldwide attention to the challenges of children's empowerment in armed conflict. One of the effects of this landmark report was the establishment of the Office of the Special Representative of the Secretary-General for Children and Armed Conflict[14] to promote and protect the rights of all children affected by armed conflict. In 2009 the 10-year strategic review of the report, "Children and Conflict in a Changing World", highlighted significant achievements but also enduring problems.[15]

As part of an emerging paradigm of human security, according to Wagnsson, Hellman and Holmberg, "a new kind of transnational morality has emerged in which the insecurity of foreign people has become everyone's concern, a universal moral obligation and not a question of defending a territory or national sovereignty. Children as a category fit right into this thinking."[16] However, as the 2012 Human Security Report notes:

> despite the increased attention, and despite the fact that wartime sexual violence against children has become a major issue for the Security Council, some 16 years after the publication of the Machel report, the UN still has no real understanding of the scope or severity of the problem worldwide. Moreover, there is little evidence that UN policies to prevent sexual violence against children in wartime, or to bring its perpetrators to justice, are having any real impact.[17]

The UN Security Council, clearly a global norm-setting body, adopted Resolution 1379 (2001) that addressed the protection of children during peacekeeping operations in armed conflicts as part of a peace agenda.[18] One of the most important requests of this comprehensive resolution was a call to "the Secretary-General to attach to his report a list of parties to armed conflict that recruit or use children in violation of the international obligations". The document prioritized "special measures to promote and protect the rights and meet the special needs of girls affected by armed conflict, and to put an end to all forms of violence and exploitation, including sexual violence, particularly rape".[19] In 2000 UN Security Council Resolution (UNSCR) 1325 highlighted the protection of girls from sexual and gender-based violence in conflict-prone societies. This groundbreaking resolution prioritized gender perspectives in peace processes, protection of women and girls from gender-based violence, including rape, and inclusion of women in DDR. Later, UNSCR 1820 (2008) recognized wartime sexual violence as a matter of international peace and security. Considering the protection of children in armed conflict, UNSCR 1612 (2005) established a monitoring and reporting mechanism on the use of child soldiers. Six specific child rights violations were distinguished: killing and maiming; abduction; attacks on schools and hospitals; sexual violence; child recruitment; and denial of humanitarian access. The document expressed deep concern "over the lack of overall progress on the ground, where parties to conflict continue to violate with impunity the relevant provisions of applicable international law relating to the rights and protection of children in armed conflict", and emphasized the key obligation of national governments "in providing effective protection and relief to all children affected by armed conflicts".[20] However, neither in this document nor in subsequent resolutions were important issues related to empowerment of children in post-conflict settings articulated in more specific terms.

The UN's concern for the protection and empowerment of children and youth has focused on their direct and indirect victimization in both conflict and post-conflict contexts. In 2011, in its eighth resolution related to children and armed conflict since 1998, the Security Council adopted Resolution 1998, which strongly condemned the recruitment and re-recruitment of children by parties to armed conflict and their denial of humanitarian access.[21] UNSCR 2068 (2012) recalled "the responsibilities of States to end impunity and to prosecute those responsible for genocide, crimes against humanity, war crimes and other egregious crimes perpetrated against children"[22] and indicated its readiness to adopt sanctions against parties that persistently violated the rights of children in armed conflict, again strongly condemning violations against children.[23]

Among the most prominent child and youth protection agencies are UNICEF (the UN Children's Fund), UNHCR (the Office of the UN High Commissioner for Refugees),[24] ILO (the International Labour

Organization) and UNESCO (the UN Educational, Scientific and Cultural Organization). Well-placed UNDP (UN Development Programme) agencies work with youth and women in post-conflict zones. Globally active human rights non-governmental organizations (NGOs) such as Save the Children, Human Rights Watch, Amnesty International, Child Rights Information Network (CRIN), Action for the Rights of Children and others are committed to the empowerment of children and youth and offer independent sources of information about violation of children's rights in conflict-prone zones. There are various successful scenarios of international and local NGOs' engagement in promoting human rights of children and youth. As Alison Watson notes, "one of the best ways to do this is through a broader inclusion of the NGOs that champion their rights during processes of postconflict resolution and reconciliation".[25]

On a practical level, UN agencies and international and local nonprofit organizations identify the key challenges that children and youth face in post-conflict societies and develop useful guides to address these issues. For instance, the ILO's "Children Formerly Associated with Armed Forces and Groups: 'How-to' Guide on Economic Reintegration" focuses on economic aims to assist organizations and individuals towards the reintegration of these young people and children in post-conflict settings.[26] International Alert, an independent peacebuilding organization, offers numerous reports related to children and youth in post-conflict settings.[27] Save the Children Norway offers "Ethical Guidelines: For Ethical, Meaningful and Inclusive Children's Participation Practice" and other relevant reports.[28] CRIN provides information on child rights, and functions as a research centre and platform for joint advocacy campaigns.[29] Child Soldiers International (formerly known as the Coalition to Stop the Use of Child Soldiers) focuses on the prevention of the military recruitment of children and their involvement in armed conflict through "a combination of targeted country work, thematic research and global monitoring".[30] As argued in Chapter 6 by David Nosworthy, local and international civil society organizations play an important role in promoting accountability and transparency on security provision, as they act as watchdogs and as an indicator of public satisfaction with security sector activity. However, in some cases particularly foreign-run or foreign-funded human rights organizations face resistance from illiberal governments when acting as champions for those without a strong formal voice, including children and youth.

Despite – and partly also because of – the multitude of actors involved (governments and intergovernmental organizations, international financial institutions and NGOs), peacebuilding interventions are criticized for cultural insensitivity, lack of coordination, duplication and over-bureaucratization. Moreover, the results, effects and impacts of the activities are difficult to assess. A US Institute of Peace report argues that "the field of international development is ahead of the peacebuilding field in regard to evaluation".[31] Even the most well-intentioned peacebuilding activities may not work as intended. As Valeria Izzi remarks:

> there is no evidence that these programmes work as intended – because evaluations are scarce, are short-term, and they normally are limited to listing the activities that were put in place and the number of young people who participated, with no regard to the long-term effect. There is also very little clarity about how they are "intended" to work, what would constitute success – in other words, about the nature of the theory of change underpinning such programmes.[32]

Peacebuilding activities supported or implemented by the donor community tend to follow liberal internationalist agendas. However, as Roger Mac Ginty notes:

> liberal internationalism is not applied uniformly in all locations. Despite its formulaic elements, especially in the implementation of post-peace accord peacebuilding programmes, liberal internationalism is contested, adapted and executed in different ways in different locations.[33]

The discussion of peacebuilding by the donor community, Western peacebuilding actors (such as the European Union) and the United Nations supposes "that the building of the state will be done along liberal democratic lines coupled with free-market economic policy",[34] as "the agencies involved in post-conflict peacebuilding programmes and reconstruction, as well as the donors who facilitate these programmes, often look for short-term solutions which are compatible with the dominant global neoliberal approach to economics and development".[35] This includes the promotion of values, norms and ideas cherished by those pushing liberal-internationalist agendas, and an inclusive approach to peacebuilding based on the participation of all parts of post-conflict society – including children and youth.

Common challenges in understanding the post-conflict realities of children and youth

Defining children and youth by age and gender

As stated in the CRC, a person under the age of 18 is considered a child. The World Health Organization (WHO) characterizes adolescence as the period "that occurs after childhood and before adulthood, from ages 10 to 19".[36] UNICEF differentiates between early adolescence (aged 10–14 years) and late adolescence (aged 15–19).[37] The UN definition of youth is a population aged 15–24. According to the UN Department of Economic and Social Affairs, although commonly children are considered to be those under the age of 14, "Article 1 of the United Nations Convention on the Rights of the Child defines 'children' as persons up to the age of 18. This was intentional, as it was hoped that the Convention would provide protection and rights to as large an age-group as possible and because there was no similar United Nations Convention on the Rights of Youth."[38] Within the category of "youth", it is also important to distinguish between teenagers (13–19) and young adults (20–24), as the sociological, psychological and health problems they face may differ.[39] Table 1.1, drawn from an inter-agency field manual produced by the UN Fund for Population Activities (UNFPA), UNHCR and WHO, offers a range of definitions of children, adolescents and youth.[40]

Definitions vary widely throughout regions, countries and communities. In Chapter 8, Valeria Izzi and Chetan Kumar note that such definitions reflect social constructs rather than fixed age categories. In Chapter 3, Kathleen Kostelny and Michael Wessells point out that "many societies consider 13-year-olds who have completed the cultural rites of passage to be adults". In his research on the Sierra Leonean experience, Stijn Smet stresses "the cultural relativity of the terms 'childhood' and 'adulthood'".[41] Alison Watson criticizes "an idealised Western conception of childhood", which is "arguably much more in line with a Western notion of children being in fulltime education, and thus at parental behest, until this time"; for "children in the South who have been looking after siblings since they were seven, or who have been working since the age of 11", these views of childhood and adulthood may be less relevant.[42] Also, male childhood definitions may significantly differ from female childhood concepts; in some societies, menstruation, motherhood, marriage or other factors affect the social roles of adolescent girls.[43]

Table 1.1 Defining children and young people

Children Convention on the Rights of the Child	0–18 years
Adolescents UNFPA, WHO, UNICEF	10–19 years
Youth UNFPA, WHO, UNICEF	15–24 years
Young people UNFPA, WHO, UNICEF	10–24 years

A diverse population of children and youth

Children should not be considered as a monolithic homogeneous group. They are diverse populations of different ages, developmental stages, sexual and gender identities and social distinctions. However, the language used in most international and national documents and reports tends to lump the diverse groups of children and youth into a single category. In that context, Valeria Izzi and Chetan Kumar criticize "the simplification of youth as a homogeneous category to fit the schemes and paradigms of external interveners" (Chapter 8). Recent research disaggregates different groups of children and youth and tends to view them as active participants with diverse needs and interests in post-conflict settings, rejecting the vision that they resemble a homogeneous group. Moreover, there are differences between boys and girls – Edward Thomas recommends:

> Say "boys and girls" or "young men and women" rather than "children" or "young people": The answers to most questions – such as the questions on incentives, ethnic backgrounds, places of recruitment or motivations – will differ significantly between males and females. It's good practice to ask separately about both, rather than grouping them together as "children".[44]

Women-and-children as a common group?

A further fallacy of overgeneralization might occur when policy reports and documents lump women and children together as helpless victims and passive beneficiaries in post-conflict peacebuilding. Nadine Puechguirbal, who is critical of this approach, argues that "Without a clear picture of the reality in the field, and with broad categories of beneficiaries like *women-and-children*, it is difficult to devise a clear strategy of humanitarian assistance that would use local resources and empower the recipients."[45] In the post-conflict context, however, there are some common features, or fates. Often, women, children and young people do not have – or are not given – the opportunities enjoyed by male adults to play active political and economic roles in efforts geared at post-conflict recovery. In keeping with pre-conflict conceptions of patriarchal hierarchy and society, they are marginalized and excluded from peacebuilding processes.

Victims and/or active agents of building peace and stability?

Children and youth – two important pillars of any post-conflict society – are often presented as mere victims and passive actors rather than as potential agents of change. On the contrary, they can and should be sources of hope. It is they who will determine to a large degree the political life and culture of their generations and their children's generations – spanning the 20–50 years in which a post-conflict society will have to achieve sustainable peace and stability if it is to be safe from further conflict and violence. As most studies and reports note, children's specific needs still tend to be frequently overlooked in post-conflict peacebuilding activities.

Perpetrators of sexual violence: Combatants or civilians?

The Human Security Report 2012, "Sexual Violence, Education, and War: Beyond the Mainstream Narrative", argues that "most sexual violence against children is perpetrated by family members or acquaintances, not members of armed groups".[46] According to the study, based on hospital data on sexual violence against children in the war-affected eastern region of the Democratic Republic of the Congo (DRC), "81 percent of the perpetrators were civilians, while only 13 percent were described as wearing a military uniform. Records about the reported relationship between the victim and the assailant revealed that 74 percent of the perpetrators were known to the family of the victim while 26 percent were strangers."[47] The report findings indicate:

> for children as well as adults, the greatest threat of sexual violence in wartime comes from family members, friends, and acquaintances, not from armed combatants. Yet, as is the case for adult survivors, the child victims of domestic sexual violence receive a disproportionately small share of attention – and assistance – from the international community.[48]

From this finding we can assume that much violence against children, not being related to armed conflict, will continue in the post-conflict period. Thus violence against children and youth might decrease a bit after the conclusion of an armed conflict, but the brunt of violent acts will likely continue, possibly with little attention from those internal and external actors involved in peacebuilding activities.

The scope of gender-based violence against girls and boys

Researchers and practitioners have debunked the myth that only girls and women are victims of sexual violence in wars and their aftermath. While sexual violence against girls and boys in post-conflict environments in general remains under-studied and under-documented, the scale and prevalence of sexual violence against boys and young men are particularly poorly understood. As a Save the Children report states, "boy survivors, and their very different experiences of sexual violence and its implications, are rarely considered at all".[49] The Canadian Human Security Report 2012 criticizes UNSCR 1325 on "Women, Peace and Security" and other UN documents that overlook "boys completely".[50] Scrutinizing the UN's policy in collecting data on sexual violence against children and adults in war-torn societies, the report assumes that this approach "cannot, by its very nature, provide reliable nationwide data on the extent of sexual violence, domestic or conflict-related".[51] Thus "the mandate of new UN peace operations should therefore include a requirement to undertake a nationwide retrospective population survey addressing the knowledge gaps noted above. Such a survey would have a violence module – including questions on sexual violence against males as well as females."[52] The field manual on reproductive health in refugee situations produced by the WHO, UNFPA and UNHCR in 1999 recommended establishing "community-based groups, commonly called anti-rape or crisis intervention teams" in order to raise awareness of sexual violence and support to victims.[53]

In some post-conflict societies, age discrimination and violence against both girls and boys may even increase. Myriam Denov underscores secondary victimization of girls in the aftermath of conflict.[54] Adolescent girls perceived as an economic liability are forcibly married off to assist their poverty-stricken families or settle a feud. For instance, in Iraq, traditionally girls had to marry "men from other tribes, as 'Diyyah' (blood money), in an attempt to settle disputes between two tribes. This form of marriage is also known as 'Fasliyah,' a sort of compensation paid for a crime that the bride's brother or a member of her tribe committed against another tribe."[55] Underage marriages reportedly are on the rise in post-conflict Afghanistan, Tajikistan, Iraq, Kyrgyzstan and Sierra Leone.[56] Annie Bunting suggests that "forced marriage" practices in Liberia, Rwanda, Uganda and the DRC "ought to be charged as 'enslavement'".[57] Families are reported to encourage adolescent girls and young women to "marry their 'bush husbands', making it more difficult for them to leave often abusive relationships".[58] A lack of attention given to gender- and age-discriminatory practices may inhibit the integration of girls and young women in post-conflict reconstruction processes and "accountability mechanisms to address the multitude of crimes and rights violations they have experienced".[59]

A hidden group: Female child soldiers

Neglect of female child soldiers in DDR is gradually drawing international attention. UNICEF reports that girl soldiers are often disregarded by DDR[60] and consequently "underrepresented in rehabilitation centers".[61] According to the Child Soldiers Global Report 2008:

> national DDR programs reflect extraordinarily low figures for girls' participation. In Liberia, 3,000 girls were officially demobilized through the formal DDR process that ended in November 2004. Around another 8,000 did not take part. In the DRC, just 3,000 or just 15 per cent of the total number of girls estimated to have been involved in the conflict had been officially demobilized by the end of 2006 when the national DDR program drew to a close.[62]

In Sierra Leone, girls and young women known as "camp followers" could not register for the DDR programme and "instead (self) demobilized far away from their place of origin".[63] A founder of the Eng Aja Eze Foundation, Ugoji Adanma, argues that "When you disarm somebody, you ask them to return their arms. Many of the female child soldiers do not carry arms. They are used as sex slaves and bush wives. From that point of view, I do not think that DDR has been successful."[64]

The forgotten population: Children born of wartime rape and orphans

Thousands of children born of armed conflict, as well as their mothers and families, face stigma and alienation.[65] Worst off are children born of wartime rape in such post-conflict societies as the DRC, Rwanda and the Balkan region.[66] Often, these children are victimized by their families and communities. The inter-agency manual produced by UN organizations recommends fostering placement and considering adoption "if the child is rejected, neglected or otherwise mistreated".[67] Children born within armed groups might be at a higher risk of abuse and discrimination by society. They "grow up knowing only this particular way of [life] and present additional challenges to the DDR process. Stigma of such children is extreme amongst the returning communities."[68] In addition, the situation of war orphans is rarely discussed.

Turning challenges into opportunities: The inclusion of children and youth in peacebuilding

Lack of physical security: Children as the targets of exploitation and abuse

Children are among the most vulnerable population groups during and after armed conflict as their political agency is very limited. In many post-conflict societies, infant, child and maternal mortality indicators "remain at the startling wartime levels, or even increase as water, power, electricity and sanitation remain severely compromised, clinics remain damaged or unstaffed, prevention programs are stalled, and health workers remain scarce".[69] Girls disproportionately suffer from gender-based violence in conflict and post-conflict settings. For instance, as in the case of the DRC, "delayed presentation, pregnancy and genital injury were more common" between the ages of 10 and 18 years than among adults and younger children.[70] Many former girl soldiers require medical attention as a result of sexual violence, including sexually transmitted infection, recto-vaginal fistulas and other injuries affecting reproductive health, in order to prevent disability and social stigmas.[71] In addition, psychosocial assistance is important, as "many former child combatants have been sexually abused by their commanding superiors and even their peers".[72] Children and young people are also particularly vulnerable to HIV/AIDS in conflict and post-conflict societies, making it important to integrate attention to HIV/AIDS education and healthcare in peacebuilding strategy.[73]

Girls and boys in post-conflict societies continue to be subjected to human trafficking and abuse.[74] In addition, they might be exploited by peacekeepers in post-conflict settings. Numerous cases are known of peacekeepers of diverse nationalities who were involved in child prostitution and trafficking for sexual exploitation, as "trafficking – especially the enslavement of women and girls for forced prostitution – follows market demand and, in post-conflict situations, that demand is often created by international peacekeepers".[75] In the DRC, for instance, most victims were between the ages of 12 and 16 years, and were "poor and illiterate; many had lost close family members and were traumatized by the sexual and other violence that characterized the conflict".[76] As Claire Morris points out, as a response to this situation:

> gender and child protection advisers must be deployed at the earliest possible stage of a peacekeeping operation to protect groups at risk of abuse and exploitation. All operations should include Conduct and Discipline Teams to oversee protection activities. They should work in co-ordination with grassroots NGOs to facilitate access to the complaints process.[77]

Disabled children and their families

In many post-conflict environments, families and communities isolate and stigmatize children with disabilities.[78] According to the UNICEF *Innocenti Digest* on the rights of children with disabilities, "a disability perspective is rarely present in assessments from the early stages of an emergency"; thus, in some cases, "humanitarian care workers revert to segregating persons with disabilities and even accommodating them only by impairment category, as happened in the Freetown amputee camp in Sierra Leone".[79] Gender-specific neglect magnifies the plight of disabled girls: Kathleen Kostelny and Michael Wessells report in Chapter 3 that in some cases "Disabled girls may have few or no options for marriage. Many disabled children do not participate in school and, lacking vocational skills or opportunities, face a life of poverty and a lack of social integration." After conflict, a number of disabled children become psychologically traumatized.

Muted voices of children and youth

Children's and youth's voices on post-conflict peacebuilding concerns are often muted. By categorizing them as vulnerable and helpless victims, both international and national actors downplay their interests and needs as low-priority issues. UNICEF notes that children "may generally lack the power of adults, but they nevertheless are social, economic and political beings – even if they cannot directly participate in political processes".[80]

Child soldiers suffer from misguided DDR programmes

According to UN estimates, around 300,000 children under 18 serve as soldiers in government armies and opposition forces involved in armed conflicts in more than 30 countries. Many soldiers under 15 are recruited by armed non-state actors.[81] Boys and girls are compelled to fight or work; for some of them participation is basically a means of survival. Numerous studies point to the failure of DDR to address the needs of child soldiers. Child Soldiers International criticizes "adult DDR planners" for their lack of awareness; "children (both boys and girls) were involved in particular conflicts in a multitude of roles and results in DDR programs that do not include provisions for children".[82] The DDR programme in Aceh (Indonesia) completely excluded child soldiers, in spite of children's participation in the Indonesian armed forces and the Free Aceh Movement.[83] Through the DDR programme in Sierra Leone in 2003, "only seven thousand of an estimated 48,000 child soldiers were demobilized, DDR interventions practiced a 'one man, one gun' policy focused on disarming adult male combatants. Women and children associated with the fighting groups were often excluded from the process."[84]

Neglected education and training

Transitions to peace cannot be effective without education and training of children and youth.

The provision of adequate education to both girls and boys is a tremendous task, as in many post-conflict countries the educational needs of children have been ignored for a long time, both during and before the outbreak of violent conflict. For instance, in pre-war Kosovo "many children, especially girls, were excluded from educational opportunities. As a result, the largest numbers of illiterate women in rural areas were in the 16–21 age group."[85] A lack of educational opportunities worsens the plight of children and youth, while adequate provision of education offers alleviation. For instance, girls "are generally vulnerable to harm and subjugation, and education can heighten and increase these vulnerabilities. However, education has the potential to provide a counterbalance to these through its resilience-enhancing aspects."[86]

Tackling youth unemployment and underemployment

Stories from various post-conflict countries demonstrate that a combination of a "youth bulge" and youth unemployment can fuel social unrest and recurrence of conflict. International Alert argues that "reintegration programmes can help break this vicious cycle if they take the specific needs and profiles of youth into account. This is of particular importance given that many former fighters were recruited as child soldiers and therefore have no previous work experience or skills."[87]

Empowering alienated adolescents

Peculiarities of adolescents frequently go unnoticed. Boys and girls come to deal with insecurity challenges differently as a function of socialization and gender identities.[88] After war, some teenagers terrorize their own communities. For instance, as Frank Faulkner writes:

> the net result of dehumanizing the children of Sierra Leone, as in similarly affected countries, is the production of a horde of insensate killers outlawed by their families, afraid of rehabilitation for fear of reprisals, and who are effectively forced to stay in the company of armed gangs – a surrogate "family". The future for young people trapped in this way is bleak, with no access to education or the normalizing influences of stable, secure family settings; they are at the mercy of quasi-military groups.[89]

The hostage crisis in Moscow in 2002, when hundreds of civilians were locked up by young Chechen radicals, both men and women, has been explained by the appearance of a new generation of youth that have lost touch with their traditions and grown up under conditions of wars in Chechnya. Analysts believe that the main problem of Chechnya lies with the children and adolescents of war who have enjoyed little general and professional education and are alienated from society. Some radicalized youth might be a recruitment basis for Islamist-inspired separatists and extremists.[90] Children and youth can transform from victims into perpetrators if their interests and needs are ignored.

Legal loopholes and the situation of children after an armed conflict

The legal status of children and youth in conflict-affected environments may change as a consequence of the war, such as through the loss of legal documents, land and property, and the restoration of local ethnic and religious traditions that discriminate against women and children. Some children are not registered at birth, depriving them of a nationality and a legal name. Among refugees and displaced persons, non-legalized children might not be able to attend kindergarten or receive official medical services.

Repairing the social fabric

Local families and communities are often not given the roles they deserve in designing peacebuilding programmes. Drawing on the situation in Uganda, Grace Maina argues that "the reintegration programmes for formerly abducted children have tended to follow a top-down approach, ignoring the input of the local communities".[91] It is therefore important that child and adolescent participation result from and are accompanied by the involvement of parents, caregivers, teachers and religious and community leaders, as well as other actors in transitional justice processes.[92] Involving children and youth in peace processes and decision-making can strengthen the ability of conflict-affected communities to restore peace. To promote intergenerational communication and traditional values and culture, meetings with elders in the community could be encouraged: when "adolescents are in a stage of search of identity, it is imperative that the values of their community are preserved [and as] fathers are often absent (many of them even involved in the fighting) the elders represent a special resource in transmitting such values".[93]

In a UNFPA study of gender-based violence in Kosovo, human rights activists articulate the social significance of engaging men and boys in empowering girls and stopping sexual violence. They recommend "positive and sustained media campaigns and gender-sensitive education, including the gender-sensitive socialization of young children, to remove stereotypes and attitudes that perpetuate traditional roles of men and women".[94]

Restoration of traditional institutions

As Kostelny and Wessels argue in Chapter 3, "Children and adults in developing societies frequently turn to traditional healers and local herbalists for support during a crisis. Religious beliefs and practices also increase resilience in many societies." Moreover, "War and post-war trauma strengthen ethnic and religious identities, revitalizing long-forgotten ethnic and religious traditions and institutions, and evoking neo-traditional beliefs in a purported 'golden age' of patriarchal social rule, which tend to embrace archaic forms of gender discrimination."[95]

Often, "the conservative backlash that takes place after war has roots in the older generation's attempt to reassert control and re-establish 'traditions' . . . In the context of re-establishing livelihood, the older generation finds it particularly important to control young women."[96] In every post-conflict society there are also positive cultural traditions that can mitigate the suffering of youth and children. For example, local customs of relatives adopting orphans and separated children "tend to be overlooked (and thus are not sufficiently supported) by Western and national aid programmes"; in such cases, "encouraging and understanding the cultural context of mutual help could facilitate a less painful return to some sense of normalcy".[97] This is a particularly delicate issue in societies that are firmly entrenched in religious belief and value systems. For instance, gender is a very sensitive issue in post-conflict Muslim states. In countries such as Iraq, Afghanistan and Tajikistan, external organizations and individuals offering assistance have to understand local customs and, in certain cases, cooperate with traditional institutions and faith-based organizations.[98] However, one needs to be cautious of highly politicized gender-sensitive activities, as even modest publicity about a successful programme can be a threat to its continuation.

Cultural activities: Sport, art, storytelling, social media

Sports activities successfully bridge gaps in divided youth communities in conflict-prone zones. Experiences in Sierra Leone[99] and Nigeria,[100] among many other countries, reveal encouraging stories of adolescents, initially a neglected group, who were empowered through sports. The Sierra Leonean case provides a good example of the healing effect of sporting activities in DDR camps. According to Christopher Dyck's study, "sport was a successful peacebuilding option and one of the most popular and satisfying activities in the camp".[101] The UN Office on Sport for Development and Peace views sport as "a driving force: contributing to development in Africa (in particular in sub-Saharan Africa); encouraging dialogue and mutual understanding in the Middle East; advancing gender equality; fostering the inclusion of persons with disabilities; and, finally, promoting youth development and supporting community role models".[102] The Council of Europe initiated a good practices handbook highlighting sport as an opportunity to strengthen social cohesion in post-conflict communities in the western Balkans and south Caucasus regions.[103]

A further successful form of rehabilitation is traditional storytelling. Kirsten Johnson and colleagues consider storytelling as:

> a powerful cultural mechanism used to pass on tradition in many African societies. The stories can create a stronger community and teach children how to behave. In addition, war chants sung by women in the local villages can be altered to highlight the dangers of children joining armed groups instead of glorifying conflict. These cultural phenomena should be utilized by communities as tools to inform their children about how to avoid recruitment by armed groups and what to do if captured.[104]

After deadly ethnic conflict in south Kyrgyzstan in 2010, the Institute for Regional Studies, along with several civil society organizations and with support of the Swiss Cooperation Office, initiated courses on psychological rehabilitation in summer camps for children aged nine to 15. Art and play therapy and storytelling proved to be especially effective tools for coping with post-conflict trauma.[105] Finally, modern technologies including cell phones, social networking sites such as Twitter and Facebook and the internet in general are becoming increasingly important factors in the mobilization, participation and empowerment of youth and children.[106]

Learning from post-conflict contexts: Chapter overviews

The first, introductory part of the book focuses on "Conceptualizing the roles of children and youth in post-conflict peacebuilding". Following this introduction, in the second chapter, entitled "Children and young people in post-conflict peacebuilding", Claire O'Kane, Clare Feinstein and Annette Giertsen show how child-centred reintegration and activities empower children as peacebuilders. The chapter provides a nuanced view of various roles of children in post-conflict reconstruction. The discussion focuses on the responsibilities of UN actors as well as international and local NGOs within the broader social institutional context. Examples include the training of military and peacekeeping forces on child rights undertaken by Save the Children in Sweden and East and West Africa. O'Kane, Feinstein and Giertsen cite an example from Uganda, where "Save the Children has signed a memorandum of understanding (2007) with the Ministry of Defence that spells out their respective roles. This includes the role of Save the Children as a 'watchdog' to monitor the military *vis-à-vis* their role in protecting and respecting children's rights, and supporting the training of the Ugandan military." With such concrete examples they emphasize the strong potential of local NGOs and community groups in empowering children in peacebuilding processes.

Part II of the book addresses "The scars of armed conflict – Children and youth as actors and victims". In Chapter 3, "Children and youth in conflict and post-conflict societies: From plights of war to paths of peacebuilding", Kathleen Kostelny and Michael Wessells consider a wider view of children empowerment in the rebuilding process than is often used. An important focus of this chapter is on the opportunities lost "through the socialization of children into systems of violence". They examine the plight of children in societies torn by armed conflict and options that engage young people as constructive contributors to peacebuilding, and outline how the changes in the nature of armed conflict have created a holistic threat to children's well-being. By linking children's well-being to that of mothers, families and communities, they analyse their situation in terms of risk, vulnerability and resilience, without offering simplistic portrayals of traumatized populations. Kostelny and Wessells argue that war-affected children are survivors with considerable resilience and coping resources and strategies. They also show that youth are influential both as soldiers and as peacemakers, and that they are powerful agents of social change. Finally, they call upon the peacebuilding community to build values, competencies and life options through which youth can participate more fully as peacemakers.

In Chapter 4, "Angry young men in Timor-Leste: Post-conflict peacebuilding and its malcontents", Henri Myrttinen focuses on the phenomenon of "angry young men". When they become threats to post-conflict settlements, this tends to be tightly linked to gender role expectations. He bases his analysis on research conducted in Timor-Leste from 2006 to 2008, but also on experiences of other conflict societies in Melanesia and Southeast Asia. His fieldwork focused mainly on interviews with members of various disaffected groups. Myrttinen finds that the propensity to violence is driven as much by a search for often-meagre economic opportunities as by grievances caused by the lack of recognition of conflict and combat experience in post-war life. He argues that although these men are perceived as threats to social stability, they are often given a certain degree of social space, if not outright encouragement and support, by other sectors of society. Myrttinen shows that while the threat to stability of this seemingly "lost generation" is manifested in the public mind as roaming groups of brooding, discontented, young, lower-class males, the phenomenon is much more complicated than this stereotype suggests. With his discussion, Myrttinen unpacks some of the issues such as gender role and class expectations inherent in the discourse of post-conflict violence and peacebuilding. For instance, he finds that some social work programmes have attempted to make gang masculinity a less attractive choice for young Timorese men. However, the core issues of "disenchantment with the state and its elites, socio-economic grievances, issues of 'respect' and, above all, gender role expectations that equate willingness to use force with masculinity" have so far not been tackled.

In Part III of the volume the discussion focuses on "Protecting and engaging children and youth in post-conflict environments". In Chapter 5, "Protection and participation of children in post-conflict peacebuilding: International law and evolving practice", Vesselin Popovski suggests incorporating broader child rights and principles developed in international humanitarian law in post-conflict peacebuilding activities. His account includes an analysis of the evolution of international humanitarian law, international criminal law and human rights law, and discusses the opportunities and shortcomings of child protection and participation in peacebuilding. He illustrates how these are reflected in UN programmes and practices. He argues that addressing children not primarily as victims, but rather as participants in post-conflict reconstruction, is the best way to help them escape from child victimhood caused by war. The process of peacebuilding is a long-term exercise and necessarily must give children, society's future generation, a significant participatory role.

In Chapter 6, "Children and security sector governance", David Nosworthy argues that children and youth – two groups especially affected by armed conflict – are rarely considered in the process of re-establishing justice and security in the post-conflict environment. Re-establishing the rule of law and respect for human rights requires that all stakeholders, including young people, be engaged in assessing and defining security priorities. Central to this is the acknowledgement that children have important contributions to make to recovery and peacebuilding processes, as well as to long-term social development. Armed conflict provides a wide range of factors with negative consequences for young people, among them insecurity, uncertainty over the future, limited or no access to services such as education, availability of small arms and general breakdown of the rule of law. Such factors are likely to be manipulated and used by peace spoilers intent on derailing stabilization efforts, whether for political or economic ends, as they push young people into violence, crime or radicalization.

In Chapter 7, "The resilience of children and youth during conflict and its contribution to post-conflict stability: The case of northern Uganda and 'night commuting'", Azar Eskandarpour focuses on the evolution of resilience among children and their families in conflict and post-conflict settings. Her analysis illuminates the age- and gender-discriminatory practices and challenges of "night commuting". Night commuting revitalizes previous links and networks and encourages a sense of community and extended family for many children in northern Uganda. She traces the evolution of night commuting from a crisis-driven strategy to a social institution of resilience that serves not only protection purposes but also the promotion of general well-being. She shows that resilience in conflict is not only a mechanism of providing protection from violence, but also a key contributing factor to maintaining and strengthening social capital, social trust and agency. All these factors strengthen Ugandan children's ability to contribute to peacebuilding – and thus show that rebuilding social cohesion and strengthening networks are a successful strategy to maximize children's contribution to protecting their rights and interests. As children and youth demonstrate their capacity to build up resilience, they show that they can contribute to social cohesion within their community and peacebuilding efforts.

The fourth part of the book offers two contributions that focus on "Children and youth as peacebuilders". In Chapter 8, "Do youth programmes contribute to peacebuilding? Some reflections on existing practice", Valeria Izzi and Chetan Kumar argue that young people are more visible in war than they are in peace. They remind us that while wars would not be possible without the youth, who typically make up the vast majority of combatants, peace negotiations remain the domain of adults. Young people rarely participate in the planning of post-conflict reconstruction and their specific needs and priorities do not generally feature in recovery plans, depriving peacebuilding activities of their relevance as the majority of the population. Izzi and Kumar explain that during conflicts, hierarchies based on age and gender are often renegotiated and shifted in complex and unpredictable ways. If post-conflict settlements ignore these changes and instead simply opt for a return to the status quo, disillusionment and frustration are bound to be the consequences. By neglecting the changes created during conflict, the sustainability of peace is threatened in the long run. Izzi and Kumar observe that, partly in recognition of this dynamic, in recent years the peacebuilding agenda has shown a new interest in youth, as policy documents have acknowledged the importance of taking into account the needs and priorities of young people. However, despite these good intentions, they find that youth programmes have not always been comprehensive and coherent, often remaining at the pilot stage, failing to produce concrete change and thus easily falling short of the high expectations of both donors and beneficiaries.

In Chapter 9, "'Conflict is a preventable disease': Recovering child soldiers teach the practice of peace", Deborah Davis shares the story of a small group of former child soldiers, called "Friends of Orphans", who train other former child soldiers to be peacebuilders in their communities. The group works in northern Uganda, where the Lord's Resistance Army (LRA) has been fighting a brutal war against members of its own ethnic group for the past 20 years. An estimated 40,000–60,000 children have been abducted by the LRA as child soldiers or other servants. While many of these children die in the bush, some manage to escape, enter an IDP camp or are rescued (or captured) by the country's army, the Uganda People's Defence Force. Many of those who manage to escape the LRA, however, are recaptured, killed or commit suicide. All depend on, but do not always receive, medical and trauma counselling to manage a sustainable reintegration into their communities.

Davis applies an ethnographic approach to examine the micro-peacebuilding method of the Friends of Orphans group in the IDP camps in northern Uganda. Her chapter is based on research conducted in the second half of 2008, during which she interviewed the group's co-founder and director, who himself was a child soldier in the LRA, as well as relief agencies which have worked with the group. Davis shows that the group's community-based initiative has made real contributions to peace and development by investing in the peacebuilding potential of former child soldiers – for instance, several former child soldiers who have found a constructive post-war role by creating successful enterprises with support from Friends of Orphans have been elected to local councils. There they advocate for the needs of child soldiers and generate support for the group's programmes. Davis recommends that donors should increasingly work with, and develop mechanisms and structures to support, such grassroots-based peacebuilding activities, "so that communities torn apart by the abduction and destruction of their children can leave their victimhood behind and become agents of their own development".

The concluding chapter by Anara Tabyshalieva and Albrecht Schnabel, entitled "Escaping and moving beyond victimhood: Children and youth as peacebuilders", revisits and compares the case studies. The chapter discusses main points of empowerment of children and youth as agents of peace, and summarizes the findings and recommendations of the case studies. Together with a brief assessment, policy recommendations developed in the case studies are suggested for practitioners and activists to advance the position of children and youth in post-conflict peacebuilding.

Notes

1. Albrecht Schnabel and Anara Tabyshalieva (eds), *Defying Victimhood: Women and Post-Conflict Peacebuilding*, Tokyo: United Nations University Press, 2012.
2. Elizabeth M. Cousens, "Introduction", in Elizabeth M. Cousens, Chetan Kumar with Karin Wermester (eds), *Peacebuilding as Politics: Cultivating Peace in Fragile Societies*, Boulder, CO: Lynne Rienner Publishers, 2001, p. 14.

3. Peacebuilding Support Office, "UN Peacebuilding: An Orientation", 2010, p. 6, www.un.org/en/peacebuilding/pbso/pdf/peacebuilding_orientation.pdf.
4. Ibid. As the report points out, this explains "the emphasis in the Secretary-General's report on the crucial window of the first 24 months after conflict".
5. Johan Galtung, "Three Approaches to Peace: Peacekeeping, Peacemaking and Peacebuilding", in Johan Galtung (ed.), *Peace, War and Defence – Essays in Peace Research*, Vol. 2, Copenhagen: Christian Ejlers, 1975, pp. 282–304.
6. Peacebuilding Support Office, "Peacebuilding & the United Nations: What Is Peacebuilding?", www.un.org/en/peacebuilding/pbso/pbun.shtml.
7. Ibid.
8. United Nations, "Report of the Panel on United Nations Peace Operations", UN Doc. A/55/305-S/2000/809, 21 August 2000, p. 3, www.un.org/documents/ga/docs/55/a55305.pdf.
9. Roger Mac Ginty, *No War, No Peace: The Rejuvenation of Stalled Peace Processes and Peace Accords*, Basingstoke: Palgrave Macmillan, 2008, p. 23.
10. Dan Snodderly (ed.) *Peace Terms: Glossary of Terms for Conflict Management and Peacebuilding*, Washington, DC: Academy for International Conflict Management and Peacebuilding/US Institute of Peace, 2011, www.usip.org/peace_terms.pdf.
11. Michelle I. Gawerc, "Peacebuilding: Theoretical and Concrete Perspectives", *Peace & Change* 31(4), 2006, p. 439, www.glencree.ie/site/documents/Gawerc-Peacebuilding-Theoretical%20and%20Concrete%20Perspectives.pdf.
12. Nadine Puechguirbal, "Discourses on Gender, Patriarchy and Resolution 1325: A Textual Analysis of UN Documents", *International Peacekeeping* 17(2), 2010, p. 179.
13. UNICEF, "Impact of Armed Conflict on Children", 1996, www.unicef.org/graca/.
14. Office of the UN Special Representative of the Secretary-General for Children and Armed Conflict, http://childrenandarmedconflict.un.org.
15. UNICEF, "Machel Study 10-Year Strategic Review: Children and Conflict in a Changing World", UNICEF and Office of the Special Representative of the Secretary-General for Children in Armed Conflict, New York, 2009, www.unicef.org/publications/files/Machel_Study_10_Year_Strategic_Review_EN_030909.pdf.
16. Charlotte Wagnsson, Maria Hellman and Arita Holmberg, "The Centrality of Non-Traditional Groups for Security in the Globalized Era: The Case of Children", *International Political Sociology* 4(1), 2010, p. 5.
17. Human Security Report Project, "Human Security Report 2012: Sexual Violence, Education, and War: Beyond the Mainstream Narrative", Human Security Press, Vancouver, BC, 2012, p. 63, www.hsrgroup.org/docs/Publications/HSR2012/HSRP2012_Chapter%203.pdf.
18. UN Security Council Resolution 1379 (2001), www.securitycouncilreport.org/atf/cf/%7B65BFCF9B-6D27-4E9C-8CD3-CF6E4FF96FF9%7D/CAC%20SRES%201379.pdf.
19. Ibid.
20. Resolution 1612 (2005), adopted by the Security Council at its 5235th meeting, 26 July 2005, www.securitycouncilreport.org/atf/cf/%7B65BFCF9B-6D27-4E9C-8CD3-CF6E4FF96FF9%7D/CAC%20SRES%201612.pdf.
21. Resolution 1998 (2011), adopted by the Security Council at its 6581st meeting, 12 July 2011, www.securitycouncilreport.org/atf/cf/%7B65BFCF9B-6D27-4E9C-8CD3-CF6E4FF96FF9%7D/CAC%20S%20RES%201998.pdf.
22. Resolution 2068 (2012), adopted by the Security Council at its 6838th meeting, 19 September 2012, www.securitycouncilreport.org/atf/cf/%7B65BFCF9B-6D27-4E9C-8CD3-CF6E4FF96FF9%7D/s_res_2068.pdf.
23. Ibid.
24. See in particular Office of the UN High Commissioner for Refugees, "Children: Protection and Building Resilience", www.unhcr.org/pages/49c3646c1e8.html.

25. Alison Watson, "Saving More than the Children: The Role of Child-Focused NGOs in the Creation of Southern Security Norms", *Third World Quarterly* 27(2), 2006, p. 235.
26. ILO, "Children Formerly Associated with Armed Forces and Groups: 'How-to' Guide on Economic Reintegration", ILO International Training Centre, Turin, 2010, http://training.itcilo.org/ils/ils_childlabour/training_materials/English/How-to%20guide_en.pdf.
27. International Alert, "Enhancing Socio-Economic Opportunities for Ex-Combatants in Post-Conflict Environments", 2010, www.international-alert.org/resources/publications/enhancing-socio-economic-opportunities-ex-combatants.
28. Clare Feinstein and Claire O'Kane, "Ethical Guidelines: For Ethical, Meaningful and Inclusive Children's Participation Practice", Save the Children Norway, Oslo, www.reddbarna.no/default.asp?V_ITEM_ID=19028.
29. Child Rights International Network, "Mission Statement", www.crin.org/join/index.asp.
30. Child Soldiers International, "Mission Statement", www.child-soldiers.org/our_work.php.
31. Andrew Blum, "Improving Peacebuilding Evaluation: A Whole-of-Field Approach", USIP, Washington, DC, 2011, p. 11, www.usip.org/files/resources/Improving_Peacebuilding_Evaluation.pdf.
32. Conversation with Valeria Izzi, a contributor to this volume.
33. Roger Mac Ginty, "The Liberal Peace at Home and Abroad: Northern Ireland and Liberal Internationalism", *British Journal of Politics & International Relations* 11(4), 2009, p. 704.
34. M. J. Williams, "(Un)Sustainable Peacebuilding: NATO's Suitability for Postconflict Reconstruction in Multiactor Environments", *Global Governance* 17(1), 2011, p. 119.
35. Beth Speake, "A Gendered Approach to Peacebuilding and Conflict Resolution", *e-International Relations*, 11 February 2013, p. 13, www.e-ir.info/2013/02/11/a-gendered-approach-to-peacebuilding-and-conflict-resolution/.
36. WHO, "Adolescent Development", 2013, www.who.int/maternal_child_adolescent/topics/adolescence/dev/en/index.html.
37. UNICEF, "The State of the World's Children 2011: Adolescence an Age of Opportunity, 2011", February 2011, p. 6, www.unicef.org/sowc2011/pdfs/SOWC-2011-Main-Report_EN_02092011.pdf.
38. Department of Economic and Social Affairs – Economic and Social Council (ECOSOC), Youth. Social Policy and Development Division, "Frequently Asked Questions: What Does the United Nations Mean by 'Youth' and 'Children'?", http://social.un.org/index/Youth/FAQs.aspx.
39. Ibid.
40. UNFPA, UNHCR and WHO, "Reproductive Health in Refugee Situations: An Inter-Agency Field Manual", New York, 1999, www.unfpa.org/emergencies/manual/8.htm.
41. Stijn Smet, "A Window of Opportunity – Improving Gender Relations in Post-Conflict Societies: The Sierra Leonean Experience", *Journal of Gender Studies* 18(2), 2009, p. 150.
42. Watson, note 25 above, p. 231.
43. UNICEF, "A Study on Violence against Girls: Report on the International Girl Child Conference, 9–10 March 2009", UNICEF, The Hague, pp. 26–27, www.unicef-irc.org/publications/pdf/violence_girls_eng.pdf.
44. Edward Thomas, "Between War and Peace: Monitoring Guidelines for Child Soldiers in Nepal's Peace Process", *Journal of Human Rights Practice* 2(1), 2010, pp. 106–107.
45. Nadine Puechguirbal, "Women and Children: Deconstructing a Paradigm", *Seton Hall Journal of Diplomacy and International Relations* V(1), 2004, p. 8.
46. Human Security Report Project, note 17 above, p. 74.

47. Ibid.
48. Ibid., p. 76.
49. Save the Children UK, "Hidden Survivors", November 2012, www.savethechildren.org.uk/sites/default/files/docs/Hidden_Survivors_1.pdf.
50. Human Security Report Project, note 17 above, p. 74.
51. Ibid., p. 77.
52. Ibid., p. 78.
53. UNFPA, UNHCR and WHO, note 40 above.
54. Myriam Denov, "Girls in Fighting Forces: Moving Beyond Victimhood", 2007, www.crin.org/docs/CIDA_Beyond_forces.pdf.
55. "The Central Organization for Statistics conducted a survey that indicated 5% of Iraqi girls under the age of 15 were married, and around 22% of those under 18 were married. Early marriages have increased at an alarming rate, although in 2010 the ministry of women's affairs warned that 'girls between 15 and 18 are twice as likely to die during pregnancy and while giving birth than women between the ages of 20 and 24'." See *AL-MONITOR Rises*, "Underage Marriage of Iraqi Girls Rises", *AL-MONITOR Rises*, 23 December 2012, www.al-monitor.com/pulse/culture/2012/12/the-underage-marriage-crisis-in-iraq.html#ixzz2MFIws200.
56. Jennifer Gong-Gershowitz, "Forced Marriage: A 'New' Crime against Humanity?", *Northwestern University Journal of International Human Rights* 8(1), 2009, p. 54, www.law.northwestern.edu/journals/jihr/v8/n1/3/Gong-Gershowitz.pdf.
57. Annie Bunting, "'Forced Marriage' in Conflict Situations: Researching and Prosecuting Old Harms and New Crimes", *Canadian Journal of Human Rights* 1(1), 2012, p. 165.
58. Smet, note 41 above, p. 157.
59. Khristopher Carlson and Dyan Mazurana, "Forced Marriage within the Lord's Resistance Army, Uganda", Feinstein International Center, Tufts University, Medford, MA, May 2008, p. 14, https://wikis.uit.tufts.edu/confluence/download/attachments/14553676/Forced+Marriage+within+the+LRA.pdf?version=1.
60. UNICEF, "The Impact of Conflict on Women and Girls in West and Central Africa and the UNICEF Response", 2005, p. 15, www.unicef.org/publications/files/Impact_final.pdf.
61. Kirsten Johnson, Gillian Morantz, Helen Seignior, Tanya Zayed and Shelly Whitman, "From Youth Affected by War to Advocates of Peace, Round Table Discussions with Former Child Combatants from Sudan, Sierra Leone and Cambodia", *Journal of International Peacekeeping* 16(1/2), 2012, p. 171.
62. Child Soldiers International, "The Child Soldiers Global Report 2008", 2008, p. 28, www.child-soldiers.org/global_report_reader.php?id=97.
63. Krijn Peters, "Reintegration Support for Young Ex-Combatants: A Right or a Privilege?", *International Migration* 45(5), 2007, p. 53.
64. Isabelle de Grave, "Former Girl Soldiers Trade One Nightmare for Another", IPS-Inter Press Service, United Nations, 14 June 2012, www.ipsnews.net/2012/06/former-girl-soldiers-trade-one-nightmare-for-another/#sthash.QZeIkrp3.dpuf; www.ipsnews.net/2012/06/former-girl-soldiers-trade-one-nightmare-for-another/#sthash.4iqBHDVo.dpuf.
65. See more in Ingvill C. Mochmann and Sabine Lee, "The Human Rights of Children Born of War: Case Analyses of Past and Present Conflicts", *Historical Social Research* 35(3), 2010, pp. 268–298.
66. See Karmen Erjavec and Zala Volèiè, "'Target', 'Cancer' and 'Warrior': Exploring Painful Metaphors of Self-Presentation Used by Girls Born of War Rape", *Discourse & Society* 21(5), 2010, pp. 524–543.
67. UNFPA, UNHCR and WHO, note 40 above.
68. Johnson et al., note 61 above, p. 170.

69. Leonards Rubenstein, "Post-Conflict Health Reconstruction: New Foundations for U.S. Policy", US Institute of Peace, Washington, DC, 2009, www.usip.org/files/resources/post-conflict_health_reconstruction.pdf.
70. Luc Malemo, Paluku Lussy Justin, Christophe Kimona, Nyavandu Kavira, Eugenie Kamabu Mukekulu, Muhindo Kasereka, Jonathan Lusi, Cöaude Kasereka Masumbuko and Michael Hawkes, "Sexual Violence toward Children and Youth in War-Torn Eastern Democratic Republic of Congo", *PLoS ONE* 6(1), 2011, www.plosone.org/article/info%3Adoi%2F10.1371%2Fjournal.pone.0015911. For similar findings in northern Uganda see Sheetal H. Patel, Herbert Muyinda, Nelson K. Sewankambo, Geoffrey Oyat, Stella Atim and Patricia M. Spittal, "In the Face of War: Examining Sexual Vulnerabilities of Acholi Adolescent Girls Living in Displacement Camps in Conflict-Affected Northern Uganda", *BMC International Health and Human Rights* 12(38), 2012, www.biomedcentral.com/1472-698X/12/38.
71. Johnson et al., note 61 above, p. 171.
72. Susanne Schaal and Thomas Elbert, "Ten Years After the Genocide: Trauma Confrontation and Posttraumatic Stress in Rwandan Adolescents", *Journal of Traumatic Stress* 19(1), 2006, p. 103, http://kops.ub.uni-konstanz.de/bitstream/handle/urn:nbn:de:bsz:352-opus-42093/Ten_years_after_the_genocide.pdf?sequence=1.
73. Johnson et al., note 61 above, p. 168.
74. Sarah Mendelson, "Barracks and Brothels: Peacekeepers and Human Trafficking in the Balkans", CSIS, Washington, DC, 2005, p. 1, www.csis.org/files/media/csis/pubs/0502_barracksbrothels.pdf.
75. Corinna Csáky, "No One to Turn to: The Under-Reporting of Child Sexual Exploitation and Abuse by Aid Workers and Peacekeepers", Save the Children UK, London, 2008, www.un.org/en/pseataskforce/docs/no_one_to_turn_under_reporting_of_child_sea_by_aid_workers.pdf.
76. Ray Murphy, "An Assessment of UN Efforts to Address Sexual Misconduct by Peacekeeping Personnel", *International Peacekeeping* 13(4), 2006, p. 536.
77. Claire Morris, "Peacekeeping and the Sexual Exploitation of Women and Girls in Post-Conflict Societies: A Serious Enigma to Establishing the Rule of Law", *Journal of International Peacekeeping* 14, 2010, p. 212.
78. N. Von der Assen, M. Euwema and H. Cornielje, "Including Disabled Children in Psychosocial Programmes in Areas Affected by Armed Conflict", *Intervention* 8(1), 2010, p. 36, www.crin.org/docs/2010introandvonderassendisabilities9355164.pdf.
79. UNICEF, "Promoting the Rights of Children with Disabilities", *Innocenti Digest* 13, 2007, p. 19, www.un.org/esa/socdev/unyin/documents/children_disability_rights.pdf.
80. UNICEF, note 43 above.
81. United Nations, "Child Soldiers", www.un.org/Pubs/CyberSchoolBus/briefing/soldiers/index.htm.
82. Child Soldiers International, note 62 above, p. 31.
83. Ibid.
84. Stephanie Hanson, "Disarmament, Demobilization, and Reintegration (DDR) in Africa", Council on Foreign Relations, February 2007, www.cfr.org/africa/disarmament-demobilization-reintegration-ddr-africa/p12650.
85. UNFPA Women, Peace and Security Initiative Technical Support Division, "Gender-Based Violence in Kosovo: A Case Study", UNFPA, New York, September 2005, p. 9.
86. Donna Sharkey, "Contradictions in Girls' Education in a Post-Conflict Setting", *Compare* 38(5), 2008, p. 577.
87. Irma Specht, "Practice Note 4: Socio-Economic Reintegration of Ex-Combatants", in Canan Gündüz and Joost van der Zwan (eds), *Peacebuilding Essentials for Economic Development Practitioners*, International Alert, London, 2010, www.international-alert.

org/sites/default/files/publications/201009PracticeNote4SocioEconomicReintegration.pdf.

88. C. G. Antonius, M. Robben and Marcelo M. Suarez-Orozco, "The Management of Collective Trauma", in C. G. Antonius, M. Robben and Marcelo M. Suarez-Orozco (eds), *Cultures under Siege*, Cambridge: Cambridge University Press, 2000, p. 46. However, according to Beneduce, "The direct participation of children and adolescents in conflicts does not always and necessarily imply psycho-pathological effects or damage to the development of the personality." Roberto Beneduce, "Contested Memories: Peace-Building and Community Rehabilitation after Violence and Mass Crimes – A Medico-Anthropological Approach", in Béatrice Pouligny, Simon Chesterman and Albrecht Schnabel (eds), *After Mass Crime: Rebuilding States and Communities*, Tokyo: United Nations University Press, 2007, p. 55.
89. Frank Faulkner, "Kindergarten Killers: Morality, Murder and Child Soldier Problems", *Third World Quarterly* 22(4), 2001, p. 499.
90. Sabrina Ravernise, "With Few Bonds to Russia, Young Chechens Join Militants", *New York Times*, 19 November 2002, p. A3. An example of international radicalization of youth is the Boston Marathon bombing (2013), when two brothers, young men of Chechen origin, committed a terror act.
91. Grace Maina, "Human Securitised Reintegration of Formerly Abducted Children in Northern Uganda", *African Security Review* 18(4), 2009, p. 118.
92. Sharanjeet Parmar, Mindy Jane Roseman, Saudamini Siegrist and Theo Sowa, "Children and Transitional Justice: Truth-Telling, Accountability and Reconciliation", UNICEF, New York, 2010, p. 412, www.unicef-irc.org/publications/587.
93. Norwegian Refugee Council, Redd Barna (Save the Children Norway) and Office of the UN High Commissioner for Refugees, "Protection of Children and Adolescents in Complex Emergencies, Oslo/Hadeland, 9–11 November 1998, Conference Report", 1999, www.unhcr.org/3ae690200.pdf.
94. UNFPA, note 85 above, p. 8.
95. Albrecht Schnabel and Anara Tabyshalieva, "Forgone Opportunities: The Marginalization of Women's Contributions to Post-Conflict Peacebuilding", in Schnabel and Tabyshalieva, note 1 above, p. 17.
96. Sheila Meintjes, Anu Pillay and Meredeth Turshen, "There Is No Aftermath for Women", in Sheila Meintjes, Anu Pillay and Meredeth Turshen (eds) *The Aftermath: Women in Post-Conflict Transformation*, London and New York: Zed Books, 2001, p. 13, cited in ibid.
97. Schnabel and Tabyshalieva, note 95 above, p. 17.
98. Ibid.
99. Christopher B. Dyck, "Football and Post-War Reintegration: Exploring the Role of Sport in DDR Processes in Sierra Leone", *Third World Quarterly* 32(3), 2011, pp. 395–415.
100. Henry Olusegun Majaro-Majesty, "Ethnicity, Conflict and Peace-Building: Effects of European Football Support in Nigeria", *Soccer & Society* 12(2), 2011, pp. 201–211.
101. Dyck, note 99 above, p. 410.
102. UN Office on Sport for Development and Peace, "Annual Report 2011", UNOSDP, Geneva, 2012, www.un.org/wcm/webdav/site/sport/shared/sport/pdfs/Reports/UNOSDP_Annual-Report_2011_FINAL_web_single-pages.pdf.
103. Olga Dorokhina, Milan Hosta and Jacco van Sterkenburg, "Targeting Social Cohesion in Post-Conflict Societies through Sport", Good Practices Handbooks No. 1, Council of Europe, Strasbourg, July 2011, www.coe.int/t/dg4/epas/publications/Handbook-1_Sport-Post-Conflict-Societies.pdf. See also UN Office on Sport for Development and Peace, ibid.

104. Johnson et al., note 61 above, p. 164.
105. Interview with Atyrkul Alisheva, director of Institute for Regional Studies (Kyrgyzstan), 20 October 2012; Swiss Agency for Development and Cooperation, "Kyrgyzstan: Children and Women in Conflict Zone Receive Psychological Support", SDC, Bern, 20 September 2010, www.swiss-cooperation.admin.ch/uzbekistan/en/Home/News/News_Detail?itemID=195298.
106. See more in J. P. Singh, "Media and Peacebuilding", in Craig Zelitzer (ed.), *Integrated Peacebuilding. Innovative Approached to Transforming Conflict*, Boulder, CO: Westview Press, 2013, pp. 242–243.

2

The active role of children and young people in post-conflict peacebuilding

Claire O'Kane, Clare Feinstein and Annette Giertsen

> We think that children are the basis of a process for searching for peace and building it. What we wanted to achieve was to inform children and help them understand that there is a much better world, and that they can make it happen with specific actions.[1]

Introduction

Children and young people under the age of 18[2] have the potential to be agents of peace, contributing to peace in their families, schools, communities and nations. As described in a UNICEF (UN Children's Fund) report:

> the period following political violence or armed conflict presents both challenges and opportunities for children and youth. New patterns of violence may emerge that directly or indirectly affect children. Young people who feel marginalized by a peace process that failed to consult them may be a source of renewed violence and unrest. The importance of engaging children and young people in justice, reconciliation and peacebuilding efforts is clear.[3]

The importance of peace and its relevance to the creation of an environment which respects children's rights have been emphasized by young people in diverse locations, especially those living in post-conflict contexts.[4] Human rights abuses, including abuse of children's rights, are both

Escaping victimhood: Children, youth and post-conflict peacebuilding, Schnabel and Tabyshalieva (eds), United Nations University Press, 2013, ISBN 978-92-808-1211-4

a cause and a symptom of conflicts, and action to tackle them is often a vital component of policies and practices to secure sustained peace.[5]

This chapter explores girls' and boys' possible roles in and contributions to conflict resolution, peacebuilding and child rights in different contexts. It also illustrates the importance of the willingness of adults (parents, teachers, local and national government officials) to recognize, engage with and support children as active citizens and agents of peace.

Support for citizenship participation and good governance, including children's participation in peacebuilding and governance mechanisms, is imperative, as many post-conflict states are left in a state of fragile peace if the root causes of conflict are not effectively addressed. Understanding how children and young people experience conflict, post-conflict and peacebuilding is vital in interpreting short- and long-term consequences for their development. What happens to children in their early years significantly determines the way they grow and develop, and, in turn, their cost or contribution to society.[6] Similarly, recognizing children and young people as social and political actors and engaging them as active citizens with a focus on their abilities, suggestions and solutions are crucial to achieving longer-term peace and security. As quoted in a study by Jessica Lenz, a formerly abducted girl associated with a rebel group in northern Uganda noted:

> I can help bring peace in Northern Uganda if only my views are heard and acted upon. I don't hold a gun anymore; I hold the power of my voice. When visitors come to see us in the centres they normally ask us about our experiences and how we managed to escape ... But, they should also be asking us how we can participate in the peace process ourselves because we also fought in the war.[7]

This chapter primarily (but not exclusively) draws upon insights and findings from a two-year research and thematic evaluation on children's participation in armed conflict and post-conflict peacebuilding activities carried out by Save the Children Norway from 2006 to 2008 in Uganda, Guatemala, Nepal and Bosnia and Herzegovina.[8] Children and young people from existing child clubs, peace clubs and children's associations were actively involved in research and evaluation as advisers, peer researchers, respondents and documenters.[9] The chapter reflects on children and young people as agents of peace, their motivations to be engaged in peacebuilding and their contributions to conflict resolution and peacebuilding. It highlights how their contributions at local and community levels are important, especially in terms of their protection and the wider process of reconciliation. It also illustrates and advocates for increased recognition and inclusion of children's representatives in national-level peacebuilding and governance processes.

Recognizing the importance of the UN Convention on the Rights of the Child (CRC) and the responsibilities of different actors, the chapter also deals with gaps in and violations of children's rights by security actors at different levels, such as the police, military and international peacekeeping forces. It presents examples of ways to prevent and reduce such gaps and violations through child rights capacity building of concerned actors and strengthening of child rights and child protection mechanisms. The chapter emphasizes how support for children's rights and their participation in emergency and post-violent-conflict situations can enhance good governance and accountability to children, and contribute to a stronger civil society which is more assertive about children's rights. It also emphasizes the importance of ethical practice which helps to support inclusive participation and identify and minimize risks faced when children participate in peacebuilding.

Recognizing children as social actors and potential agents of peace

This section emphasizes the importance of recognizing children and young people as social actors – understanding and responding to the political and social reality of their lives.[10] Western concepts of childhood as a time of innocence, dependency and powerlessness need to be challenged if we are to find ways to divert children and young people from violent action to non-violent action for positive social change.[11]

While some children are forced into association with armed forces through violence, threats or abduction, or are compelled due to poverty, Lori Drummond-Mundal and Guy Cave stress how it must not be assumed that all children involved in armed conflict are manipulated by adults. In situations of violent conflict, faced by threats to their survival from which adults may not be able to protect them, children and young people may resort to a range of strategies, including engagement in political-military action.[12] Young people's role in the political change in the Middle East today is a vivid illustration of this. While some young people choose to engage in non-violent forms of action and social change, including the increasing use of social media for mobilization and awareness raising, others choose violent forms of protest.

In a further example Jason Hart describes how children in the Occupied Palestine Territories are "often willing participants in the national struggle. Their political consciousness is developed to an extent and from an age that commonly takes outsiders by surprise. They also display great awareness of their role, as children, in the effort to influence public opinion through the media."[13] Pamela Reynolds makes a similar observation in relation to children in South Africa choosing to take part in the struggle against apartheid – she stresses that they took "profoundly serious political and moral decisions in relation to their own safety and interests of their families".[14]

Children and young people may engage in a variety of other actions to protect themselves and their families, peers and communities; and they may choose to engage in non-violent peacebuilding and child rights initiatives to improve their communities and nations, especially if they are informed and aware of such opportunities.

There are many examples that illustrate how living through violent times has strengthened girls' and boys' aspirations for peace, as documented in this chapter.[15] In many contexts, particularly through child club group initiatives, children condemn violence and urge that it be replaced by peaceful and caring ways of resolving conflict. Some researchers have suggested that children and youth may have unique contributions to make to peacebuilding by virtue of their stage of development.[16] In the words of Kemper, the "transitional state [of youth] is regarded as valuable for initiating change at the grassroots level, which can, in turn, affect peace processes on higher levels".[17]

Also, as articulated by Lori Drummond-Mundal and Guy Cave, social and political inclusion of children, in particular youth, in conflict transformation and peacebuilding makes pragmatic and constructive sense. These young people may have experience and capacities that can work either for or against new social and political constructions. For peace to be sustainable, the adults of tomorrow need to feel a sense of ownership and responsibility for the creation and maintenance of a climate of peace.[18]

As highlighted in the Machel Study 10-Year Strategic Review:

> In many countries afflicted by armed conflict, engagement in public decision-making is denied to all citizens regardless of their age. Such exclusion can give rise to frustration – including among the young – that can ignite or further fuel conflict. The challenge is thus two-fold. First, to address the systems and structures that inhibit the full functioning of civil society; and second, to transform relationships between adults and children and among children and youth in order to open up avenues for all to be engaged as actors in civil society processes.[19]

Thus governments, UN agencies and civil society organizations need to increase opportunities to support children's role as active citizens and agents of peace.

There is growing awareness within the international community of the limited efforts made by governments to support the participation of children in peacebuilding processes, and of the need of promoting it. This is addressed by, among others, the UN Committee on the Rights of the Child:[20]

> There is a growing body of evidence of the significant contribution that children are able to make in conflict, post-conflict and reconstruction processes following emergencies. Thus, the Committee emphasised in its recommendations that children affected by emergencies should be encouraged and enabled to participate in analysing their situation and future prospects.

In continuation, the committee encourages "States parties to support mechanisms which enable children, in particular adolescents, to play an active part in both post-emergency, reconstruction and post-conflict resolution processes".[21] It suggests that:

> Their views should be elicited in the assessment, design, implementation, monitoring and evaluation of programmes. For example, children in refugee camps can be encouraged to contribute to their own safety and well-being through the establishment of children's forums. Support needs to be given to enable children to establish such forums, while ensuring that their operation is consistent with children's best interests and their right to protection from harmful experiences.[22]

Promoting a culture of peace

In 2001 UNESCO (the UN Educational, Scientific and Cultural Organization) declared the period 2001–2010 the International Decade for a Culture of Peace and Non-Violence for the Children of the World. As defined by the United Nations, the "Culture of Peace" is a set of values, attitudes, modes of behaviour and ways of life that reject violence and prevent conflicts by tackling their root causes to solve problems through dialogue and negotiation among individuals, groups and nations.[23] As described by children's representatives from conflict-affected countries who were participating in a global workshop about peace:

> Peace is life and survival. It is to live in our houses and sleep without being displaced. It is reflected in how we treat each other and how we work and live. It is to respect each other's silence and to listen to each other's song; to respect and realise that every single human being has got a worth. It is having social order and freedom of opinion; and having a government.[24]

Children's role in peacebuilding takes different forms in different socio-political, cultural, religious and geographic contexts. Their contributions also vary according to their age, interest, time availability and levels of support mobilized from their peers, parents, community members and other actors in civil society and the state government.[25] Young people can actively contribute to peace in a myriad of ways, such as by promoting peaceful relations in their own families, among their peers and community members; by promoting child rights; through rebuilding social relationships that contribute to a culture of peace; and by rebuilding social structures. Through their own child clubs, groups and/or associations in Uganda, Nepal, Guatemala and Bosnia and Herzegovina, which are supported by Save the Children and partner non-governmental organizations (NGOs) with training programmes on child rights and peacebuilding, children have regular space to meet together, share their views, plan and implement actions which increase realization of their rights, and participate in peace initiatives. Their peacebuilding efforts include:

- organizing children's meetings – how to live, relate to and respect each other, and protect themselves better
- preparing poems, songs, dance, drama, debates and (wall) magazines to sensitize peers, family, school and community members on child rights and peace
- using local and district-level radio programmes to raise awareness, spread messages and encourage dialogue on peace and child rights
- promoting conflict transformation, dialogue and peer advice, peer support, peer education and peer counselling
- encouraging all girls and boys to go to school and study (including children who were formerly associated with armed forces and children with disabilities)
- raising their voices to tackle discrimination, abuse, violence and corruption within school and community settings; and promoting children's participation in school governance, local governance and policy and practice developments to address issues which affect them.[26]

In some countries children have also participated in truth commissions, contributing to the restoration of justice.

Children's participation in truth commissions

As reported in a UNICEF study on children and truth commissions:

> The role of children in truth commissions has evolved gradually. In the 1980s and early 1990s, commissions in Chile, El Salvador and Haiti documented violations against children. Subsequent truth commissions in Guatemala (1997–1999) and South Africa (1995–2002) investigated and reported a substantially higher number of child and adolescent victims. The final report of Peru's truth commission (2001–2003) included a chapter on children, and the truth commission in Timor-Leste (2002–2005) had a chapter on children in its final report as well as a public hearing dedicated to children. The commission in Sierra Leone

> (2002–2004) was the first to explicitly mention children in its mandate and to recognize the rights and protection governing children's involvement. The Liberia commission (2005–2009) went further, systematically including children in its activities throughout the country.[27]

UNICEF reports how truth commissions "whose work is human rights-based can help provide accountability for violations against children and engage young people, offering a safe space for them to recount their experiences and contribute to community healing. Effective and mutually supportive participation and protection can help to break the cycle of violence and prevent future conflict and instability."[28] The UNICEF study also calls attention to the importance of addressing:

> different challenges faced by girls and boys, adolescents and younger children, refugee and internally displaced children, children recruited into armed forces and groups, children orphaned by war, children from different religious and ethnic backgrounds, and children with disabilities. When assessing the risks of child and adolescent participation in a truth commission, the potential risks of excluding young people from the process must also be considered. Furthermore, for their participation to be meaningful, children must have access to psychosocial assistance throughout the process, and provisions must be made for their physical safety and long-term community support.[29]

The Sierra Leone Truth and Reconciliation Commission (TRC) of 2002–2004 was the first to explicitly mention children in its mandate, in recognition of the serious impact the armed conflict had on children.[30] Furthermore:

> The commission decided that children would not be categorized as victims, witnesses or alleged perpetrators. Instead, all children would be treated by the commission only as victims and witnesses. Children participated in statement-taking and in closed and thematic hearings. With the help of child protection agencies, children prepared an official submission to the TRC and participated in preparing the first-ever child-friendly version of a truth commission report.[31]

Children promoting child rights and peace

Northern Uganda has been affected by conflict for over 20 years. As described in a Save the Children report:

> The conflict has resulted in: gross violations of human rights and children's rights – including killing; massive ongoing abductions of children, young people and adults to join the fighting forces; sexual abuse, exploitation and slavery – especially of girls who have been abducted and forced to "marry" commanders; and, forcing the abducted children to kill, maim, and injure civilians, including

> their own family members. Abduction of children from villages, and the wider conflict has resulted in massive population displacement into camps; the breakdown of infrastructure; dependence on food and other humanitarian supplies; a deteriorating education and health situation; loss of culture, and decreasing life expectancy.[32]

Formal peace talk processes were under way in 2006–2008 in Juba, southern Sudan, but despite the drafting of a peace agreement it was never signed and the talks broke down in 2008.

In Gulu district, one of the conflict-affected regions of northern Uganda, children's peace clubs and associations have been established within both primary and secondary schools and in communities. They involve children's representatives from different grades who are interested in promoting child rights and peace, and are supported by teachers who have received training on children's rights and participation from a child-focused international agency, such as Save the Children in Uganda (SCIU). These associations are community-based and tend to involve out-of-school children (including child mothers), as well as schoolchildren. They are supported by a facilitator from a local NGO and/or a child-focused international organization. Members are both girls and boys, including former child soldiers abducted by the Lord's Resistance Army (LRA). The children's peace clubs and associations use song, traditional dance, debates and radio programmes to create messages and action for peace. These child-led initiatives have meant a great deal to the members, as they allow them to share and reflect on experiences, and play an active role in getting their peace messages across to their communities and schools through creative drumming and artistic activities, with the help of a local radio programme.

Reconciliation and rebuilding of social relationships

Since 1995, also in Uganda's Gulu district, the local NGO Gulu Support the Children Organisation (GUSCO), in collaboration with SCIU and World Vision, has supported the rehabilitation and reintegration of released or rescued child soldiers. Save the Children and GUSCO have also supported the formation and strengthening of peace clubs and children's associations. Meaningful participation and space to come together with peers can give children strength and increase their life skills and self-confidence. Especially for children and young people whose rights have been violated during armed conflict, participation and association are part of a process that helps them promote their rights and fight for social justice.[33] As expressed by a formerly abducted child solider in northern Uganda:

> I stayed alone, with no parents. I used to think about the past. It was difficult to forget what happened to me in the bush. I felt alone. No-one wanted to stay with me, to share with me. I then joined an association and began to find peace within myself. My family came back to me. I have friends and I have learned from others. These days I am fine. I know what to do at the right time and right place.[34]

The association members support reintegration activities by helping to prepare families and communities to receive sons or daughters who had been abducted and released, or had been able to escape. One of the key messages was that the young people who return belong to the communities just like anybody else living there, and they had the right to live with their families. The contributions of the children's associations were important in convincing some family and community members that they should accept their children back, although they did not succeed in all circumstances. Some community members feared new attacks from the LRA rebel group to reclaim their soldiers if formerly abducted persons were accepted back into their communities. Young mothers who had returned with babies and small children fathered by LRA commanders have faced particular difficulty in reintegrating. Many of these young mothers felt that their only option was to leave their communities again due to the stigmatization and discrimination they have faced, based on community fears that the fathers of these children would soon join their wives and children in the villages and the children would grow up to become rebels themselves.

Keeping up the memory of the violent conflict

In Guatemala it was first and foremost the indigenous Mayan communities who suffered death, displacement, disappearances and torture during 36 years of internal armed conflict. Children suffered the same treatment as adults, as they were viewed as future guerrilla members by the militaries and paramilitaries.[35] Despite the fact that peace accords were signed in 1996 by the government and Unidad Revolucionaria Nacional Guatemalteca (Guatemalan National Revolutionary Unity), the current generation is still affected by the experiences of conflict. During the thematic research and evaluation process children and young people who were involved in children's groups supported by Save the Children Guatemala shared their concerns about the lack of teaching of recent history and the armed conflict in the public primary education curriculum. They felt it to be important to understand the history and causes of the conflict, as this would contribute to a better understanding of what is needed to secure a lasting peace. In local and national workshops they also emphasized the importance of "rebuilding memory" to ensure that the cultural identity and practices of indigenous groups, which were threatened and repressed during the periods of internal conflict, are remembered, valued and maintained.

Some young people from an organization participating in the evaluation had learnt the technique of mural painting, and decided to create a mural of the history of the violent conflict to ensure that its memory would not be lost. They prepared the painting in a municipality in the Department of Guatemala. As they were painting a young man came up and threatened them, arguing that the mural would generate feelings of fear and confrontation in the community. When the participants explained that they had secured permission from the school authorities and the neighbourhood committee, the young man reacted violently. A little later his father appeared and accused the young people of having attacked his son. He expressed his willingness to defend his community from those who kept alive the idea of the war. Accompanied by the neighbourhood committee, the young people were later able to go back and finish their painting, as they felt strongly about completing their peacebuilding work. In discussions with the neighbourhood committee the young people shared their concerns about gang violence and insecurity in the area, as well as the importance of their peacebuilding initiatives. The committee members shared similar concerns about local insecurity and violence, and stated their appreciation of the children's and young people's efforts in promoting peace. Based on this experience, the committee decided to engage in other peacebuilding initiatives with the young people.[36]

Searching for protection and rights – Networking among adults and children

> In Nepal, the conflict between the Government and Maoist rebels since 1995 has negatively impacted children and adults in communities, particularly in the period between 2001 and 2006. In October 2006 a peace agreement was reached and processes are underway to establish a federal government.[37]

Efforts to develop and finalize a constitution have been ongoing for more than five years. In February 2011 newly elected Prime Minister Jhalanath Khanal called upon competing political parties to cooperate in drafting a new constitution. However, changes in political leadership and conflicts between various groups have delayed its development.

There is a long history of support to child clubs in Nepal. Since the late 1980s child-focused agencies have supported the development of more than 12,000 clubs in the country, among them over 7,000 community-based and over 5,000 school-based clubs.[38] The clubs have been organized in rural as well as urban communities, providing a space for children to share their views and plan and undertake activities on issues affecting them. Children aged eight to 18 years join clubs whose sizes range from 15 to over 300 members. Some clubs have an explicit focus on child rights and peacebuilding, while others focus more on other issues, such as the environment.

Together with adult partners, including government officials, children have implemented the concept of "children as zones of peace" (CZOP) during the armed conflict.[39] CZOP is a movement that advocates children's basic rights to survival, development and protection, especially during conflict. Child-focused agencies and child clubs are involved in the campaign. CZOP has led to various initiatives, including the formation of a national coalition for CZOP; a public commitment by five major political parties to respect CZOP; the issuance of child protection guidelines for security forces by the Prime Minister's Office; and the announcement by the government that schools are also zones of peace.[40] Such initiatives were developed because Maoist rebels had been targeting schools and child clubs to organize propaganda programmes and lure students and teachers to their cause. At the community level children and child clubs have successfully negotiated with both warring parties (with Maoist leaders, and police or army officials) not to involve children, not to use or involve schools in the conflict, and not to interfere in the work of child clubs.[41]

One example illustrates how child club members in the Tanahun district of Nepal were able to use dialogue to negotiate with the Maoists to allow their initiatives to promote child rights to go ahead without negative disturbance. During a campaign on compulsory school enrolment organized by child clubs in Tanahun, in one community the club members had hung a banner with the name of the campaign – *Milijuli* (meaning in cooperation with each other) – in the middle of the village. After one day the Maoists took the banner away, as the child club had not informed them in advance about the campaign. The club members immediately held a children's meeting to discuss what to do. They decided to organize a tripartite meeting involving parents, the Maoist area commander and child club members. During the meeting the children explained how the school enrolment campaign was part of their child rights work, as education is a child's right. They negotiated with the Maoists and explained that 100 child clubs in the district were part of the campaign. The following day the Maoists put the banner back in the same place and promised they would cooperate in more positive ways in the future. This shows children's capacity for dialogue and negotiation when they receive support from their parents, teachers or people in their community.[42]

Institutionalizing protection for children

The CZOP initiative in Nepal involves coordination between government and civil society, including international NGOs and child clubs. These efforts to reduce and prevent violence also contribute to efforts by the government to establish comprehensive child protection systems (from community to district and national levels). Village child protection committees have been formed to identify and address issues at the local level.[43] Children's representatives from the child clubs are part of such committees. At the district level child club forums have been established to share information, undertake joint advocacy and elect representatives for district-level structures, including the district child welfare boards. Nationally, processes have been provided to give space for children's voices and children's rights to be heard and reflected in the development of the constitution.[44] Children's participation in the constitution development process started in 2007 at the village development committee and district levels, and culminated in a national children's conference, entitled "Children's Rights in the New Constitution: Children's Participation in the Constitution-making Process", in December 2007. The process was supported by UNICEF, Save the Children Alliance and other child rights partners as part of the Consortium of the Organizations Working for Child Participation and Child Clubs.[45]

During this national conference, which brought together child club representatives from 48 districts of Nepal, children discussed and developed a 12-point declaration based on recommendations and suggestions generated during consultation and discussions conducted at local and national levels. Their declaration covered issues concerning education, health facilities, child clubs, children as zones of peace, banning use of children by armed groups, protection of orphans, addressing gender discrimination, child marriage and trafficking of children, supporting the participation of children in all levels of planning and policy-making, and guaranteeing the participation of children in the constitution-making process by respecting children's right to participate.[46]

As shared by UNICEF:

> In 2008, prior to elections, the children's 12-point declaration was incorporated into the Children's Manifesto, targeting political parties. The manifesto sought to make the political parties aware of the situation of children in the country and need to give priority to children's issues. Lobbying with members of political parties was undertaken prior to the elections to build support for the Children's Manifesto and to ensure that children's issues were incorporated into their own election manifestos ... On 20 March 2008, representatives of political parties came together in Kathmandu for a unique event where they signed a

Joint Declaration of Commitment to Children, pledging to "ensure that the state will allocate resources to the maximum extent possible to meet the basic needs and fulfil the rights of children." Thirty-two political parties signed the commitment that day.[47]

Adults supporting children's peace initiatives

Adult support to children's contributions to peacebuilding and to the development and strengthening of their own initiatives is crucial. Children benefit from encouragement and practical support from their parents, teachers, community elders, NGOs and government, including security actors. As outlined in the examples above, adults can support the establishment and strengthening of structures such as children's peace clubs, child protection committees and CZOP. This support can take place at different levels. At the local level, adults from local NGOs, local government and schools, as well as community leaders, can facilitate children's groups and networks to meet together and develop peace initiatives. NGOs can provide children with practical resources (for example, basic funds for materials and transport), information (for example, a child-friendly version of relevant government policies or legislation) and skills training (for example, training on children's rights, life skills or conflict resolution). Links to media such as radio stations or news journalists can support the development and integration of child-led media initiatives (for example, radio programmes, newsletters or children's articles in mainstream newspapers) to increase dissemination of children's views and advocacy messages. One such initiative – the Children's Radio Manifesto[48] – builds on the understanding that radio can help transform conflict and support children's and young people's efforts as peacebuilders within their communities. Children's contributions and impact at local and community levels are very important, especially in terms of protection responses and reconciliation processes. As Nosworthy suggests:

> Civil society and local authorities will be the prime actors in recognising and responding to [young people's] protection needs. The notion of "local ownership", central to security sector governance, means encouraging pro-active engagement and dialogue, including with youth, in the identification and resolution of local security problems ... This engagement in local security agendas between young people, civil society and the local authorities can subsequently be directed and used in informing and influencing national security agendas in a meaningful way.[49]

Experience shows that children's peacebuilding initiatives first and foremost take place within local communities, or within the operational areas of an organization. For example, Save the Children (in country offices across Asia, Africa, Southeast Europe and the Middle East) and NGO partners support capacity building of children on child rights, protection and participation through workshops, the use of participatory tools and life skills, theatre for development, drama and advocacy. The children's representatives then go back to their clubs, schools and communities and share what they have learnt so that collective efforts can be strengthened. Broader initiatives to support children's role as active citizens in society, taking action on a range of issues that directly affect them, are supported by Save the Children and other child-focused agencies in diverse societies, not only countries characterized by conflict or post-conflict situations.[50] In several countries (Bangladesh, India, Cambodia, Serbia, Montenegro, Moldova and Peru) children and young people have submitted their own supplementary reports to the UN Committee on the Rights of the Child. However, the issues and concerns that affect young people most clearly manifest at the local level. Many of the examples shared above illustrate how children's more direct contributions to peace and to their own protection have mostly taken place in local projects and are rarely scaled up to the national level, generally due to a lack of political support from the concerned national authorities. This limits the impact of children's contributions in terms of political process, and should be seen as a missed opportunity in contributing to sustainable peace.

Children's contributions have to build on social relationships of mutual trust and respect at all levels – in families and communities, in schools and workplaces, and at district and regional levels. An example from Uganda of how children influenced Agenda 3 of the draft peace agreement shows what can be achieved when such trust and respect are in place.[51] During Save the Children Norway's thematic evaluation, a group of 20 young people were involved in initial consultations on justice and accountability in Gulu. Wider consultations with children and young people in the northern region of Uganda were then organized by several NGOs (including Concerned Parents Association, Trans-cultural Psychosocial Organization, SCIU and UNICEF) as a means of listening to their views and feeding these to key parties engaged in the Juba peace process. In September 2007 over 200 children and young people from peace clubs in four districts of northern Uganda and Teso region were invited by the organizing agencies[52] to take part in the consultations on Agenda 3 of the formal peace talks concerning reconciliation and accountability.[53] The outcomes of the consultations were presented to government representatives who were involved in the peace talks; these officials also met directly with children's representatives to gain further insight into their perspectives. In the emerging agreement there is a special section on children that includes the need to consider the experiences and concerns of all children; protect the dignity and security of children in any reconciliation proceedings; ensure children are not subject to criminal justice proceedings, yet are invited to participate in reconciliation processes; and facilitate children's participation in implementing the agreement.

This example shows how children can participate in national policy processes in a meaningful and authentic way, and how their views can contribute to a more comprehensive and inclusive agreement. It also demonstrates the need for children to be prepared, and for adults to facilitate children's documentation and research, include them in processes and meetings, be ready to listen to and recognize children's messages, and use decisive opportunities to include children.[54]

The challenge remains to ensure that government policy-makers and all security actors respond to requests from children to involve them in peace processes at every level, including the national level.

Adult civil society organizations can cooperate in identifying and providing the arrangements and conditions needed to enable children and young people to speak with decision-makers at various levels. They can find ways to build and strengthen children's and young people's groups at local, subnational and national levels so that regular or permanent cross-generational dialogue forums can be established between government agencies and groups of young people's representatives, which, in turn, can create ongoing national intergenerational dialogues. Such forums may take different forms. For example, in Nepal child club networks have their fixed representatives on village and district welfare committees, which allows them to influence planning and budgeting. In Nicaragua municipal child commissions offer the opportunity for representatives of children's associations to be involved in developing municipal policies on children. Among the most common demands expressed in these commissions are those related to rights to recreation, such as construction and expansion of parks and sport fields, improved quality in education and infrastructure improvements, such as requests to repair access roads to schools and school roofs, as well as improvements to drinking water and sanitation systems. Various countries, including Ethiopia, Zimbabwe and Mozambique, have established child parliaments giving young people opportunities to address priority issues to local and national authorities. While it may take some time before concrete outcomes are seen from such initiatives, some positive results have already emerged: for instance, in a national meeting children in Mozambique complained about the declining quality of education and managed to increase the required number of years of teacher training and limit the number of students per class. Children in Nicaragua took part in the validation of a citizenship participation strategy; as a result of their participation, school curricula, pedagogical approaches and methods were improved, with emphasis being placed on educational games, reflection and action research.[55] Through such representative structures, children's views can begin to influence more systematically the development of peace agreements, comprehensive peace plans and/or efforts to monitor and report back on progress made towards the implementation of such agreements or plans.

Understanding and responding to children's priorities and perspectives

Children have their own priorities

In situations of armed conflict and insecurity children may have been identified and acknowledged as victims, but increased efforts are needed by their communities, wider civil society, governments, security actors and the UN system to engage with them as social actors with their own views, perspectives and contributions. Girls' and boys' roles and contributions to their families, communities and nations are generally unrecognized by adults.[56] In efforts to protect children and families, or to make communities safe, security actors have neglected to take into account the different perspectives that children and young people have on security and priority issues of particular relevance to them. However, in the past 15 years the importance of engaging children as social actors and the need to understand and respond to the political and social reality of children's lives have been highlighted by a number of practitioners and academics.[57]

It is increasingly recognized that children have their own very valuable perspectives and priorities – which are often very different to those of adults.[58] For example, during a rapid assessment of child protection concerns in northern Uganda in 2006, carried out by SCIU, children living in camps for internally displaced persons (IDPs) expressed greater fear of abuse and harassment at the hands of the government army, which was supposed to protect them, than they did of the LRA rebel forces.[59] In 2002 and 2003 in post-Taliban Afghanistan, children explored dangers, risks and options for creating a safer environment in Kabul. They prioritized concerns over road safety, and subsequently received support in child-led initiatives to train traffic police and raise awareness of road safety among children.[60] In Sri Lanka and Zambia groups of children prioritized concerns over insecurity and domestic violence, which resulted from their parents' (mostly fathers') excessive use of alcohol. They subsequently lobbied for restrictions on the opening hours of bars.[61] Children tend to prioritize concerns and challenges grounded in their day-to-day reality over more distant fears or worries.

Capturing the perspectives of children

Listening to children, taking their views seriously and recognizing the various roles and responsibilities taken on by girls and boys (within their families, communities and in broader society) require a change in the way that most adults perceive and engage with children. Adults need to recognize the capacities and contributions that girls and boys (of different ages, abilities and backgrounds) can make, and be prepared to share information and engage with them in more constructive ways. During situations of violent conflict children may face increased risks, such as sexual harassment, abduction into armed forces and/or the danger of landmines. Some may be obliged to take on additional roles and responsibilities, such as economic responsibility for the family if the adult (usually male) head of the household is absent. In addition, as highlighted above, children may choose to be directly involved in various socio-political armed activities in their communities and broader society.

Genuine children's participation generally requires a commitment of time to a process in which girls and boys are given space at times that suit them to express their views on matters that concern them – first with their peers and then with adults (parents, teachers, government officials), who should treat them with respect and take them and their views seriously. When supported by adults, opportunities for children's participation abound. An example from Nepal illustrates how children have contributed to inclusiveness and non-discrimination in their community. Members of a child club noticed that some peers had either dropped out of school or were about to drop out because of family pressures to contribute to the family income. The club members offered educational support for homework and catching up with missed class work to help these children return to the grade in which they belonged. The members offered such support one hour ahead of the weekly child club meeting. When teachers in the community heard about this initiative, they proposed supporting the young people who assisted their peers by raising their teaching skills in a number of subjects. This is an example of children's capacity to care and take responsibility for each other, to find practical solutions and to take the initiative to address problems faced by them and their peers. It also shows how adults found ways to support children in their project without taking over and dominating the initiative as originally conceived by the children.[62]

A further example from Nicaragua illustrates how children have organized their participation at local and municipal levels in presidential and mayoral election campaigns. The initiative came from child groups, which began to map and assess the human rights situation in their village or neighbourhood. Based on that information, analyses were prepared at municipal or national levels and presented at open meetings with representatives from civil society, local authorities and the media. They specifically invited the mayoral and presidential candidates. The young people chaired the meetings and presented their analyses, culminating in two separate documents, one summarizing their personal commitment to the fulfilment of their rights in their communities and at the national level, while the second summarized the respective commitments required from the electoral candidates. The documents were read to the audience; the child representatives signed their document and invited the candidates to sign theirs. In this way the children managed to put their rights on the political agenda of at least some candidates, although it proved to be difficult to secure the attendance of the most important. This initiative was supported by a network of mayors who are trained in and committed to children's rights.[63]

Children's role in "keeping safe"

Providing children with a regular space to organize their own groups and initiatives can enhance their confidence and skills to identify, analyse and initiate action and advocacy initiatives around concerns affecting their security and protection. Through their collective initiatives children are also in a stronger position to negotiate with adults regarding any roles that are inappropriate to their age or damaging to their development.[64]

For example, girls in Nepal have identified unsafe places and sought support and protection from community leaders to create safer places in their neighbourhood and schools. This project was conceived by a group of girls from various ethnic backgrounds, with the support of adult facilitators from NGOs.[65] Initially the girls were supported to undertake surveys to map the places in their community that they felt were unsafe for them. The school, the road, public transport, the cinema and the public tap where they drew water on a daily basis were all found to be unsafe. The girls collected evidence of harassment and its impacts on them. They also received some training in facilitation, communication and leadership skills from the NGO facilitators. The girls developed recommendations to make these places safer and then used them to negotiate with key persons – such as the cinema manager – to improve safety in the spaces. They also provided psychosocial support to other girls who had suffered abuse or harassment to ensure they were not made to feel guilty or isolated. Such peer support was crucial in helping to rebuild self-esteem, confidence and morale. Building upon the success of this initial project, it was subsequently implemented through schools in other districts with the involvement of both boys and girls. Adult support groups, including guardians, teachers, locally elected officials and representatives of governmental and non-governmental organizations, have been formed in the project areas and in the schools to respond to children's concerns.[66]

In many different contexts creative participatory tools, such as risk mapping to understand where girls and boys feel safe and unsafe, and body mapping to explore children's experiences of conflict or post-conflict situations, can also be used to help children's perspectives to be shared and acted upon.[67] For example, risk mapping undertaken by a girls' representative from conflict-affected northern Uganda highlighted the dangers of walking to the well to collect water due to fears of abduction or landmines (see Figure 2.1).[68] In contrast, the girls felt safest in schools, as many children are present there, and are able to share their experiences and support each other.

The situation of children can be a sensitive indicator of change, and should be of direct interest to adults at all levels. For example, if children and their parents feel it is too unsafe to travel to and/or to remain in school, this may be an early warning sign of other security problems (such as risks of abduction, sexual harassment or the presence of landmines).

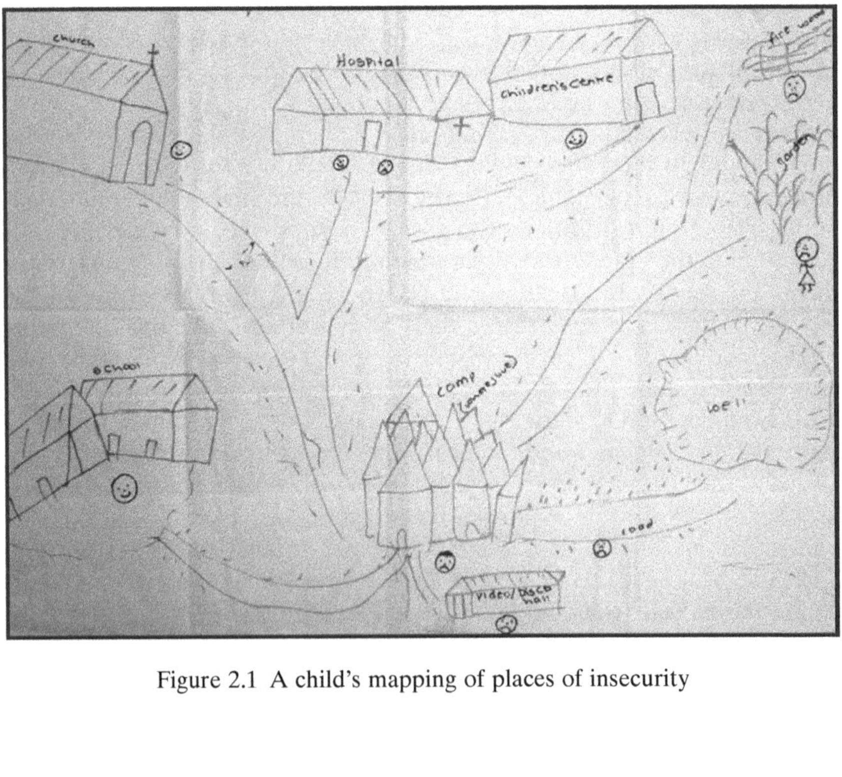

Figure 2.1 A child's mapping of places of insecurity

Ethical issues and challenges

In any participation process there are many ethical issues and challenges involved in working with children in participatory ways. Jason Hart and Bex Tyrer note how the "environment of armed conflict poses particular challenges for safe, ethically responsible research involving children".[69] They emphasize the importance of thorough preparation and the need to be aware of and anticipate possible risks beforehand – and to have strategies readily available to deal with them. Ethical issues can be better understood and addressed by listening and responding to the ideas of local people – both children and adults – that build on their understanding of the local socio-cultural and political contexts. In this way, strengthening local ownership of participatory initiatives contributes to ethical practice.

At the beginning of any process, a framework to ensure ethical, meaningful, inclusive and participatory practice with and for girls and boys should be established. For example, drawing on years of experience in supporting children's participation at local, national and global levels, in 2005 a global Save the Children working group developed practice standards in children's participation.[70] The primary purpose of these standards is to ensure consistent, high-quality child participation practice. They aim to provide a framework that gives guidance and direction first and foremost to field staff and partners in continuously improving their participatory practice.

These standards recognize unequal power relationships between adults and children. They ensure that issues reflecting or reinforcing child-adult power relations are addressed, for instance by ensuring that children have the space to express their own views without adults dominating, dictating or manipulating them. The practice standards encourage reflection on patterns of discrimination among children and young people (based on age, gender, disability, ethnicity, religion or income), and encourage efforts to ensure that non-discrimination is practised. The standards also ensure that child safety issues are dealt with appropriately and sensitively. This includes the careful consideration of potential risks of working with children in conflict situations and efforts to ensure that children are not harmed as a result of their participation, to the extent possible.

Child safety goes hand in hand with and is integral to the practice standards. The use of codes of conduct,[71] particularly when developed in consultation with girls and boys as well as their parents and guardians within the community, can help to identify behaviour and good practice to ensure that children's participation takes place within safe and respectful environments. Such codes of conduct should include procedures to protect children from risks and potential exploitation and abuse, as well as sensitive approaches in dealing properly and effectively with possible disclosures of harm or abuse. These include the need to identify in advance local organizations and/or individuals who have skills to provide psychosocial support to children who have faced traumatic experiences – particularly when working with those who live in insecure post-conflict environments. In all situations the principle of "the best interests of the child", defined by the children and their parents or guardians, should guide decisions as to what are and are not appropriate activities for children of different ages and abilities to engage in.

Ethical issues also relate to the mode of interaction with children: it is important that information is conveyed to them in an easily understandable, child-friendly manner, by applying participatory tools and using local forms of cultural expression such as poetry, drama and songs. This approach ensures that the full diversity and range of children's experiences can be captured.

Experiences of childhood are diverse and affected by gender, dis/-ability, level of family income, ethnicity, culture, geography, socio-political context and related factors. In addition, children's evolving capacities mean that the level and nature of participation of a five-year-old will be very different to that of a 17-year-old. Although the CRC refers to the importance of "due weight" (giving weight to the child's view in accordance with the age and maturity of the child), the views of a five-year-old on what makes her/him feel safe and unsafe are equally important to the views of an older child and can equally be elicited and acted upon.[72] The diversity of children's lives in armed conflict and post-conflict situations needs to be adequately explored and reflected in order to gain a better understanding of the experiences, reflections, views and aspirations of both boys and girls in different contexts, and ensure that even the most marginalized groups are supported to share their experiences and views. These most marginalized groups typically consist of those who suffer from discrimination, such as non-school-going children; those with different abilities or disabilities; those from poor families; refugee and internally displaced children and asylum seekers; children formerly associated with armed or military groups; those with minority background and unrecognized authorities; and children belonging to nomads and migrant families.

Additional efforts may be required to ensure equal opportunity for participation of marginalized children. Children in all settings (home, school, community, national processes) should be encouraged by adult facilitators, parents, teachers and government officials to reflect on who is included in, and excluded from, participatory peace initiatives.

A process of continuous reflection and action planning supports quality, ethical and inclusive child participation practice, whereby children's perspectives inform action planning at local levels (where impact may be more immediate for some children) and at national policy and practice levels. It also embraces wider accountability – preparing adults to acknowledge the capacities of children and to respond and act upon them.

Local NGOs and community groups are often in the best position to engage regularly with children and young people. They are better placed to support them in raising their issues with local authorities or security institutions. Local and international NGOs and the United Nations can also support opportunities for children's voices to be heard in peace processes and efforts to develop comprehensive plans of action to fulfil children's rights in peace agreements. This requires the establishment of child-friendly structures and processes for communication and dialogue between children and adult actors (including in particular government officials, UN representatives and civil society representatives).

Security actors responding to children's perspectives and experiences

The 1989 UN CRC is the most ratified convention in the world.[73] It outlines the responsibility of the state and other duty bearers, including a wide range of security institutions, to uphold children's rights to survival, protection, development and participation. According to the CRC, child rights are human rights, and apply to all children regardless of age, gender, race, colour, country of origin, religion, physical or mental dis/ability and socio-economic background. The CRC deals with principles (the right to life, non-discrimination, participation and decision-making in the best interests of the child) and how to put them into practice, by embracing all children regardless of the circumstances or societies in which they live. Children's rights, like human rights or women's rights, are a complete package and cannot be "cherry-picked" according to what is convenient, palatable or preferred in a particular situation. Each of the rights set out in the CRC interrelates to the others. Participation goes hand in hand with protection, development and survival. The full set of children's rights is equally applicable whether during times of violent conflict or in peace.

A range of security institutions, directly involved in conflict, post-conflict and peacebuilding, have roles and responsibilities to respect and protect children's rights. In their efforts to secure protection for all civilians and meet security governance benchmarks it is crucial that these actors give increased recognition to children and young people.[74] As children in Afghanistan remind us, their role as agents of peace can be best fostered when the younger generation are engaged, with a focus on their potential and their priorities:

> If you are involved in bringing security to Afghanistan, talk to us to hear why we feel afraid or why we feel safe in a place ... If you are involved in community development, make sure you listen to what we think our communities need. We look forward to contributing to a greater society, where adults and children work together and are respected by one another.[75]

Awareness-raising, training and capacity-building initiatives with different security actors are critical, as paradoxically the rights of the most marginalized groups of children living in insecure contexts, including internally displaced, refugee, street, working and trafficked children, are often violated by those security actors who are supposed to protect them – such as the military, police and border security guards. For instance, in government camps, squatter areas and relocation areas for IDPs in Khartoum, Sudan, the lives of children and their families are characterized by insecurity and marginalization, with gross violation and denial of their rights by state security actors. During an inter-agency situation assessment[76] in which focus group discussions and mind-map drawings were used to elicit children's views, girls and boys highlighted the manner in which their IDP families were subjected to regular raids, harassment, demolition and forced relocation by law enforcement agencies. Some older children, women and men were also arbitrarily arrested and unlawfully detained during the demolitions.

The implications that today's security actions can have for tomorrow's security situation need to be more clearly understood and given careful consideration, especially in terms of their impact on children. Demolition of shelters and forced relocations have had a detrimental impact on livelihoods, family integrity, and children's education and general well-being, interfering with their rights to life, dignity, liberty and security. The agencies involved in the Save the Children assessment are undertaking advocacy efforts with relevant government ministries to try to address children's concerns.

In understanding situations of armed conflict and insecurity from children's perspectives, and the role of security institutions in either perpetuating or mitigating violence, the significance of gang and gun cultures has been highlighted by children and young people in different parts of the world, particularly in South, Central and North America. A cycle of violence and insecurity is perpetuated by gang and gun culture, as children have to be tough in order to survive.[77] In Honduras a community-based model for the prevention of violence has been developed to support gang members' reintegration and rehabilitation in the city of San Pedro Sula.[78] Together with partner organizations, Save the Children UK has set out to address the lack of understanding and mechanisms to promote a positive community response to the gang phenomenon and support gang members who want to withdraw from their gangs. Awareness-raising is being undertaken with key actors – including the government, police, judiciary and the public – to support reintegration efforts and stop the killing of young people by police and security forces. Generation X, a youth-led organization, has been developed to enable peer support and give ex-gang members access to education, vocational training, employment opportunities and psychosocial support programmes. Training has also been provided for community police, which are a relatively new department of the Honduran Preventive Police.

Strengthening the role of the local police to protect children's rights and creating positive linkages between the police and child-focused community-level initiatives are required to improve security sector interventions – particularly in terms of harnessing children's perspectives on security and developing appropriate responses. Save the Children has been involved in triggering initiatives to establish child protection units (CPUs) in local police stations in Ethiopia and Kenya. These units are made up of specially trained police and social workers to deal with all cases involving children, as both victims and perpetrators. In this way, violations of children's rights are taken seriously and treated with respect. The CPUs are encouraged to develop strong links (and referral mechanisms) to local community-based structures, local and international NGOs and relevant government ministries.[79] They have been effective in ensuring appropriate responses to children's care and protection needs, particularly when working with those who have been in conflict with the law. In Kenya, better relationships between children and the police were reported – according to Martin and Parry-Williams:

> In the four CPUs, police officers treat children more humanely, pay more respect to their rights and opinions and provide better separate facilities for boys and girls. CPU officers wear civilian clothes, use friendly language, are more child-focused and do not assume children are criminals.[80]

Understanding and responding to the diversity of children's perspectives and experiences are a step towards addressing their specific needs and rights. Children living in armed conflict and post-conflict situations will have their own priorities. For example, during a global evaluation of children affected by armed conflict, displacement or disaster, the priorities identified by children included protection from abduction and being used as soldiers and sex slaves; protection from other forms of abuse, hunger and disease; the importance of access to education and health services at all times (even in the midst of conflict); peace and reconciliation; projects that build on children's self-esteem, provide hope and reduce stigma; support to families to relieve poverty and conflict; fair distribution of aid; and opportunities to participate in decisions affecting them and be heard.[81]

International military peacekeeping forces, UN observers and UN civilian police have an important mandate to monitor, prevent, report and respond to abuse and exploitation faced by girls and boys during conflict.[82] Protecting civilians is one of the most important tasks of peacekeeping forces. However, protection issues geared at children are often neglected. To address such neglect, training opportunities for armed peacekeepers, observers and civilian police on issues relating to children's rights have grown in recent years.[83] For example, training of military and peacekeeping forces on child rights and protection has been undertaken by Save the Children in Sweden and East and West Africa. As one soldier in southern Sudan noted, "Before we took part in the Save the Children Sweden's training programme we always referred to civilians as a single entity, without seeing children as a group in need of special protection."[84]

Some international NGOs have similar roles. In Uganda, Save the Children has signed a memorandum of understanding (2007) with the Ministry of Defence that spells out their respective roles. This includes the role of Save the Children as a "watchdog" to monitor the military *vis-à-vis* its role in protecting and respecting children's rights, and in supporting the training of the Ugandan military (Uganda People's Defence Force – UPDF).[85] SCIU has undertaken training on child rights, including the CRC optional protocol on the involvement of children in armed conflict, and child protection; it has trained hundreds of senior army officers and more than 10,000 soldiers from the local defence units. The overall aim of cooperation with the military has been to strengthen the UPDF's capacity to protect children, respect their rights and mainstream these rights into the policies and structures of the UPDF. The main achievements have included the establishment of a human rights desk within the UPDF structure at the national level and CPUs at local levels to respond in practical ways to child protection issues, including the needs of children abducted by rebel forces.

In terms of the "watchdog" role, SCIU and its NGO partner staff have been involved in monitoring cases of child rights violations by UPDF forces, especially at local levels. There have been instances in which SCIU has identified underage children employed as soldiers within the UPDF; here SCIU, in collaboration with UNICEF, has taken action to ensure that the young person is removed from the army. However, in general the task of monitoring and reporting is very sensitive, as local staff may be intimidated by UPDF soldiers. To ensure anonymity in reporting and responses from high-level management, reports by local staff are shared with the SCIU head office in Kampala, which reports directly to senior staff within the government. However, a lack of effective documentation of cases and fears of intimidation remain a challenge. In addition, accountability mechanisms in terms of how the government responds to and follows up on the reports need to be substantially strengthened.

At a global level, the UN Security Council has followed up advocacy recommendations to appoint child protection advisers (CPAs) in peacekeeping missions. CPAs operate in some of Africa's most war-affected countries, including Sierra Leone, the Democratic Republic of the Congo and Angola. The role of CPAs includes the provision of training for all mission personnel on child rights and protection, as explicitly requested by the Security Council, as well as systematic reporting on children's concerns in all country-specific reports to the Security Council. On issues related to children, the CPA serves also as a contact point and interlocutor between peacekeeping operations and UN country teams, NGOs working to protect children, national governments and civil society groups. S/he supports and complements their work on the ground, particularly as it relates to UNICEF.

In child rights terms, accountability to children and young people means that adult decision-makers take action that responds to children's concerns, priorities and recommendations about violence, security and peace. They also ensure the fulfilment of children's rights to protection, participation, development and survival. Adult duty bearers (including parents, teachers, civil society organizations, government officials, police, military, private security actors, UN officials, etc.) have responsibilities to protect children's rights. Increasing the opportunities available for listening to children, sharing information with them in accessible ways and providing feedback about how their views and recommendations have (or have not) been addressed are mechanisms that reflect this accountability.

In post-conflict societies such mechanisms need to be specifically identified and developed within the process of security sector reform to involve and sensitize security sector actors and strengthen their accountability towards children and young people. Adherence to international human rights treaties, including the CRC, must be integral to such efforts, as experience shows that children's needs and rights are not adequately considered. The development of clear reporting and complaints mechanisms is essential to ensure systems that may hold to account any security actor (private or state) who violates human rights or child rights standards.[86]

As illustrated earlier, the training of security institutions – the police, judiciary, border control officers, military groups and private security actors

– on children's rights, child protection, gender awareness and children's participation is very important. It helps to ensure recognition of children and enhances security sector actors' knowledge, skills and values about the fulfilment of children's rights and the importance of taking their views into consideration. Child-focused NGOs, local or international, can play an important role in providing such training and monitoring its impact. Advocacy to institutionalize children's rights within the training curricula for all military, police, border control and security guard personnel should continue so that such efforts are mainstreamed. Existing good practice mechanisms could be scaled up and expanded, including the appointment of CPAs in peacekeeping missions and the training of key security sector actors.

In addition to training security institutions and the appointment of CPAs, the establishment of child-friendly complaints procedures could contribute to accountability mechanisms – allowing child or adult civilians to report any complaints about violations of their rights by security actors, which would be systematically and sensitively followed up. The Third Optional Protocol to the CRC, on a complaints mechanism for violations of children's rights, can be crucial to this, as it will allow individual children to submit complaints regarding specific violations of their rights on the sale of children, child prostitution and child pornography and the involvement of children in armed conflict.[87]

In addition, the CPAs should undertake proactive efforts to ensure that the views and experiences of girls and boys are incorporated in reports of the UN special representatives and special rapporteurs, to be heard in the UN Security Council.

The development of comprehensive child protection systems, including the formation of child protection committees in communities and at district and national levels and the strengthening of their links with other more informal community-based child protection mechanisms, would also enhance holistic, sustainable efforts towards children's care, protection and participation. At each level young people should be supported to form their own groups and initiatives (including peace initiatives), so that girls and boys of different ages and backgrounds can identify and address key security and protection issues affecting them, and elect their own representatives to the protection committees at each level. In particular, children and young people can identify and ensure a response to protection, security and peace issues that affect them locally. A review of national legislation, policies and practice should be undertaken in order to build a more effective child protection system that, informed by children themselves, offers better protection of girls and boys and holds perpetrators of violence against children accountable.

Capacity-building initiatives with children and young people on life skills, conflict resolution, organizational development and peacebuilding could also be scaled up to support the strengthening of child-led organizations and initiatives. Child-led media initiatives and partnerships with mainstream media institutions (including radio, newspapers and television) can also be proactively supported to increase awareness raising with and by children and young people around their concerns and messages. Media can be a practical and powerful way to raise and amplify the voices of young people and help adults recognize children's capacities and potential as change agents. Increasing use of social media (Facebook, Twitter and other online and mobile phone communications) among young people also provides an important way for their voices, concerns and aspirations to be heard, and for them to share information and mobilize others to join their social cause to improve the society they live in. This merits further exploration and championing. Linkages and partnerships between children's groups and other civil society groups that engage in security, protection and peace initiatives (at local, subnational and national levels) should also be encouraged to exchange knowledge and strategies that promote and support young people's roles as agents of peace. As highlighted in this chapter, local civil society organizations are often best placed to support practical responses to children's priority concerns, especially when partnerships with local authorities have been established.

In addition, entry points for dialogue with both government and security providers should be explored and key interlocutors identified and engaged. Intergenerational dialogue forums between the government and groups of children's representatives should be established at local, district and national levels. These would allow children and young people to influence the development, implementation and monitoring of government policies and practices that affect their security, including peacebuilding activities and national action plans. In countries affected by armed conflict, good governance initiatives, including efforts to protect and empower children and young people as active citizens, are closely related to and may be pursued alongside other peacebuilding practices.

Concluding remarks

Although they are bearers of specific rights and represent a significant proportion of the population, in any society children and young people under the age of 18 years have little or no access to political processes. It is therefore incumbent on those in positions of authority to acknowledge and respond to the concerns of children and begin to transform relationships between adults and children. Only then can children and child-led groups be recognized and engaged as important civil society actors and contribute to governance processes at local, district and national levels. When children and young people are recognized as civil society actors, when they feel that their views are being listened to and taken into account, and when they feel their concerns and aspirations are being addressed, their full potential as active agents within society can be fulfilled.

Children's and young people's role as active citizens is relevant to all societies, including contexts characterized by conflict, instability, post-conflict or peace. There is increasing evidence – some of which has been presented in this chapter – to illustrate the enthusiasm with which children and young people are ready to take on responsibilities as active citizens. They use creativity and innovation to address issues affecting them, ranging from peace and protection to the environment and climate change.[88] Thus it is imperative that government, UN and civil society actors make systematic efforts to support children's role as active citizens.[89] These must involve creating genuine opportunities for children to inform, influence and monitor all peace-related initiatives and actions at local, national and global levels, including formal peacebuilding processes.

Acknowledgements

This chapter builds on an earlier version of this text, published as Claire O'Kane, Clare Feinstein and Annette Giertsen, "Children and Young People in Post-conflict Peacebuilding", in David Nosworthy (ed.), *Seen, But Not Heard: Placing Children and Youth on the Security Governance Agenda*, Münster: LIT, 2009. We would like to acknowledge contributions from Save the Children's Practice Exchange Network on children's participation and child protection in emergencies, as well as country teams participating in Save the Children Norway's thematic evaluation on Children's Participation in Armed Conflict, Post-Conflict and Peacebuilding in Guatemala, Uganda, Bosnia and Herzegovina and Nepal. We also appreciated information from Elizabeth Jareg, and useful feedback from Jo de Berry, David Nosworthy, reviewers and the editors.

Notes

1. Comment by children of the Asociación Cristiana de Jóvenes ACJ (Young People's Christian Association) in Guatemala City, quoted in Clare Feinstein and Claire O'Kane, "I Painted Peace: Handbook on Peace Building with and for Children and Young

People", Save the Children, Oslo, 2008, p. 4, http://tn.reddbarna.no/default.asp?HMFILE=130236.

2. The UN Convention on the Rights of the Child defines a child as under the age of 18 years. This chapter refers to children and young people under the age of 18.
3. UNICEF, "Children and Truth Commissions", UNICEF Innocenti Research Centre, Florence, 2010, p. 65, www.unicef-irc.org/publications/pdf/truth_commissions_eng.pdf.
4. Clare Feinstein and Claire O'Kane, "Adults' War and Young Generation's Peace: Children's Participation in Armed Conflict, Post Conflict and Peace Building", Save the Children, Oslo, 2008, http://tn.reddbarna.no/default.asp?HMFILE=130235.
5. Christine Bell, *Negotiating Justice? Human Rights and Peace Agreements*, Versoix: International Council on Human Rights Policy, 2006, p. 11.
6. Elizabeth Jareg, "Children in War and Peace", in "Building Peace Out of War", workshop report, Save the Children Norway, Oslo, 2005, attachment 1, p. 45, www.reddbarna.no/default.asp?HMFILE=42817.
7. Quoted in Jessica Lenz, "Armed with Resilience – A Study Addressing the Issues of Reintegration and Resiliency of Formerly Abducted Girl Child Soldiers in Northern Uganda and Their Potential Role as Peace Builders", MSc thesis, Centre for Development and Emergency Practice, Oxford Brookes University, 2004.
8. Feinstein and O'Kane, note 4 above.
9. Ibid.
10. See, for example, Jason Hart, *The Participation of Conflict-Affected Children in Humanitarian Action: Learning from Zones of Armed Conflict*, Oxford: University of Oxford Refugees Studies Centre, 2004; Jane Lowicki, "Untapped Potential: Adolescents Affected by Armed Conflict", Women's Commission for Refugee Women and Children, New York, 2000, www.unicef.org/emergencies/files/adolescents_armed_conflict.pdf; Yvonne Kemper, "Youth in War-to-Peace Transitions", Berghof Handbook for Conflict Transformation, Berghof Research Centre, Berlin, 2005, www.berghof-handbook.net; Jason Hart and Bex Tyrer, "Research with Children Living in Conflict Situations: Concept, Ethics and Methods", Refugee Studies Centre Working Paper Series No. 30, University of Oxford, 2006; Claire O'Kane, Clare Feinstein and Annette Giertsen, "Children and Young People in Post-Conflict Peacebuilding", in David Nosworthy (ed.), *Seen, But Not Heard: Placing Children and Youth on the Security Governance Agenda*, Münster: LIT, 2009, pp. 259–284.
11. Lori Drummond-Mundal and Guy Cave, "Children as 'the Seeds of Peace': Exploring Children's Potential Contribution to Conflict Transformation and Peacebuilding", unpublished paper, 2006, http://tn.reddbarna.no/default.asp?HMFILE=45723.
12. Hart and Tyrer, note 10 above.
13. Jason Hart, "Children's Participation in Humanitarian Action: Learning from Zones of Armed Conflict", document prepared for Canadian International Development Agency, Ottawa, February 2004, www.acdi-cida.gc.ca/inet/images.nsf/vLUImages/Childprotection/$file/E05.pdf.
14. Pamela Reynolds, "Activism, Politics and the Punishment of Children", in Geraldine Van Bueren (ed.), *Childhood Abused*, Basingstoke: Ashgate, 1998, p. 45.
15. Ibid.
16. Drummond-Mundal and Cave, note 11 above, quoted in Kemper, note 10 above.
17. Kemper, note 10 above, p. 43.
18. Drummond-Mundal and Cave, note 11 above.
19. Jason Hart and Claire O'Kane, "Children as Peace Makers", in *Children and Conflict in a Changing World*, Machel Study 10-Year Strategic Review, New York: UNICEF, 2009, p. 36.

20. Committee on the Rights of the Child, "General Comment No. 12", CRC/C/GC/12, New York, United Nations, 20 July 2009, p. 125.
21. Ibid., p. 126.
22. Ibid.
23. UN General Assembly Resolution, "Culture of Peace", UN Doc. A/RES/52/13, New York, 15 January 1998; UN General Assembly Resolution, "Declaration and Programme of Action on a Culture of Peace", UN Doc. A/RES/53/243, New York, 6 October 1999.
24. Quoted in Save the Children Norway, "Building Peace Out of War", workshop report, Save the Children Norway, Oslo, 2005, p. 6, www.reddbarna.no/default.asp?HMFILE=42817.
25. Feinstein and O'Kane, note 4 above.
26. Ibid.
27. UNICEF, note 3 above, p. x.
28. Ibid.
29. Ibid., p. xiii.
30. Ibid., p. x.
31. Ibid.
32. Clare Feinstein and Claire O'Kane, "Global Report – Adults' War and Young Generation's Peace: Children's Participation in Armed Conflict, Post Conflict and Peace Building", Save the Children Norway, Oslo, 2008, p. 66, http://tn.reddbarna.no/default.asp?HMFILE=130235.
33. See Maggie Brown, "Global Evaluation: Children Affected by Armed Conflict, Displacement or Disaster (CACD)", Save the Children Norway, Oslo, 2005; Claire O'Kane, "Children and Young People as Citizens: Partners for Social Change", Save the Children South and Central Asia, Kathmandu, 2003, www.savethechildren.net/nepal/citizens.html; Hart, note 10 above; Hart and Tyrer, note 10 above.
34. Drummond-Mundal and Cave, note 11 above.
35. Oficina de Derechos Humanos del Arzobispado de Guatemala, *Guatemala Nunca Más: I Impactos de la Violencia*, Guatemala: Archdiozese of Guatemala, 1998, p. 81.
36. Ubaldo Ruiz, "Evaluation of the Participation of Children in Armed Conflict, Post-Conflict and Peacebuilding, Country Report, Second Version", August, Save the Children Norway, Guatemala, 2008.
37. ARC, "Child-led Organisations and Adult-Child Partnerships: Case Studies", in Foundation Module 4: Participation and Inclusion, ARC Resource Pack 2009, ARC-ModF44H32009, p. 2, www.arc-online.org/modules/foundation/participationinclusion/pdfs/ARC-ModF4-4-H3-2009.pdf.
38. Kavita Ratna, "Child Clubs Strategic Review", PowerPoint presentation, Kathmandu, 10 January 2012 (shared with authors by Kavita Ratna).
39. ARC, note 37 above.
40. Save the Children Norway, note 24 above.
41. Ibid. This is in line with UN Security Council Resolution 1882, based on Resolution 1612.
42. Feinstein and O'Kane, note 4 above.
43. Clare Feinstein and Claire O'Kane developed the module on participation and inclusion for ARC. See www@arc-online.org and www.arc-online.org/modules/.../word/ARC-ModF4-4-H3-2009.doc.
44. UNICEF, "Nepal: Children's Manifesto (Innovation)", in "Evaluation and Lessons Learned", UNICEF, New York, 2008, www.unicef.org/evaluation/index_57404.html.
45. Ibid.
46. The authors thank a colleague at Save the Children Nepal for sharing this information.
47. UNICEF, note 44 above.

48. Copies of the Children's Radio Manifesto can be downloaded in French, English or Portuguese from the World Radio Forum, www.worldradioforum.org.
49. David Nosworthy, "Children's Security in Post-Conflict Peacebuilding: Discussion Paper – A Contribution to the 10-Year Review of the Machel Study", DCAF, Geneva, 2007.
50. O'Kane, note 33 above; Inter-Agency Working Group on Children's Participation, "Children as Active Citizens: A Policy and Programme Guide", Inter-Agency Working Group, Bangkok, 2008, www.unicef.org/eapro/Children_as_Active_Citizens_A4_book.pdf.
51. Concerned Parents Association, "Accountability & Reconciliation: Perspectives from Children and Youth in Northern & Eastern Uganda", Concerned Parents Association in association with Trans-cultural Psychosocial Organisation/SCIU/UNICEF, Kampala, 2007.
52. Ibid.
53. Ibid.
54. The authors thank Kato Nkimba for this assessment.
55. Save the Children Nicaragua, "Internal Annual Report to Save the Children Norway's Head Office", Save the Children, Oslo, 2011.
56. Gerison Lansdown, "The Evolving Capacities of the Child", Innocenti Insight 5/18, Save the Children/UNICEF, Florence, 2005; O'Kane, note 33 above.
57. Drummond-Mundal and Cave, note 11 above; Hart and Tyrer, note 10 above; Jo Boyden, "Childhood and the Policy Makers: A Comparative Perspective on the Globalisation of Childhood", in Alison James and Alan Prout (eds), *Constructing and Reconstructing Childhood: Contemporary Issues in the Sociological Study of Childhood*, London: Falmer Press, 1997, pp. 190–229; Gerison Lansdown, "Can You Hear Me? The Right of Young Children to Participate in Decisions Affecting Them", Working Paper 36, Bernard van Leer Foundation, The Hague, May 2005; Cairo Arafat and Neil Boothby, "A Psychosocial Assessment of Palestinian Children", Save the Children, Washington, DC, 2003, http://resourcecentre.savethechildren.se/content/library/documents/psychosocial-assessment-palestinian-children; Kemper, note 10 above; Claire O'Kane, "Supporting the Development of Children's Groups and Networks in Afghanistan: Reflections on Practice and Possibilities", *Children, Youth and Environments* 17(1), 2007, pp. 222–237, www.child-soldiers.org/psycho-social/Linked_Guyot_2007.pdf.
58. O'Kane, note 33 above; Lansdown, note 56 above.
59. Informal discussion between Save the Children assessment team members and one of the authors, autumn 2006.
60. Jo de Berry, "The Children of Kabul: Discussions with Afghan Families", Save the Children US, Kabul, 2003, p. 61.
61. Brown, note 33 above. Zambia case example shared by a Children's Christian Fund adviser with one of the authors, March 2007.
62. Chandrika Khatiwada, "Child Morning Class – Child Clubs Helping Community Children in Their Education", unpublished paper, 2004.
63. Authors' personal experiences.
64. Herman Ketel, "Proud to Work and Happy to be Organised: Working Children in West Africa and Their Participation in Their Own Movement", Save the Children Sweden, Stockholm, 2002; O'Kane, note 33 above.
65. Clare Feinstein and Claire O'Kane, "A Kit of Tools for Participatory Research and Evaluation with Children, Young People and Adults", Save the Children Norway, Oslo, 2008, http://tn.reddbarna.no/default.asp?V_ITEM_ID=19028.
66. International Save the Children Alliance, "Global Submission to the UN Study: Listen and Speak Out against Sexual Abuse of Girls and Boys", Save the Children Sweden,

Stockholm, 2005, www.rb.se/NR/rdonlyres/004E96E7-B0E0-4802-979F-5A9FFC1457CD/0/UNStudyonViolenceAlliance_executivesummary.pdf.

67. Feinstein and O'Kane, note 4 above.
68. Ibid. The risk map is reproduced in this chapter with permission of the young person representative.
69. Hart and Tyrer, note 10 above, p. 18.
70. Save the Children, "Practice Standards in Children's Participation", Save the Children UK, London, 2005.
71. See, for example, Save the Children, "Code of Conduct for Save the Children Staff", Save the Children UK, London, 2005.
72. See Judy Miller, "Never Too Young: How Children Can Take Responsibility and Make Decisions", Save the Children UK, London, 1997; Alison Clark, "Spaces to Play: Gathering the Perspectives of Young Children", Thomas Coram Research Unit, Institute of Education, London, 2006; Lansdown, note 56 above.
73. The CRC has been ratified by all countries in the world except the United States, Somalia and South Sudan.
74. OECD, *The DAC Guidelines: Helping Prevent Violent Conflict*, Paris: OECD, 2001.
75. Extract from "Children's Declaration: Northern Gathering of Children's Group Representatives", Save the Children, Afghanistan, August 2004, unpublished. Claire O'Kane was one of the facilitators.
76. Save the Children UK, "Interagency Situation Analysis of Child Protection and Education in Jabal-Awlia IDP Camp, Fateh-el Moubin 3 New IDP Relocation Area, Soba Arradi and Shigla Haj Yusuf Squatter Areas", Save the Children UK, Sudan, 24 October–6 December 2005.
77. Florence Martin and John Parry-Williams, "The Right Not to Lose Hope: Children in Conflict with the Law. A Policy Analysis and Examples of Good Practice. A Contribution to the UN Study on Violence against Children from the International Save the Children Alliance", Save the Children, London, 2003.
78. Ibid.
79. Ibid.
80. Ibid.
81. Brown, note 33 above.
82. Since 2000 peacekeepers have had a mandate concerning human rights and child protection. See Security Council Resolution 1291 (2000).
83. Save the Children Sweden, "Training Peacekeepers and Military Forces in Child Rights and Protection", Save the Children Sweden, Stockholm, 2004.
84. Ibid., p. 4.
85. Information received by e-mail from Save the Children Denmark colleague Lene Steffen, May 2007.
86. The increasing privatization of security services by government agencies could further complicate the process of ensuring accountability. It can be foreseen that responsibility for some security actions becomes diluted between the contracting party and the security service. In situations of vagueness and confusion of responsibility for actions, more time, efforts and resources will be needed to sort out such issues, and the possibility of identifying accountability may get lost.
87. The Third Optional Protocol to the CRC, which was adopted on 19 December 2011 by the UN General Assembly, opened for signature on 28 February 2012 in Geneva, where states were able to sign and ratify the new protocol. It allows individual children to submit complaints regarding specific violations of their rights under the CRC and its first two optional protocols on the sale of children, child prostitution and child pornography, and on the involvement of children in armed conflict. It is the only complaint mecha-

nism covering the full range of rights guaranteed under the CRC, and should significantly contribute to empowering victims whose rights have been violated in seeking remedies. By ratifying the new protocol, states provide a crucial contribution to complement measures for respecting and protecting the rights of the child worldwide.

88. See Roger Hart, *Children's Participation: The Theory and Practice of Involving Young Citizens in Community Development and Environmental Care*, London: Earthscan, 1997; International Institute for Child Rights and Development, *Children as Partners: Children's Participation Promoting Social Change*, Victoria, BC: IICRD, 2004; O'Kane, note 33 above.
89. See Inter-Agency Working Group on Children's Participation, note 50 above.

Part II

The scars of armed conflict – Children and youth as actors and victims

3

Children and youth in conflict and post-conflict societies: From plights of war to paths of peacebuilding

Kathleen Kostelny and Michael Wessells

Contemporary armed conflicts, which are fought mostly within state boundaries by rival ethnic groups, have ravaged human rights, divided societies and created systems of violence in families, communities and societies. Over 40 per cent of armed conflicts last 10 or more years.[1] The challenges to peacebuilding in these contexts are enormous and entail a constellation of interrelated political, social, economic and psychological changes. In short, peacebuilding requires the conversion of systems of violence into cultures of peace.[2]

Children's issues are intimately connected with issues of peacebuilding. Defined in international law as people under 18 years of age, children are a key part of the human capital in any society and typically comprise half the population in war-torn countries. Contemporary conflicts damage this precious source of human capital by subjecting large numbers of children to attack, displacement, loss of parents and homes, landmines and sexual violence. Women also suffer extensively, and this negatively impacts children, whose well-being is inseparable from that of their mothers and other caregivers. Damage to human capital adds to the resource scarcity, instability and desperation that enable armed conflict.[3] Growing up amid normalized violence, many children learn values, competencies and behaviour patterns related to violence. Some become combatants who are willing to continue cycles of violence and have few skills relevant to civilian life, tolerance or peace.[4]

Important opportunities for peacebuilding are lost through the socialization of children into systems of violence. By nature, peacebuilding is a

Escaping victimhood: Children, youth and post-conflict peacebuilding, Schnabel and Tabyshalieva (eds), United Nations University Press, 2013, ISBN 978-92-808-1211-4

long-term process that requires commitment of the energy, creativity and vision of rising generations. In contrast to traditional views of children as innocents, victims or vulnerable, a growing literature attests to children's agency and their potential and impact as actors.[5] Teenagers in particular have enormous capacity to do good or harm in their society. A key challenge of peacebuilding, then, is to create life pathways that engage young people in activities that contribute to peace.

The purpose of this chapter is to analyse the plight of children in societies torn by armed conflict and examine options that engage young people as constructive contributors to peacebuilding. Drawing on both the scholarly literature from a social ecological framework and the authors' field experiences, the chapter has three sections. The first outlines how changes in the nature of armed conflict have created a holistic threat to children's well-being. The second section situates children's plight in an ecological perspective that links their well-being to that of mothers, families and communities. Analysing children's situation in terms of risk, vulnerability and resilience, it cautions against simplistic portrayals of traumatized populations –rather, war-affected children are survivors who exhibit considerable resilience and have a variety of coping resources and strategies. The third section focuses on youth, examining their role and impact as actors in contemporary conflict and post-conflict situations. It shows that youth are influential as both soldiers and peacemakers, and are powerful agents of social change. From this perspective, a key challenge of peacebuilding is to build the values, competencies and life options that will enable youth to participate fully as peacemakers.

The holistic threat to children

Contemporary armed conflicts are often lethal to children, as much of the fighting occurs in and around communities. Civilians are often targeted directly in struggles between warlords or government armies and armed opposition groups. Although accurate quantitative data are sparse, it is estimated that during the 1990s armed conflicts claimed the lives of over 2 million children.[6] Even after a ceasefire has been signed, significant dangers to children continue owing to shortages of food and other basic materials. Also, the term "post-conflict" belies the reality that waves of political violence are typically followed by waves of banditry and criminal violence, thereby blurring the lines between war and peace and creating situations harmful to children. This harm extends far beyond physical damage to include emotional wounds, damage to social and cultural systems and lost opportunities for having a positive childhood experience. Further, these effects interact: the effects of physical harm and social harm cannot be understood in isolation but must be viewed in a dynamic, interactional perspective.

The UN Convention on the Rights of the Child (CRC) is a useful framework for analysing the holistic threat to children (see also Chapter 5 in this volume). The CRC promotes four basic categories of children's rights. Survival rights include the right to life and to fulfilment of basic needs for food, shelter, healthcare and other necessities. Protection rights provide safeguards against diverse forms of abuse, neglect and exploitation, including the various forms of exploitation that typically arise in war zones. Development rights provide for children's positive development by guaranteeing the right to education, play, cultural activities and identity, and freedom of religion, among others. Participation rights enable a positive, participatory role in community life through freedom to express one's views, join associations and have a voice in matters affecting one's life. A thorough analysis of the ways in which armed conflict shatters children's rights is the 1996 global study "Impact of Armed Conflict on Children", led by Graça Machel. The following subsections draw on this landmark study and its 10-year strategic review.[7]

Health and nutrition

Although large numbers of children are injured or killed by bullets, shrapnel and landmines, the greatest toll on their physical well-being comes from food insecurity, inadequate nutrition and damage to infrastructure such as roads, sanitation systems and healthcare facilities. Rising malnutrition heightens disease susceptibility, enabling the spread of diarrhoeal problems and preventable diseases such as measles, tuberculosis, malaria and acute respiratory infections. In addition, deficiencies of micronutrients such as vitamin A lead to high rates of child blindness, while mental retardation is attributable to deficiencies of iodine. Chronic war zones such as Iraq and the Democratic Republic of the Congo have high rates of infant and under-five mortality, and survivors' quality of life is often reduced by hunger, illness and inadequate healthcare.

Children's health is also undermined by environmental damage. Environmental damage erodes the overall quality of life, reduces the abundance of necessities such as food and clean water, leads many children to walk long distances daily in search of firewood and makes communities increasingly susceptible to catastrophes from drought, floods or landslides.

HIV/AIDS

Armed conflict and HIV/AIDS intertwine in a deadly cycle. Conflict often contributes to the spread of HIV/AIDS, as soldiers – many of whom have sexually transmitted infections – exploit young women through either forced sex or demands for sex in exchange for gifts or money. The resulting spread of HIV/AIDS, which occurs most rapidly among people between the ages of 10 and 24 years, leads to the birth of children who themselves carry the disease or acquire it through breast-feeding from an HIV-positive mother. As of 2011, 3.3 million children under the age of 15 were living with HIV. Moreover, 230,000 children under 18 years of age had died in 2011 alone of HIV/AIDS-related illnesses.[8]

In addition, 17.3 million children had lost one or both parents to AIDS.[9] Many children, watching their parents die, carry enormous emotional burdens as well as the responsibilities of caring for the dying. Following their parents' deaths, children are at increased risk of becoming heads of households, face increasingly difficult economic circumstances and may have to drop out of school or work long hours, often in dangerous jobs. Horribly, the spread of HIV/AIDS amplifies conflict by destabilizing communities, killing large numbers of productive people and increasing poverty, which is among the root causes of armed conflict.[10]

Displacement

Armed conflict displaces masses of people, many of whom have seen their homes, properties and livelihoods destroyed. Worldwide there were an estimated 37 million displaced people in 2011, approximately half of whom were children.[11] Those who cross an international border to seek asylum often become refugees, who typically suffer lack of basic materials and cultural identity, discrimination, alienation and difficulties earning a livelihood and negotiating the complexities of their new social system.[12] Refugee camps, where living conditions are very difficult, often become hotbeds of radicalism that help fuel continued armed conflict. In the Afghan war, for example, which at its peak created nearly 6 million refugees, the camps in Pakistan became frequent sources for Taliban recruitment of young people as soldiers.[13]

In addition, armed conflicts displace large numbers of people who stay within the borders of their country. These internally displaced persons (IDPs) often live in or near zones of active fighting and face daily insecurity. For example, the 40-year-old war in Angola had by 2001 displaced nearly one-third of the population, significant numbers of whom were terrorized by the opposition group, UNITA (União Nacional para a Independência Total de Angola, or National Union for the Total Independence of Angola).[14] Many people live in camps or settlement areas that lack adequate sanitation, shelter, healthcare, food and education. Particularly during flight, displaced children face increased risks of many kinds, such as separation from parents, abduction, sexual violence and exposure to landmines.

Landmines and unexploded ordnance

In approximately 80 countries children face the ongoing threat of uncleared landmines and unexploded ordnance such as bombs, shells or grenades. Afghanistan, which is believed to have millions of landmines, provides a portrait of the damage done to children. During the mujahidin era, the former Soviet Union dropped from the air "butterfly" landmines that looked like toys and invited children to pick them up. In the fighting between the Northern Alliance and Taliban forces, both sides implanted large numbers of new landmines, resulting in 5–10 casualties per day in 1999.[15] Many of the casualties were children who had tended animals or played in mined areas, and are now amputees who must deal with disability, stigma and reduced economic and social opportunities.

Child soldiers

Worldwide, government forces, opposition groups, warlords and other groups use large numbers of children, both girls and boys, as soldiers.[16] In some conflicts girls comprise up to 40 per cent of the child soldiers.[17] Most child soldiers are teenagers, although children as young as six or seven years of age have been reported. In the military, children may perform roles such as porters, cooks, spies and combatants. Typically, girls are given as "wives" to male soldiers, serving as sex slaves. Even after the conflict, the girls and their children suffer an enormous burden of stigma and isolation.[18]

Sexual violence, exploitation and trafficking

In conflicts such as those in the former Yugoslavia, mass rape has been used as an instrument of terror. In conservative societies, this practice can lead to women being seen as damaged goods and having dishonoured the family. During and following armed conflict, children are at heightened risk of sexual exploitation. The entry of peacekeepers into an area frequently spawns a cottage industry of prostitution, as poverty drives girls to take desperate measures to feed their families. In IDP camps sex often becomes a way for girls and boys to obtain food, plastic sheeting and other needed items.

Girls and women are often damaged through structural violence such as gendered inequities in healthcare that lead to inadequate access to maternal and child health services, thereby causing high rates of maternal mortality. Increased poverty leads families to marry off daughters at progressively younger ages as a means of obtaining a bride price. Marriage of young girls, however, often leads to higher rates of spousal abuse of girls and increased risk of health problems during pregnancy and childbirth.

Worldwide, sex trafficking of young girls and boys is a significant problem. Conflict zones are a major source of sex trafficking, as children are abducted and sold as wives or forced into prostitution.[19]

Education

Armed conflict destroys schools and disrupts the education that is every child's right and is necessary for building the human capital of societies. During conflicts, large amounts of money are poured into military pursuits rather than civilian services such as education. In post-conflict situations, poverty and decreased government capacities often make it difficult for governments to rebuild schools or pay teachers. Families may be unable to afford to send their children to school; and many children have to work in order to feed themselves or help support their families. Gender inequities in education also exist. In refugee camps globally, nine girls are enrolled in primary school for every 10 boys.[20] In many societies, girls are not allowed to walk the long distances required to reach school.

Psychosocial effects

In conflict and post-conflict environments, nearly all children are affected emotionally and socially.[21] Losses of family members, home and belongings can produce trauma, fear, anxiety, depression and other reactions that leave emotional wounds or create feelings of being overwhelmed. In addition, war often changes children's social and economic status, moving families from high status and relative economic security to living on the margins in abject poverty. Multiple losses and lack of positive options can lead adolescents to feel depressed, hopeless or pessimistic about their future. Displaced children often live in camps lacking the adult supervision, support and routines that aid protection and emotional well-being. After a ceasefire, economic stresses may boost levels of family violence, which often produces some of the worst outcomes for children. Moreover, everyday distress, such as discrimination and humiliation, continues post-conflict and can have significant psychosocial effects.[22]

Although children are affected by war and violence, it is important to resist the temptation to impose Western labels such as post-traumatic stress disorder.[23] Local people in non-Western societies have their own idioms of illness and health that constitute the lens through which they interpret their experience. These indigenous idioms, which typically integrate psychological stresses with physical ailments and material losses and hardships such as poverty, may provide greater insight into local people's reactions and modes of coping.[24] Not uncommonly, children report that some of their greatest stresses are spiritual, stemming from problems such as having been unable to conduct a culturally appropriate burial for dead relatives. In this respect, the plight of children should not be universalized excessively, as cultural particularities and meanings must be taken into account. In addition, it can be stigmatizing to label children as "traumatized" or imply that they are a "lost generation". As discussed in the next section, children exhibit considerable resilience, making it advisable to focus not only on their deficits but also on their resources.

Risk, resilience and vulnerability

War zones expose children to a mixture of discrete stressors such as attack and chronic stressors such as poverty. These stressors comprise risk factors that can have adverse emotional, social, spiritual or physical impacts. Because of the urgency of meeting basic needs in emergency situations, attention is usually focused on physical risk factors such as illness, lack of shelter or danger of attack. In fact, however, children are also affected powerfully by emotional and social risk factors. A child who witnessed his parents being killed is at risk of emotional damage, as is a child who has been raped. A very poor teenage mother who wonders whether she will obtain sufficient food to feed her family faces profound emotional uncertainties and also the social burdens of being unable to care adequately for her children.

Risk accumulation and protective factors

Because war zones present multiple risks to children, their situation cannot be understood in terms of single events such as displacement or attack. A useful way to conceptualize their plight is a risk accumulation model, which asserts that as risks accumulate, the likelihood of damage to children increases.[25]

The damage may be physical, as health risks such as malnutrition, infection by a dangerous disease and lack of access to healthcare accumulate. Damage may also be emotional or behavioural. For example, a child who had lost a parent, seen his home destroyed and been sexually exploited would be more likely to exhibit greater emotional problems or difficulties learning in school than would a child who had encountered fewer risk factors. A key point is that damage to children increases exponentially as risk factors accumulate. The accumulation of three or more risks can produce 10 times as much damage or negative outcome than results from the presence of a single risk factor.[26]

Fortunately, risk accumulation is only part of the story of children's lives in war zones. Even under the worst conditions, many children continue to play, relate well to others and function in ways suited to their culture and situation. In this respect, children exhibit resilience: the ability to adapt and function effectively in the face of adversity. To say that children are resilient is not to imply they are unaffected, but rather that they have coped effectively with their experiences. For example, a girl whose parents have been killed but who lives with extended family and functions well is said to exhibit resilience, although she still may carry emotional burdens from the loss of her parents.

Children's resilience has individual, social and cultural sources.[27] Children exhibit significant individual variation in temperament, as some readily tolerate and adapt to changes in their environment. In addition, children learn coping skills and strategies that enable them to adapt and manage adversity. Children who are upset may seek time with friends or immerse themselves in play or work that helps them avoid fixation on painful memories. Similarly, children who are hungry may learn to do small jobs that help them secure some extra food. Or a child who had lost a parent but had not conducted the necessary burial ritual might seek support from a local healer or spiritual leader who could conduct a ritual that would help to restore spiritual harmony. Every community contains local supports and sources of resilience for children. These might include informal networks of women, youth groups and religious organizations. These coping skills and strategies and social support can be thought of as protective factors, as they protect children against the adverse effects of risk accumulation.

In addition, cultural and spiritual support often enhances protection and resilience. Each culture creates traditions, rhythms of life and normal daily practices that confer a sense of meaning and continuity in life. The practice of traditions in difficult situations can offer strong emotional and spiritual support. In Angola, for example, conducting a burial ritual for one's parents can reduce anxiety and restore a sense of spiritual harmony.[28] Children and adults in developing societies frequently turn to traditional healers and local herbalists for support during a crisis. Religious beliefs and practices also increase resilience in many societies. In Afghanistan, for example, youth say that their Islamic faith gave them comfort in times of great stress and they often go to local mullahs for support.[29]

In conflict zones, then, children's well-being and level of resilience depend on the balance of risks and protective factors.[30] From this standpoint, it is an oversimplification to portray all displaced children as either traumatized or resilient. Two children who experience similar events such as attack or displacement may react very differently. If a displaced child is in the care of a competent mother or caretaker, then the child might function relatively well, exhibit resilience and not be in immediate danger. In contrast, a displaced child who is separated from her parents and not in the care of a supportive, protective adult might function much less well, show less resilience and ability to cope effectively with her circumstances, and be in danger of abduction, sexual exploitation and further risk accumulation.

How children react to stressful events depends also on their interpretations of what they have experienced. The meanings they assign to the events are culturally scripted. For example, a girl who had been raped in a highly conservative Islamic society might have catastrophic interpretations of the situation as having ruined her chances for marriage and a normal life, and having relegated her to a state of family dishonour and rejection. Viewing herself as "damaged goods", she might consider suicide as her only option. In contrast, a raped girl from a less conservative society might not have such catastrophic interpretations of her situation and may not consider suicide as the sole option. As this example illustrates, exposure to traumatic, life-threatening events does not produce a universal reaction. All people living in war zones may be affected by the displacement, poverty and family violence that typically flourish in such environments, but it is an oversimplification to think that such events inevitably produce trauma and extreme reactions. Analyses of children's plight in war zones need to move beyond universalized stereotypes and take into account the importance of individual differences, social situations and support, and culturally constructed meanings.

Sources of vulnerability

Although children's level of resilience depends on the balance of risks and protective factors, there are particular sources of vulnerability that simultaneously increase risks to children yet usually offer few protective factors to offset the risks. An important point is that exposure to particular sources of vulnerability does not automatically translate into harm to children. In fact, some children may do quite well even following exposure to a major source of vulnerability if they have offsetting protective factors. This is why there is a trend away from talking about "vulnerable groups" of children, which can mislead one into thinking that all children within a category are equally vulnerable. In most conflicts, the following factors are particularly potent in boosting children's vulnerability.

Displacement

During flight, displacement increases children's risk of exposure to landmines, attack, abduction, recruitment and poor health and nutrition, among other ills. Even following flight, displaced children often experience fear, anxiety and uncertainties about the well-being of friends and extended family members. Many have traumatic memories of having seen their homes and communities destroyed. Moreover, they are often in the care of parents or adults who are not in a good position to provide quality emotional support to children as they themselves have been affected by their experiences and are often overwhelmed trying to meet basic needs for their families.

Separation

Family separation leaves children not in the care of their parents, thereby depriving them of a crucial source of protection, particularly the protection usually provided by a mother. Separation often stems from poverty. For example, single parents such as war widows may be unable to feed all their children, some of whom may subsequently be forced to leave home. Separated children include orphans, who may be placed in orphanages which typically are overcrowded and cannot provide adequately for children's healthy development. Not uncommonly, separated children live with extended families in the care of relatives such as aunts or uncles, who by custom may be very important figures in the lives of most children. If, however, extended families are too poor to take in additional children, the separated child may have no option besides local institutions or the streets. Children may live and sleep on the streets by necessity or by choice; either way, they are subject to exploitation such as abduction for sexual trafficking. Still other separated children are in prisons, as many countries lack legal constraints against the imprisonment of even young children or have few options for handling children in conflict with the law.

Disability

In addition to physical challenges, disabled children face issues of loss, disfigurement, social isolation and, in many societies, stigmatization. Child landmine victims often lack access to quality medical care, and amputees may not have access to prosthetics, physical rehabilitation and psychosocial support. In some societies disabilities are viewed as a family or community dishonour, leading families to keep disabled children locked away at home. Disabled girls may have few or no options for marriage. Many disabled children do not participate in school and, lacking vocational skills or opportunities, face a life of poverty and poor social integration.

Child labour

Caught in a downward spiral of poverty, families often rely on children to work to feed themselves or boost family income. Children may be exposed to hazardous work that can produce long-term damage. Even non-hazardous labour keeps children out of school, prevents the development of appropriate competencies and robs them of their childhood. Labour is also a source of family separation, as very poor families may send their children to live with and work for wealthier families. Since these children often become invisible, they may be subject to sexual abuse and other kinds of exploitation.

Sexual exploitation

In conflict and post-conflict situations both boys and girls are subject to rape, involvement in prostitution or pornography, and sexual trafficking. Among the damaging results are separation from family, undermining of social trust and contraction of sexually transmitted infections, including HIV/AIDS. Young girls who become pregnant also face high risk of complications in pregnancy and delivery. In many countries sexual exploitation is part of wider patterns of discrimination against women.

Minority status

Many conflict situations entail blatant discrimination against and mistreatment of minority groups. Amid the lawlessness that often pervades conflicts, minority children may be subjected to attacks, harassments, threats and other forms of mistreatment in a context that provides little support or protection. For example, after the conflict in Kosovo, although education was officially open to all ethnic groups, Serb children were reported to have been attacked while walking to school by Kosovar Albanians, who were the ethnic majority. And while school buses were available to Kosovar Albanians, they were not available to Serb children.[31]

Child soldiers

Child soldiers are at grave risk of physical harm not only from fighting or landmines but also from poor health, endurance of physical hardships and sexually transmitted infections. Emotionally, child soldiers may suffer guilt, trauma, fear, depression and spiritual distress. In sub-Saharan Africa, for example, child soldiers may believe they are haunted by the spirits of the people they have killed, and that this spiritual contamination makes them unable to reintegrate into their communities.[32] Socially, former child soldiers are at risk because communities may fear or reject them. Teenage former soldiers in particular may have military identities and find it difficult to re-enter civilian life. Many of those who do try lack the jobs, education and life skills necessary for a sustainable return.

Youth as warriors and peacebuilders

Although this chapter has thus far emphasized the enormous burdens that war imposes on children, it would be a mistake to conclude that war-affected children are somehow a "lost generation" who cannot develop into contributing citizens. This section focuses on youth – specifically adolescents – and how the social environment influences their actions as either soldiers or peacebuilders.

Among children, teenagers have a special place in regard to issues of war and peace. For one thing, adolescents are immersed in the life task of identity formation and often try out various roles and modes of behaviour. Still at an early stage in life, they are making important choices about which paths to pursue. In addition, they have enormous energy and significant capacities to do good or harm. Sadly, in many conflict and post-conflict situations youth feel invisible, marginalized or impotent. This leaves them undecided about whether to go the way of violence or the way of peace. In post-independence Timor-Leste (East Timor), for example, youth spoke of how frustrating it was to have played a key role in the liberation struggle only to find that in the post-conflict situation they had little voice, influence or sources of support. A key insight for the international community is that youth comprise the next generation of either warriors or peacebuilders. In a post-conflict environment, it is young people who will, in the long run, either lead a country to peace or help plunge it back into war.

In this context, it is useful to analyse the roles, values, behaviour patterns and life options of youth, focusing on the disparate poles of young soldiers and peacebuilders. The analysis here suggests some of the key differences in socialization processes that are required to enable youths to be agents of peace rather than warriors. Although the term "youth" is used to refer to teenagers, mainly 13–18-year-olds, it also refers to people up to 24 years of age who are in transition. Further, it is recognized that the concept of youth is not universal. In fact, many societies consider 13-year-olds who have completed the cultural rites of passage to be adults.

Youth soldiers

In many war zones, children grow up in societies transformed by the militarization of daily life, normalization of violence and blurring of boundaries between war, crime and fighting between warlords. Children in such societies often learn values, competencies and behaviour patterns related to violence. At an early age they may act out war scenarios with sticks and look up to the older boys who wear a uniform and carry a gun in the streets. Watching the actions of their government and local warlords, they learn the power of the gun and come to see violence as an acceptable means of achieving goals. By the time young children in such societies become teenagers, they view soldiering as a normal activity and an extension of their life pathways. Animated by poverty or wanting the prestige and power of wearing a military uniform and carrying a gun, they may be willing warriors. It is not surprising, then, that increasingly youth are the fighters of wars on the sides of both government and opposition forces.[33]

Youths' entry into military activity varies according to the conflict[34] and the situation, although forced recruitment is the dominant mode of entry in many situations. In northern Uganda, for example, the euphemistically named Lord's Resistance Army recruited children and youth through abduction, often in public places through press-ganging or roundup at gunpoint. Similarly, in northern Afghanistan in the fighting between the Taliban and the Northern Alliance in the 1990s, the Northern Alliance recruited youth forcibly, as powerful local commanders visited homes and told boys to come with them.[35]

Shortage of troops is the dominant reason given for the forced recruitment of youth. Some commanders, however, report that they favour youth over adult soldiers because youths do not recognize their mortality, are highly obedient and are thus willing to accept very dangerous assignments.

Worldwide, a mixture of forced and voluntary recruitment also occurs.[36] In Sierra Leone the rebel Revolutionary United Front (RUF) forced children into soldiering at gunpoint; to prevent them from trying to return home, they sometimes forced children to kill members of their own village or family. To protect themselves against the RUF, villages used their traditional hunters' societies, called *kamajors*. Youth often entered the *kamajors* voluntarily when a family member or peer joined. They viewed their activities as fulfilling an obligation to their families and communities. Youth also join militaries for reasons related to power and ideology. Afghan youth have reported that wearing the uniform and carrying a gun give them a sense of power and prestige they would not otherwise achieve. In the liberation struggle against apartheid, South African youth reported that they fought for the cause and for political freedom.[37] In many conflicts, youth join the military to earn money, meet basic needs such as healthcare or gain protection. Because entry is often grounded in desperation and inability to meet basic needs, the phrase "voluntary recruitment" is best regarded with caution.

Youth's experiences in armed groups reflect both general patterns and particularities of the situation and the group. In all armed groups, youth learn obedience, camaraderie, endurance of hardship and skills related to killing and military operations. In contrast to sanitized images of professional soldiers who obey international law, commanders in many armed forces use terror tactics to teach patterns of ruthlessness and butchery. In Sierra Leone, for example, young soldiers were fed drugs and encouraged or ordered to terrorize villagers by cutting off their arms or hands. In northern Uganda abducted youths were forced to engage in progressive violence, a technique known to numb people to killing and remove any moral qualms. One boy reported that following his abduction, another boy tried to escape. The commander ordered the youths to surround the escapee and beat him to death lest they be beaten themselves. This horrific process was clever psychologically, in that it used peer activity to encourage participation but left it unclear who had actually dealt the death blow. The next time a boy tried to escape, the boys were required to impale him with a bayonet, exposing each boy to blood and the realization that his actions alone would have killed the escapee. In other contexts, youth recruits have been forced to drink the blood of the person they kill and perform various mutilations and atrocities.[38] Through brutal indoctrination and participation in forced killing, youth begin a process of learning to kill, devaluing the sanctity of life and throwing off previously learned moral restraints. The process continues as youth soldiers receive promotions for toughness and brutality, and through fearlessness win the respect of those whom they command. In conflicts in sub-Saharan Africa it is not uncommon to meet 15-year-olds who have killed many people and made life-and-death decisions that affect the lives of hundreds more people. Typically, such youths see themselves as soldiers and have difficulty imagining how they could return to school and take orders from a teacher who had never faced death or made life-and-death decisions.

Even for those who are not commanders, soldiering can produce a constellation of effects that work against reintegration into civilian life. Many youth acquire drug habits, while others learn patterns of excessively aggressive behaviour that impede a return home and successful reintegration. Some youth carry deep emotional scars associated with what they have seen and done, and will probably have difficulty concentrating, sleeping or establishing trustful relationships. Few youth soldiers are literate or have job skills that could enable them to earn a living. Even following a demobilization process, these youth may see few opportunities for re-entering civilian life and starting a family. Fearing community rejection, which is a very real possibility for youth who have done bad things in their own communities, many former youth soldiers stay in the bush, using banditry and crime to meet their needs.

Despite these challenges, it is inappropriate to think of former child soldiers as damaged goods or destined for lives as troublemakers. Numerous successful programme models and options for achieving post-conflict integration exist. These link cultural practices such as communal purification rituals with family integration, economic development, psychosocial assistance and literacy and life skills, including skills of nonviolent conflict resolution.[39] Even this brief overview, however, suggests that it is better to prevent youth from becoming soldiers than to try to reintegrate experienced soldiers, some of whom have seen or done horrible things, into civilian life. A key step in the prevention of youth soldiering is to engage young people in positive roles as peacebuilders.

Youth peacebuilders

Adolescents have often suffered from stereotypes that they are troublemakers or disobedient. Analyses of child soldiers have sometimes promoted images of youth as hardened killers and damaged goods.

Such stereotypes, however, do not fit with the reality that youth often play positive roles in their communities and are themselves important agents of peace. Following Serb attacks on Kosovars in 1999, for example, hundreds of thousands of Kosovars lived as refugees in Albania. The camps were overcrowded and the mood was bleak, since many people had suffered trauma and losses and were uncertain about the future. Apathy pervaded the camps, which offered few activities for youth and children. Fortunately, Kosovar youth councils, led by youths and people between the ages of 19 and 25 years, organized themselves and worked to clean the camps, and assisted newly arrived and poor families by conducting fundraising campaigns. These activities are well in line with the principle that empowerment and self-help are key parts of emergency psychosocial assistance.[40] The youth councils also organized concerts and sports activities such as football games that helped to reduce the grimness and apathy of the camps, and organized recreational activities for children. These activities, which aided the social integration of youth and children, won them the respect of the camp elders and gave youth a highly positive role in their community. This pattern continued following the return home, where the youth councils became consistent voices for peace and organized positive youth activities that contributed to demilitarization, thereby enabling post-conflict transition.

In active conflict situations, too, youth have significant potential for peacebuilding. Colombian children, for example, created in 1996 a grand exhibit for peace that displayed children's drawings, poems and letters expressing their collective desire for peace. This event spawned the Children's National Movement for Peace, which constructed a national children's referendum in which 3 million children voted for their rights to survival, freedom from abuse and peace. Mayerly Sanchez, a 14-year-old leader of the organization, stated, "Children are the seeds of a new Colombia. We are the seeds that will stop the war."[41]

Two important venues in which youth contribute to peacebuilding are radio and schools. In South Africa youth groups have organized and produced their own radio shows as part of community-based programming. Through dialogues, they explore a wide range of issues concerning reconciliation and the reconstruction of South Africa for peace and social justice. Youth report that as a result of these activities, they are regarded in a more favourable light and are seen as having an important role in their communities. Similarly, youth in Sierra Leone participate in a regular radio show called *Talking Drum*, produced by Search for Common Ground, which uses dialogue, story and drama to take peace messages to public audiences.[42]

Schools, too, give youth a powerful forum for peace. In partnership with UNICEF, UNESCO (the UN Educational, Scientific and Cultural Organization) and other international agencies, many local schools are building peace education and non-violent conflict resolution into their curricula. Designed well, these include participatory activities such as peer mediation wherein trained youth serve as facilitators who help students solve their conflicts.

Due in part to these and other accomplishments, youth participation rights and leadership are receiving greater attention. Many actors, including government, local communities and civil society and faith-based groups, that formerly had youth participate in projects mostly as beneficiaries are now beginning to view them as partners and decision-makers who ought to be intimately involved at all project stages, from design to evaluation. For example, in Sierra Leone, Uganda and Liberia adolescent girl mothers who had been part of armed conflicts have successfully implemented their own interventions and evaluated the impact in community projects that promote peace.[43] Further, the importance of cultivating and enabling youth leadership is increasingly recognized. Since youth often have the vision and energy required to help move a peace process forward, it makes sense to support them through training, building of organizational and technical skills and provision of resources. It is vital to share power with youth, as their empowerment is a prerequisite for them becoming effective agents of peacebuilding rather than tools of the war system.

Conclusion

The plight of children in conflict and post-conflict situations entails too much suffering and destruction of human capital to be ignored. It clearly warrants strong, well-coordinated efforts to protect children, mothers and families from the massive rights violations that every conflict creates.

However, it is not enough to wait for the conflicts to erupt and pick up the pieces afterwards. Strong efforts in conflict prevention are necessary.

Since youth are important actors in conflicts, effective prevention and post-conflict peacebuilding require work on behalf of youth and children at many different levels. The increasing visibility of youth on the international security agenda – as evidenced in Security Council resolutions such as Resolution 1379[44] – is a positive step towards integrating children's well-being into policy discussions about peace. A longer-term step is to strengthen the legal, cultural and community-level protections that prevent child soldiering, and vigorously prosecute offenders. Perhaps the most important long-term challenge is to change the socialization patterns and roles of youth. Slowly, the international community, including governments and bilateral donors, and national, regional and local communities are realizing that war zones create powerful socialization for youth violence and soldiering. Equally powerful socialization for peacebuilding is a prerequisite for peace. The question now is whether youth will receive ongoing support as warriors or whether the international community will nourish youth as leaders in peacebuilding.

Notes

1. Dan Smith with Kristin Ingstad Sandberg, Pavel Baev and Wenche Hauge, *The State of War and Peace Atlas*, London: Penguin, 1997.
2. Ablardo Brenes and Michael Wessells, "Building Cultures of Peace", *Peace and Conflict: Journal of Peace Psychology* 7(2), 2001, pp. 99–107.
3. Paul Collier, V. L. Elliott, Havard Hegre, Anke Hoeffler, Marta Reynal-Querol and Nicholas Sambanis, "Breaking the Conflict Trap: Civil War and Development Policy", World Bank/Oxford University Press, Washington, DC, 2003, www-wds.worldbank.org/external/default/WDSContentServer/IW3P/IB/2003/06/30/000094946_0306190405396/Rendered/PDF/multi0page.pdf.
4. Michael Wessells, *Child Soldiers: From Violence to Protection*, Cambridge, MA: Harvard University Press, 2006.
5. Michael Wessells, "Children, Armed Conflict, and Peace", *Journal of Peace Research* 35(5), 1998, pp. 635–646; Jason Hart (ed.), *Adolescence, Political Violence and Displacement*, New York: Berghahn Books, 2008.
6. Graça Machel, *The Impact of War on Children: A Review of Progress since the 1996 United Nations Report on the Impact of Armed Conflict on Children*, London: Hurst, 2001.
7. Graça Machel, "Impact of Armed Conflict on Children", UN Doc. A/51/306, New York, 26 August 1996, www.unicef.org/graca/a51-306_en.pdf; UNICEF, "Machel Plus Ten Strategic Review", UNICEF, New York, 2007.
8. UNAIDS, "Global Report: UNAIDS Report on the Global AIDS Epidemic", 2012, www.unaids.org/en/media/unaids/contentassets/documents/epidemiology/2012/gr2012/20121120_UNAIDS_Global_Report_2012_en.pdf.
9. Ibid.

10. Andrew T. Price-Smith and John L. Daly, "Downward Spiral: HIV/AIDS, State Capacity, and Political Conflict in Zimbabwe", Peaceworks No. 53, US Institute of Peace, Washington, DC, 2004, www-previous.usip.org/files/resources/pwks53.pdf.
11. UNHCR, "A Year of Crises: UNHCR Global Trends 2011", Office of the UN High Commissioner for Refugees, Geneva, 2012, www.unhcr.org/4fd6f87f9.
12. Kenneth Miller and Lisa Rasco, *From Clinic to Community: Ecological Approaches to Refugee Mental Health*, Mahwah, NJ: Lawrence Erlbaum, 2004.
13. Ahmed Rashid, *Taliban*, New Haven, CT: Yale University Press, 2000.
14. Michael Wessells and Carlinda Monteiro, "Healing Wounds of War in Angola: A Community-Based Approach", in David Donald, Andrew Dawes and Johann Louw (eds), *Addressing Childhood Adversity*, Cape Town: David Philip, 2000, pp. 176–201.
15. International Campaign to Ban Landmines, "Landmine Monitor Report 2000", www.the-monitor.org/index.php/publications/display?url=lm/2000/.
16. Wessells, note 4 above; Rachel Brett and Irma Specht, *Young Soldiers: Why They Choose to Fight*, Boulder, CO: Lynne Rienner, 2004.
17. Human Rights Watch, *You'll Learn Not to Cry*, New York: Human Rights Watch, 2003; Jean-Claude Legrand, "Lessons Learned from UNICEF Field Programmes for the Prevention of Recruitment, Demobilization, and Reintegration of Child Soldiers", UNICEF, New York, 1999.
18. Charlie Carpenter (ed.), *Born of War: Protecting Children of Sexual Violence – Survivors in Conflict Zones*, Bloomfield, CT: Kumarian Press, 2007.
19. Ralph Regan, "Background Briefing: International Trafficking of Women and Children: Testimony before the Senate Committee on Foreign Relations Subcommittee on Near Eastern and South Asian Affairs", Human Rights Watch, New York, 22 February 2000, www.hrw.org/news/2000/02/21/international-trafficking-women-and-children.
20. Sarah Dryden-Peterson, "Refugee Education: A Global Review, 2011", Policy Development and Evaluation Service, Office of the UN High Commissioner for Refugees, November 2011, www.unhcr.org/4fe31759.pdf, p. 29.
21. Neil Boothby, Alison Strang and Michael Wessells (eds), *A World Turned Upside Down: Social Ecological Approaches to Children in War Zones*, Bloomfield, CT: Kumarian Press, 2006.
22. James Garbarino, Kathleen Kostelny and Nancy Dubrow, *No Place to Be a Child: Growing Up in a War Zone*, San Francisco: Jossey-Bass, 1991; James Garbarino and Kathleen Kostelny, "The Effects of Political Violence on Palestinian Children's Behavioral Problems: A Risk Accumulation Model", *Child Development* 67, 1996, pp. 33–45; Michael Wessells and Kathleen Kostelny, "Everyday Distress: Psychosocial and Economic Impact of Forced Migration on Children and Families", in Valerie Maholmes and Rosalind King (eds), *The Oxford Handbook of Poverty and Child Development*, London: Oxford University Press, 2012, pp. 640–655.
23. Patrick Bracken and Celia Petty (eds), *Rethinking the Trauma of War*, London: Free Association Books, 1998.
24. Wessells, note 4 above. See also Alcinda Honwana, "Non-Western Concepts of Mental Health", in Maryanne Loughry and Alastair Ager (eds), *The Refugee Experience*, Vol. 1, Oxford: Oxford University Refugee Studies Programme, 1999, pp. 103–119.
25. Michael Rutter, "Protective Factors in Children's Response to Stress and Disadvantage", in Martha W. Kent and Jon E. Rolf (eds), *Primary Prevention of Psychopathology, Vol. 3, Social Competence in Children*, Hanover, NH: University Press of New England, 1979, pp. 49–74.
26. Ibid.
27. James Garbarino, Kathleen Kostelny and Frank Barry, "Neighborhood-Based Programs", in Penelope K. Trickett and Cynthia J. Schellenbach (eds), *Violence against*

Children in the Family and the Community, Washington, DC: American Psychological Association, 1998, pp. 287–314; Kathleen Kostelny, "A Culture-based Integrative Approach: Helping War-Affected Children", in Boothby, Strang and Wessells, note 21 above, pp. 19–37.

28. Michael Wessells and Carlinda Monteiro, "Psychosocial Interventions and Post-War Reconstruction in Angola: Interweaving Western and Traditional Approaches", in Daniel Christie, Richard Wagner and Debra Winter (eds), *Peace, Conflict, and Violence: Peace Psychology for the 21st Century*, Upper Saddle River, NJ: Prentice-Hall, 2001, pp. 262–275.
29. Michael Wessells and Allison Strang, "Religion as Resource and Risk: The Double-Edged Sword for Children in Situations of Armed Conflict", in Boothby, Strang and Wessells, note 21 above, pp. 199–222.
30. Michael Rutter, "Resilience in the Face of Adversity: Protective Factors and Resistance to Psychological Disorder", *British Journal of Psychiatry* 147, 1985, pp. 598–611.
31. Michael Wessells, personal communication, Kosovo, 1999.
32. Wessells, note 4 above.
33. Brett and Specht, note 16 above; Wessells, ibid.
34. Michael Wessells, "Recruitment of Children as Soldiers in Sub-Saharan Africa: An Ecological Analysis", in Lars Mjoset and Stephen E. Van Holde (eds), *The Comparative Study of Conscription in the Armed Forces*, Comparative Social Research Vol. 20, Amsterdam: Elsevier, 2002, pp. 237–254.
35. Michael Wessells and Kathleen Kostelny, "After the Taliban: A Child-Focused Assessment of Afghan Children in the Northern Provinces of Kunduz, Takhar, and Badikshan", Christian Children's Fund, Richmond, VA, 2002.
36. Wessells, note 4 above.
37. Gillian Straker, *Faces in the Revolution*, Cape Town: David Philip, 1992.
38. Rachel Brett and Margaret McCallin, *Children: The Invisible Soldiers*, Vaxjo: Rädda Barnen, 1996; Ilene Cohn and Guy Goodwin-Gill, *Child Soldiers: The Role of Children in Armed Conflicts*, Oxford: Clarendon Press, 1994.
39. Wessells and Monteiro, note 28 above; Michael Wessells and Kathleen Kostelny, "Youth Soldiering: An Integrated Framework for Understanding Psychosocial Impact", in Brian K. Barber (ed.), *Adolescents and War: How Youth Deal with Political Violence*, New York: Oxford University Press, 2009, pp. 105–122; Wessells, note 4 above.
40. Inter-Agency Standing Committee, "IASC Guidelines on Mental Health and Psychosocial Support in Emergency Settings", IASC, Geneva, 2007.
41. UNICEF, "The State of the World's Children 2000", UNICEF, New York, 1999, www.unicef.org/sowc00/.
42. See radiopeaceafrica.org.
43. Susan McKay, Angela Veale, Miranda Worthen and Michael Wessells, "Building Meaningful Participation in Reintegration among War-Affected Young Mothers in Liberia, Sierra Leone and Northern Uganda", *Intervention* 9(2), 2011, pp. 108–124.
44. Security Council Resolution 1379, adopted in November 2001, asks the Secretary-General to prepare a list of parties to armed conflict that violate their international obligations by recruiting or using children as soldiers.

4

Angry young men in Timor-Leste: Post-conflict peacebuilding and its malcontents

Henri Myrttinen

Introduction

In the fragile setting of post-conflict or transitional societies, the volatile "youth demographic" is often cast as a major potential threat to either peace processes or societal peace as such.[1] "The youth", often taken implicitly to mean young un- or underemployed men of lower social strata, are seen as an instability factor, an uncontrollable force, dangerous and brooding, contemptuous of existing mores and lacking respect for elders. In post-conflict societies many of these young men will have had combat experience of some sort, and may possibly still have access to weapons and be integrated into clandestine networks of other ex-combatants, often under the leadership of their former mid-level field commanders. While they may have been physically and legally demobilized, their mind-sets often are not. The qualities which had been inculcated in them during the years of conflict, such as readiness to use violence, sworn secrecy or risk-prone behaviour, are in the post-conflict context seen as liabilities. As Thokozani Xaba describes for South Africa, "the struggle heroes of yesteryear . . . [became] the villains and felons of today. The 'young lions' or 'the foot soldiers of the revolution' have become marginalised and some have become full-time gangsters."[2] Their "struggle masculinity" leaves them ill equipped to deal with the challenges of the post-conflict order:

Escaping victimhood: Children, youth and post-conflict peacebuilding, Schnabel and Tabyshalieva (eds), United Nations University Press, 2013, ISBN 978-92-808-1211-4

> When the gender norms of a society change, boys who modelled themselves in terms of an earlier, "struggle" version of masculinity may grow up to become unhappy men. Those who cannot change together with the society or who do not possess the skills to make it in the new social environment find themselves strangers in their own country.[3]

Often especially the lower-ranking (and therefore younger) members of fighting forces feel a sense of loss and resentment at the post-conflict settlement: they may think they do not receive the societal recognition they feel they deserve for having risked or sacrificed their lives "for the cause", there is resentment at their former superiors reaping economic and political benefits from the post-conflict settlement while they themselves feel socio-economically marginalized, or they may feel swamped in the mundane drudgery of everyday civilian life, having lost the sense of purpose (and adventure) which they had during the struggle. Furthermore, together with their peers, they can find themselves in what Henrik Vigh in his study of young male ex-combatants in Guinea-Bissau calls the "social moratorium of youth": unable to fulfil either the traditional or the modern prerequisites for being regarded as adult men (e.g. having employment with a steady income, being able to pay dowry and thus marry and have legitimate children, set up one's own household), they remain trapped in the socially marginalized category of "youth" well beyond their generational age.[4]

This chapter seeks to unpack some of the issues, such as gender role and class expectations, inherent in these discourses. It is mostly based on my research in Timor-Leste during the crisis years of 2006–2008 and thereafter, but I also draw comparisons to other conflicted societies, mainly in Melanesia and Southeast Asia. The fieldwork consisted of 45 interviews with members of various disaffected groups.[5] The interviewees were, for the most part, in their teens or early 20s, although some group leaders were older, in their late 20s to early 30s. Although most groups claimed to be open to female members, the interviewees were exclusively male and I did not come across any female members in the course of my fieldwork. Most interviews were conducted in the capital, Dili, mainly in the poorer *bairros* (neighbourhoods) of the city or the internally displaced person (IDP) camps which had sprung up in the capital after the violent political crisis of 2006. Additional interviews with members of these groups were conducted in some smaller cities. Supplemental interviews were carried out with East Timorese and international law enforcement officials, government agencies, civil society organizations, academia and media representatives. At the risk of stating the obvious, I would like to point out that although the chapter focuses on young men acting violently, by far not all young men in Timor-Leste are violent. Even those active in violence-prone groups can act as peacebuilders. For example, several local NGOs such as Ba Futuro and Belun have been successfully engaging with young men at the village and community levels to act as agents for positive change.

My argument is that the phenomenon of "angry young men" as a threat to post-conflict settlements is tightly linked to gender role expectations, among other factors such as past historical experiences and the socio-economic environment. Although these men are perceived as a threat to social stability, they are nonetheless often given a certain degree of social space if not outright encouragement and support by other sectors of society in their violent activities. While the threat to stability by the "lost generation" is manifested in the public mind in groups of brooding, discontented, young, lower-class males, the phenomenon is more complicated than the stereotype. Accepting and understanding the complexity of the phenomenon can be a first step towards finding constructive ways of integrating the young men into society.

After a brief examination of the historical background and socio-economic situation in Timor-Leste, I discuss how local notions of gender, age and class interact in the constructions, expectations, displays and readings of male youth violence. A central point I reiterate here is that in Timor-Leste, as in many other societies, "youth" problems are often equated with the problems of young men. Without wanting to continue to marginalize young women in the youth discourse, I mostly refer to young men and their issues in this chapter, mainly as the terminology in the literature I use here is based on equating youth with young men. The following section therefore looks, albeit far too briefly, at the role of women in the post-independence violence in the context of the social space given for violent enactments of masculinity. I then briefly outline some of the efforts undertaken by the Timor-Leste government and civil society to address "the youth problem".

Timor-Leste – An introduction

Today, the Democratic Republic of Timor-Leste is a country of slightly more than a million people, and this number is rapidly growing. With one of the world's highest birth rates, the population is expected to double to over 2 million by the year 2025.[6] According to the UN Development Programme, the country is one of the poorest in all the Asia-Pacific region, with the majority of people living on less than a dollar a day. Unemployment is high and the population is young – in 2006 43.5 per cent of East Timorese were less than 15 years old, and given the high birth rate this percentage is expanding rapidly.[7] It is estimated that one-third of the labour force of Dili aged between 25 and 29 years of age are unemployed or not actively seeking employment. This figure rises to 60 per cent among male teenagers, and around 50 per cent in the age group of 20–24 years.[8] The figures need to be seen in the specific socio-cultural context in which unemployment becomes an urban, male phenomenon. Young men are often released from domestic duties by their sisters, mothers and female partners, with the latter often not expected or able to seek formal employment outside the home. In a rural setting, most men and women work as subsistence farmers rather than seeking jobs in the formal economy.[9]

For almost two years, from April 2006 to February 2008, Timor-Leste and its capital city were plagued by instability caused by continuous low-level violence attributed, to a great part, to violence-prone youth groups. The initial outbreak of the *krize*, as it soon came to be known in the national language Tetum, was mainly due to a complete breakdown in the national security forces. However, it was the disaffected groups consisting mainly of young men (often collectively labelled "gangs") which soon became the main perpetrators of violence.[10] One of the initial dividing lines between communities in Dili was that of regional origin, with "westerners" attacking "easterners" and to a lesser extent the other way around. Acts of violence included killings, arson, stoning of houses, IDP camps and vehicles, rapes, extortion and public shows of force. The history of this political conflict which erupted in 2006 is closely tied to the nation's quarter-century armed struggle for independence and the post-conflict settlement.

Much of what has happened in the past 35 years in Timor-Leste's conflicted history can be traced back to the Portuguese Carnation Revolution, which on 24 April 1974 overthrew the fascist dictatorship of António de Oliveira Salazar and Marcello Caetano and kick-started a rapid decolonization process. For the previous 450 years or so Timor-Leste had been a Portuguese colony. The territory was ill prepared for independence and quickly caught up in Cold War international politics. A brief but bloody civil war between the two biggest of the newly formed East Timorese political parties saw the rise of the left leaning party Fretilin (Revolutionary Front for an Independent Timor-Leste) to power. Fearing a further Southeast Asian "domino" falling into the leftist camp, the United States and Australia encouraged Indonesia to invade on 7 December 1975.

What ensued was an exceptionally bloody 24-year struggle against Indonesian military occupation, which left an estimated 102,800 East Timorese dead, for the most part civilians.[11] The military part of the struggle was carried out by the Falintil (Armed Forces of the National Liberation of Timor-Leste) guerrilla movement, and was supported by a clandestine civilian resistance movement. Following the fall of the Suharto dictatorship in Indonesia in 1998, the new Indonesian government offered the East Timorese the possibility of determining the status of the territory in a UN-supervised referendum.

The run-up to the referendum on independence saw a new level of violence, with Indonesian armed forces setting up and arming Timorese pro-Indonesian militias as proxies. Immediately after the announcement of the result of the ballot in favour of independence, the militias, supported by the Indonesian security forces, began an unprecedented rampage. A common estimate is that around 1,500 unarmed civilians died in this phase.[12] Utilizing a "scorched earth" policy, the infrastructure of the territory was systematically destroyed. Over a third of the population, about 250,000 people, were forcibly deported, mainly to militia-run camps in Indonesian West Timor.[13]

In reaction to the international outcry over this brutal campaign of destruction, an international peacekeeping force was dispatched, and until May 2002 the territory was under the administration of the UN Transitional Administration in East Timor (UNTAET).

During the UNTAET period, Falintil was demobilized and partially integrated into the new armed forces, Falintil-Forças de Defesa de Timor-Leste, and, to a much lesser extent, the new police force (Policía Nacional de Timor-Leste). This disarmament, demobilization and reintegration (DDR) process was carried out in a relatively *ad hoc* manner, reflecting the fact that it had not been part of the initial UNTAET mandate and sowing the seeds for future discontent.[14]

The relationship between the two security forces was tense from the outset, and grew worse in the years following independence. Turf battles at times turned into actual battles. Events came to a head in January 2006 when almost 600 soldiers, mainly from the western part of the country, signed a petition claiming discrimination based on their regional origin. Feeling that they were not given a proper response, the "petitioners" left their barracks in February 2006 and were dismissed from the army a few weeks later. Events turned violent at the end of April 2006, with a protest by the petitioners ending with several deaths. The tensions mounted over the following weeks, ending in full-scale street battles in Dili and environs at the end of May 2006 that caused at least 37 deaths and 150,000 IDPs. Weapons were distributed to civilians by members of the security forces as well as by key political figures, and found their way into the hands of the various disaffected groups.

In the aftermath of the 2006 crisis, responsibility for internal (and, in part, external) security was transferred from the East Timorese security forces to international peacekeepers and a beefed-up UN mission. In spite of this, "gang" violence (involving not only gangs but also martial arts and ritual arts groups) continued on a daily basis in Dili for the next two years or so, with varying intensity and in varying locations, often paralysing both the city and the nation. Though no exact overall figures are available, my estimate based on incomplete UN, police and press reports is that perhaps up to 100 people were killed, scores more wounded, dozens of houses burned and hundreds of acts of vandalism (mostly stonings) carried out in this period.[15] In spite of the presence of UN agencies, international non-governmental organizations (NGOs) and local women's organizations, no data on the probable increase in gender-based violence (GBV) during this period seem to be available.[16]

A key role in the events of April–May 2006 was played by renegade Major Alfredo Reinado, who quickly became a youth idol, with his name emblazoning walls across Dili and young gang members emulating his "look".[17] In his perceived quest for "justice" he became a repository of hopes and dreams of those who felt frustrated with and marginalized by the post-conflict settlement.

On the morning of 11 February 2008, Major Reinado and his followers precipitated a series of violent events by arriving armed at the house of President José Ramos-Horta. The exact details and sequence of events remain unclear in spite of a court case on the matter, but by the end of the stand-off Reinado and one of his followers had been shot dead and President Ramos-Horta critically wounded. The other attackers managed to escape, but surrendered on 27 April 2008. Despite Reinado's popularity as a millenarian figure among disaffected groups and previous vows that "Dili would burn"[18] if something happened to him, "the youth" did not react violently to the sudden loss of their idol. Why this is so remains unclear. Reinado might have been seen as overplaying his hand, with the attack taking the nation so close to the brink of violent disaster that it was necessary to step back.[19] In the aftermath calm slowly returned to the streets of Dili, and has held for the following years at least, although acts of violence perpetrated by the gangs and martial arts and ritual arts groups continued at a lower and more sporadic level.

An overview of the disaffected groups

The crisis of 2006 brought to the fore a phenomenon that had already been causing some headaches for the previous five years – that of potentially violent, disaffected groups, some with clear political agendas and others with a more diffuse feeling of resentment and often a degree of criminal energy. They describe themselves as either martial arts groups (MAGs), traditional or ritual arts groups (RAGs), gangs or veterans' groups.[20] They vary in size and composition: reliable figures are difficult to obtain, as groups may exaggerate their membership numbers and include "hang-around" members. My conservative estimate is that there are several thousand active members in the groups, with a smaller hard core. Members do, however, drift in and out of the groups.

Martial arts groups

These groups derive their common identity from practising a particular form of martial arts, such as karate, *pencak silat* or kung fu. While some groups concentrate strictly on practising martial arts for sports, others have taken more interest in "extracurricular" activities such as street-fighting, assault, murder, arson and extortion. The main MAGs are Persaudaraan Setia Hati Terate (PSHT), Kera Sakti and Kung Fu Master; these have often fought each other for influence and control of territory. PSHT is the largest and most influential MAG in Timor-Leste.

Many of the MAGs started up during the years of the Indonesian occupation and learned their martial arts skills from Indonesian teachers, often members of the military. This does not, however, mean they were tied to the Indonesian security apparatus in the same way as the pro-Indonesian militias of 1998–1999. Rather, the connections tend to have been of a personal nature, and some have survived over the years. PSHT in Timor-Leste, for example, is at least theoretically a branch of the Indonesian (and, as many members claim, global) PSHT "brotherhood". While the claims to membership in transnational networks need perhaps be taken with a grain of salt, there is undoubtedly an "international" character to these groups, as they often have not only been originally taught by outside (read Indonesian) teachers but also draw on martial arts icons and iconography popularized by global media culture, e.g. figures such as Bruce Lee, Jet Li or the Shaolin monks. With the exception of *bona fide* sports organizations such as the Timor-Leste judo and taekwondo associations, many MAGs have been involved in street and criminal violence, often fighting against other groups.

Ritual arts groups

Unlike the MAGs, which the RAGs see as drawing on "imported" skills and arts, these groups claim to base their identity on traditional Timorese rituals, though it seems highly likely that many of these are "invented" traditions. A number of the RAGs formed an informal coalition called Rai Nain (Owners of the Land – thus casting the tradition-oriented RAGs as "more East Timorese" than the MAGs) to fight PSHT. However, this has not prevented RAGs from fighting each other as well. The main RAGs are "numbers" or *kakalok* groups such as 7-7 and 5-5, Colimau 2000 and KORK (Kmanek Oan Rai Klaran – Wise Children of the Land, also occasionally called Korka).

Many of the RAGs tend to draw their following from disaffected former members of the "clandestine front" who felt left out by the post-conflict DDR process which seemed, at least in their eyes, to favour well-connected ex-Falintil combatants over other members of the resistance movement.[21] The RAGs are arguably also more political in their outlook than the MAGs in general, and stress the need for "real independence".[22]

More than the MAGs or the gangs, the RAGs claim to have access to magical powers, endowed upon them by their connections to ancestral spirits, the use of amulets and magic powders. The "numbers" groups such as 5-5, 7-7 and 9-9 use scarification in their initiation rituals, in which magic powder is inserted subcutaneously into parallel rows of scars corresponding to the group's number.[23] While much of this is based on traditional East Timorese beliefs, many elements in these beliefs have been imported from outside Timor-Leste via popular culture. Given their focus on "Timoreseness", the RAGs are arguably more political than the gangs or MAGs, although all the groups maintain connections to key political parties and figures.

Gangs

In the East Timorese context, the term "gang" can refer to a range of groups, mostly based in and organized around a certain neighbourhood. Some are harmless youth groups of friends hanging out, while others have a more clearly criminal intent.

A number of the gangs are led by former members or supporters of the clandestine front during the Indonesian occupation, and their illegal activities were in part seen as supporting the independence struggle. The gangs tend to be named after either their leaders or the particular part of town they hail from. Some, however, have adopted other names, in part imported, such as Gang Hitler, PLUR (which can be interpreted as either "Peace, Love, Unity and Respect" or the title of an eponymous song by the popular Indonesian band Slank), Blok M (which can be read as referring either to a lower-class neighbourhood of Jakarta or to its *clandestino* roots as "independence block", with M standing for *merdeka*) or Fudidu (literally "the fucked ones").

The influence of international and Indonesian pop culture is perhaps most visible in the case of the gangs. Gang houses and streets controlled by gangs are often painted in graffiti referring to popular musical idols seen as icons of (male) rebellion, especially Bob Marley (often with marijuana leaves), Che Guevara, Bruce Lee or the above-mentioned band Slank, but occasionally also heavy-metal bands.[24]

Veterans' organizations

Prior to the 2006 crisis one of the major sources of potential instability was the veterans' organizations, which consisted of disenchanted former Falintil fighters and members of the clandestine opposition movement who felt marginalized by the DDR process. These groups include the Sagrada Familia, CPD-RDTL and SF-75.[25] They are reported to have connections to various RAGs and MAGs, especially those with high numbers of former *clandestinos*, and have been suspected of involvement in several incidents of public unrest in Timor-Leste. These connections remain vague, however, and some older men active in RAGs and the veterans' organizations have sought to distance themselves from the activities of the younger, more volatile members.[26]

During their main period of activity, from mid-2006 to early 2008, the allegiances and alliances between the various groups were continuously shifting and the "official" reasons for fighting changed as rapidly: from "ethnic/regional"[27] to political to group A versus group B, riots due to a lack of rice and grievances against activities of the peacekeeping forces. In the latter case, even sworn enemies such as the two main rival gangs, 7-7 and PSHT, could and would cooperate politically and practically, temporarily, against the common foreign "enemy" before taking up arms against each other again.

The overall structure, especially of the larger groups, is somewhat amorphous but hierarchical. For the overwhelming part the members are men, with a wide age span within the groups, ranging from boys in their young teens to leaders who can be in their 50s or even 60s. In general, the hierarchy in the gangs tends to be based on age, with the majority of the "foot soldiers" being in their early to mid-teens, mid-level leaders in their 20s and the higher-up leaders, at times with coveted white-collar jobs or tertiary degrees, in their late 20s to late 30s.

While some gangs trace their "lineage" to the Portuguese colonial era and others to the times of the Indonesian occupation, many seem to be more recent creations.[28] Regardless of their historical background, many of the gangs seem to include former members of the pro-Indonesian militias, ex-Falintil guerrillas and former or currently serving members of the security forces. The widespread disappointment with the DDR process for former combatants was a major factor in fuelling discontent and motivating them to join the various groups.[29]

The various groups described above have played an ambivalent role in East Timorese society since independence. On the one hand they have been a key factor of instability, causing deaths and displacement, especially during the crisis years of 2006–2008. On the other hand they have also acted as receptacles for young (and some not so young) men disorientated by the post-conflict settlement, thus serving a – possibly stabilizing – societal purpose.

Masculinity and violence

Masculine role expectations in Timor-Leste are closely linked to hierarchies based on age and membership in (and thus loyalty to) various, at times competing, networks of patronage. Furthermore, the young men forming the core constituency of the disaffected groups described here find themselves trying to navigate a complex web of expectations – those of society as well as their own. By joining the groups, they are on the one hand protesting against traditional, hegemonic expectations of masculinity, but simultaneously creating new forms of hegemonic masculinity. Similar to the South African coloured *skollies* described by Steffen Jensen, they are caught in a paradox: through their agency in joining the various groups they can be seen as trying to escape the stereotypes levelled against them, yet ending up reproducing these negative stereotypes.[30] These imaginings of urban, poor young men are similar in South Africa and Timor-Leste, and echoed elsewhere on the planet. As outlined in a Plan Timor-Leste survey carried out at the height of the crisis, local residents saw the young men as "stupid", "lazy", "violent" and "uneducated".[31] In my own interviews the men saw themselves differently, stressing the positive aspects of joining – being part of a "brotherhood", protecting the community, finding and creating one's identity and spiritual home. Many felt unfairly discriminated against by the dominant public discourse, which focused too little on the positive and constructive societal aspects of these groups.[32]

On deference

As de Silva noted for constructions of masculinities in Sinhala society in Sri Lanka:

> While deference is to a code of seniority, senior members will also defer to others defined as somehow "more" senior, even as they receive the deference of those construed as "younger" or "social inferiors". Still, a withdrawal of deference creates anxiety and unvoiced rage. It implies an – unspoken – challenge to one's status ... hegemonic masculinity requires constant displays of deference from "lesser" masculinities and femininities, even while it defers to authority or others seen to be "more" senior.[33]

Similarly, in traditional East Timorese society more senior members have automatically expected deference from younger men and all women. However, the experience of a quarter-century of war, coupled with the twin processes of urbanization and modernization, as well as the influx of new, globalized ideals and idols, has changed this situation profoundly. Many of the young men active in the disaffected groups do still abide by codes of seniority within the organizations and *vis-à-vis* respected elders, but this is perhaps more out of a sense of propriety (in the case of venerated elders) than an indication of subjugation to a code of seniority. On the contrary, "to the man" all my interviewees were scathing in their views of the older *ema bo'ot* (literally "big people"), who traditionally would have expected the deference of the younger. Socially, most of the men I interviewed remain in the "social moratorium" of *joventude*, of youth, even when they have passed the age of 35, as they have not been able to fulfil the societal requirements for becoming adult men. While the status of youth gives the men a certain degree of *Narrenfreiheit* (fool's freedom), e.g. to go out drinking, hang around, create mischief, it also means that they are not considered to be or respected as full adults. This seems to be an impediment to peacebuilding measures: given the premium placed on seniority, the support and involvement of more senior and older figures are required for these measures to gain the necessary traction. However, older men in the groups complained that they were no longer able to control their younger members.[34]

Networks of patronage

As in many other countries in the region, male identity in Timor-Leste is in part constructed socially through complex networks of loyalty and patronage. Rather than this meaning merely a lack of loyalty to the state institutions, loyalty to the state or nation competes with other, often stronger, ties and obligations that form an older basis for society. As Sinclair Dinnen has argued for a number of Melanesian societies, rather than "anarchy", i.e. the lack of authority being the driving force behind conflicts, there are "many competing sources of authority and allegiance at local levels, with the claims of the state being merely one among many".[35] Thus, in a sense, especially male identity (and the range of responses available to an individual in any given situation) becomes "overdetermined" by obligations of the individual male to various competing clientelist networks of patronage controlled by *ema bo'ot* to whom he owes his loyalty. In the context of peacebuilding this can work both ways – if the leaders make peace, their followers will, or at least should, follow. Equally, lower-ranking members might find it difficult to push for peace if their leaders are unwilling to do so.

The various networks of patronage and obligation include the extended family/clan, party membership, regional or "ethnic" origin, belonging to a certain neighbourhood, membership in the Catholic Church or other religious organization, previous or continuing membership in a gang or martial/ritual arts group, membership in a veterans' organization and employment in state structures/private enterprises. As these networks of allegiance are often overlapping and contradictory, they pose dilemmas of competing loyalties for both individuals and networks, including the security sector institutions.[36]

The futile search for modernity

The young men in the urban and peri-urban areas of Timor-Leste are caught between several, mostly unattainable, visions of masculinity: that of the traditional, rural, subsistence-agriculture-based traditional Timorese society which they have left behind as city dwellers; that of the imagined urban modernity of the male breadwinner, working in a white-collar job with modern conveniences and perks to go with it; and that of the heroic freedom fighter.[37] Having left the countryside behind, the traditional/rural model of masculine respectability is far removed from the reality of the young men, not necessarily attractive and also extremely expensive, as ritual expenses, including dowries, can be several months' worth of wages. With little education and few connections, white-collar jobs are beyond the reach of most members of the groups, with the notable exception of some of the well-connected leaders. While the youngest members would have been too young to participate personally in the independence struggle, most mid-level members as well as a number of the leaders actively took part in the resistance. All will, however, be imbued with tales of heroic warrior masculinity from both the independence struggle and earlier revolts against the Portuguese colonial power. In the post-conflict settlement, however, heroic warrior status is of course far more difficult to achieve. Caught between these unattainable tropes, the disaffected groups simultaneously act as an avenue for asserting one's masculinity as being apart from these unattainable visions, a source of identity and respect (if only through instilling fear) and a way out of the tedium of an everyday life of under- and unemployment.

The younger generations, through the years of resistance and instability following independence, have also learned the lesson that violence pays, that committing violent acts has become the most effective way of achieving results for what are often legitimate socio-economic or political grievances and airing one's frustrations. This "legitimization" of violence as a tool to gain respect and achieve one's goals is visible both on the streets and at home – GBV is the most reported crime in the country by a wide margin, and even then only a fraction of the overall cases will have been reported.[38]

Patterns of violence

Localizing violence in class and "in the hood"

The local and international media, public opinion, government authorities and researchers often have a tendency to link "youth" violence in Dili with the poorer neighbourhoods or the IDP camps. In 1999 many Timorese I spoke to tended to dismiss members of the militias as being either non-Timorese or from the lowest classes of society. A similar sentiment was evident in 2006–2008 with respect to gang violence. As the blog Return to Rai Ketak records it:

> The Timorese diaspora, or educated class with good jobs here in Dili, tend to blame the *ema beik*, the stupid people who have come from the districts and live in these shitty peripheral neighborhoods in Dili. Why do they resort to violence? They are ignorant. *Beik*.[39]

Similar sentiments were recorded by the Plan Timor-Leste survey mentioned above. The gang violence has thus led to a stigmatization of the poorer *bairros* of Dili as being "hotbeds" of criminal activities and their inhabitants as being inherently prone to crime and violence. These neighbourhoods have also therefore been targeted by occasional and often heavy-handed crackdowns by the security forces. Most residents of the "problem areas" are, however, not involved in criminal activities; they seek, where and when possible, to find regular employment, and are more often the victims rather than the perpetrators of criminal activities.

Focusing on the socio-economic problems, important and pressing as they are, also obscures many of the complexities of the issue. The various disaffected groups in Timor-Leste do recruit many of their members from what Marx might have termed the *Lumpenproletariat*, but the groups also have strong links to members of the economic and political elite as well as the security forces. A relatively high number of members of the East Timorese security forces maintain ties with the disaffected groups, and some police officers have even been arrested by the international security forces as suspects in cases of serious crimes, including murders.[40]

Class is an important and often neglected factor in the equation. There is a clear class-based discourse between the "leaders" (or "big people", *ema bo'ot* in Tetum) versus the commoners (or "little" people, *ema ki'ik* in Tetum) in Timor-Leste.[41] Even those in positions of power and influence may refer to themselves as being a part of the "little people", shifting all responsibility for the current problems from themselves to "those up there in the positions of power". A random incident gave me an indication of the political connections of these disaffected groups: when I asked an East Timorese go-between for some indication as to where I might possibly find one of the better-known RAG leaders as well as a well-known gang leader, I was told that Fretilin party headquarters usually knew where the former could be found, while the latter was usually at the parliamentary office of the Partido Democrático.[42]

Attire, appearance and "attitude"

In terms of their appearance, the gang members of Dili and Port Moresby, Papua New Guinea, share many commonalities, and I therefore take the liberty of quoting at length from Dinnen and Thompson's description of the youthful gangsters, or *raskols*, in Tok Pisin, Port Moresby:

> From its inception, the *raskol* gang has been a predominantly male preserve. Gangs have become an important vehicle for the initiation of young, disenchanted, urban men into the ambivalent space of [Papua New Guinea's] rapidly expanding towns. As well as drawing on older Melanesian models of masculinity, they draw increasingly on models provided by global culture. Prominent among these are the macho heroes of the action videos that are watched avidly in settlements, villages and private homes. The violent masculinity of Rambo and his many imitators is reflected in the popular culture of urban youth. Militaristic clothing is highly valued, as are dreadlocks or shaven heads, and the ubiquitous dark shades. Media images from distant conflicts, including the "war on terror", are scrutinized with great interest and used selectively to replenish a vibrant street style. In late 2002, Osama Bin Laden t-shirts became the latest accoutrement of young male fashion in Port Moresby.[43]

The attire, the names (such as Rambo, Van Damme, *ninjas*, etc.) and the "gangsta" swagger displayed by gang members in Dili as well as in Port Moresby are artefacts, symbols and mannerisms of a globalized gang masculinity, often hegemonic in the local context but a form of protest masculinity in the wider societal picture. Following on from the above quotation from Dinnen and Thompson, it is interesting to note the way the security forces use similar imagery. The globalized impact of this can be seen in Dili, where some members of the local and international forces also seem to have a predisposition towards similar paraphernalia (shades, black t-shirts, ostentatious display of weapons, swagger).[44]

Dinnen and Thompson mention Bin Laden, who was a popular icon in Catholic Timor-Leste and other parts of the region, be it Muslim Indonesia or the Protestant Solomon Islands. Another popular icon is Ernesto "Che" Guevara, whose picture is held up even by ultra-Catholic, virulently anti-communist youth gangs in Dili. Both icons, and others such as Bob Marley, are detached from their political and historical contexts, which are often unknown to the young men sporting their name or portrait, having become icons of masculine rebellion. The Iraq war has brought its own phraseology into the violence – possibly as a pun on the term *firaku* (easterner) and possibly as a reference to the Arab heritage of former Fretilin Prime Minister Mari Alkatiri, western gangs began calling easterners "Iraqis" and, taking things a step further, adopting Stars of David and pro-Israel slogans to demarcate westerner-controlled areas. This imported dichotomy was "supported" by the perceived anti-Fretilin sentiment of the Australian peacekeepers who, simultaneously, had also been deployed to Iraq. A further imported "pun" was calling *firakus* "Figos" in reference to the Portuguese footballer, as the Portuguese UN Police (UNPOL) contingent was perceived at least initially as being more pro-Fretilin and hence, in accordance with the reductivist logic, more pro-eastern.[45]

Magic, mystics and millenarianism

In addition to the icons and symbols borrowed from globalized mass culture, gang members draw on local influences, often merging these with the global ones. An array of icons of male resistance are called upon, sometimes in a literal sense.[46] These include nineteenth-century resistance hero Dom Bonaventura as well as newer icons such as military leaders Rai Los and Alfredo Reinado. What is interesting is the way these icons are depicted in paintings or murals – usually with a certain resemblance to depictions of both Che and Jesus.

Belief in ritual magic and supernatural skills (which are often strikingly reminiscent of the feats performed by the protagonists of popular Indonesian and Chinese action movies) is especially widespread among RAGs, but also claimed by other groups. One of the RAGs, KORK, has developed its own secret language based, according to a senior member, on "ancient" Timorese languages and "global" terms taken from influences as far and wide as Arabic, Mandarin, Sanskrit and contemporary English. The founders of Colimau 2000, on the other hand, claim that independence hero Nicolau Lobato, along with similar figures, is hiding in an underground city in the mountains, waiting for the appropriate time to make his return to save the nation.[47]

Substance abuse

In Timor-Leste male violence, public or private, is often linked to substance abuse. Usually this tends to be alcohol (both commercial and home made), with an additional kick coming from betel nut – and perhaps more significantly from peer pressure within the gangs once the drinking, smoking and chewing begins.

The use of "harder" drugs is often alleged but statistics are rather hard to come by. Australian media reports[48] have raised the spectre of "ice" (methamphetamine, called *shabu-shabu* in Indonesia) as an additional factor in gang violence. This is not necessarily far-fetched, as *shabu-shabu* is the drug of choice in Indonesian provincial towns. Preliminary investigations in Dili would indicate, however, that the drug issue seems to have been played up by the Australian media with relatively little evidence of it on the streets, at least for now. While harder drugs may be an issue in Timor-Leste (or will in all likelihood become one in the near future), it seems that palm wine and beer are usually enough to help the young men tap into their personal and social frustrations.

The spectacle of violence

The disaffected groups in Timor-Leste have preferred using what were termed "offensive weapons" by the UN administration, such as machetes, *rama ambon*,[49] spears and swords. From interviews with law enforcement officials and personal experience, it is clear that during the breakdown of the state security apparatus the groups gained state-of-the-art firearms, such as assault rifles and automatic pistols.[50] In addition, they have access to home-made handguns (*rakitan*) capable of firing standard ammunition and hand-grenades. But in spite of this arsenal, even during the heyday of the crisis the groups were very reluctant to display their weapons, let alone put them to use, at least during daylight hours.[51]

Instead, the violence in Timor-Leste seems to be more about spectacle and intimidation than actual killing. As during the Indonesian-sponsored militia activities in 1998 1999, the public spectacle of "controlled mayhem", of bringing a large, frenzied yet disciplined group of young men displaying their readiness to use violence on to the streets, seems to be more important than actually using this potentially violent force. This pattern is similar to traditional Timorese and, more broadly, Melanesian group warfare, which tended to avoid individual and direct combat. There was also "method in the madness" with regard to the seemingly spontaneous outbreaks of violence, which give the impression of it being able to be "turned on and off" as well as following a geographical pattern.[52]

Social space for violence

As is often the case with young men, one of the key motivational factors for gang members is "respect", be it personally for oneself, within the gang or within the broader community. Some of the social acceptability of these groups stems from their dual functions as protectors of the neighbourhood in question (though the line to extortion may be thin) and their self-assumed role as seekers of justice and vengeance for the injustices of the past. Similar to the ethnic militia and youth gangs in Indonesia, the groups take over state functions such as security provision as "state proxies" while addressing and feeding off group feelings of resentment for real or alleged wrongs.[53]

While women and girls often suffer disproportionately from the public violence of these groups, and even more so from GBV in the private sphere, they are not merely passive victims. Many women "buy into" the violent enactments of masculinity, be it involuntarily or in some cases voluntarily. Mothers, sisters, wives and girlfriends provide what can be seen as logistical support for the young men: washing laundry, cooking food, caring for wounds and giving emotional support. At times women in communities have actively and publicly urged their young men to attack UNPOL in Dili and protected them from police searches.[54] In a sense, women and girls also form, wittingly or unwittingly, the "audience" for whom many of the displays of masculinity are ultimately meant. This is not to say that all or even a majority of women condone the violence. However, during the height of the violence, neither non-violent women nor men were able to find the social space or clout to act against it.

Addressing the violence

Given the debilitating instability caused by the disaffected groups, a number of efforts to address the issue have been made by the East Timorese government, UN agencies and local and international NGOs – including, among many others, the local NGOs Ba Futuro (Towards the Future), Belun (Friend) and Asosiasaun Mane Kontra Violensia (Association of Men against Violence), international agencies such as the Norwegian Ministry of Foreign Affairs, the German GTZ, IrishAid, AusAid, NZAID, USAID and at least eight different UN agencies, as well as grassroots initiatives. In addition to numerous moderately successful dialogues, these efforts have included basic social work programmes such as sports and leisure activities, non-violence training and limited occupational training. The East Timorese government under Prime Minister Xanana Gusmão has also sought to integrate the various groups into society by creating oversight bodies for MAGs as well as "buying off" potential spoilers by offering them lucrative contracting deals.[55]

Following the events of 11 February 2008, when Major Reinado and one of his men were killed in a gun battle and President Ramos-Horta was seriously wounded, the security forces have taken a more forceful stance against the groups. The net effect has been a significant reduction of violence, which has held for four years at the time of writing, although violent gang, MAG and RAG street-fights continue to occur on a regular basis. However, while the social-work-type programmes have temporarily been able to tie in some of the less hard-core members of the groups, the key underlying issues which have made "gang masculinity" an attractive, viable choice for young Timorese men have not been addressed. These core issues include disenchantment with the state and its elites, socio-economic grievances, issues of "respect" and, above all, gender role expectations that equate willingness to use force with masculinity. Given the difficulties of gaining the status of a respectable man through the imagined hegemonic traditional/rural or modern/urban ways, joining a gang, MAG or RAG offers a seeming route out of the social offside position of being a young, urban, poor male.

Conclusion

In this chapter I try to argue, based on my experiences from Timor-Leste, that while young, marginalized men often do form one of the most restless sections of a post-conflict society, the phenomenon tends to be more complex than a simple equating of youth and masculinity with violence. Young men join potentially violent pressure groups for a number of reasons: membership helps alleviate a social crisis linked to the need to adapt to a post-conflict settlement where the clarity of the conflict situation no longer exists; the pressure groups address personal and group grievances; and membership gives the young men a sense of purpose and, for some, economic, social and political advancement. The new identities adopted are amalgamations or hybridizations bringing together local traditional elements of masculinity with idealized concepts of militarized masculinity from the years of struggle and newly imported set-piece masculinities from globalized popular culture. Violent male behaviour has often been normalized in the struggle as a legitimate way to reach socio-economic and political goals – and "private", gender-based violence is far too often seen as acceptable male behaviour.

The disaffected young men do not, however, act out their violence in a vacuum. They are given social space as well as financial and logistical support by those who are "capitalizing" on their violent behaviour: on the one hand, the political and socio-economic elites who are willing to use the groups to further their own goals; and on the other hand, the communities where the young men live and where the disillusionment with the failure of the state and its elites to deliver leads to these groups taking on a role as "state proxies".

The approaches of the East Timorese government, the UN mission and agencies in the country, local civil society and international donors have covered of a wide spectrum of different measures, ranging from "hard" policing to buying off potential spoilers, and from traditional social work to attempts at encouraging young men to reconceptualize their approaches to masculinity and violence. Some of the most ambitious projects, holding both the greatest promise but also the greatest risk of failure, seek to use the groups as positive resources. The various groups do carry out important personal and societal functions for the men involved – functions which can ideally be harnessed productively. These include the sense of identity and belonging which the groups give to their members and their stated ethos of doing something for the greater good. A nurturing of these positive aspects will, however, need to be accompanied by other measures, such as an improvement of the socio-economic situation of the young men, weaning the groups off violence as a tool for addressing grievances and fostering a culture of tolerance.

Notes

1. Studies from other contexts include Manuela Camus, "Primero de Julio: Urban Experiences of Class Decline and Violence", in Kevin Lewis O'Neill and Kedron Thomas (eds), *Securing the City: Neoliberalism, Space, and Insecurity in Postwar Guatemala*, Durham, NC: Duke University Press, 2011, pp. 49–66 (for Guatemala); Danny Hoffman, *The War Machines – Young Men and Violence in Sierra Leone and Liberia*, Durham, NC: Duke University Press, 2011 (for Liberia and Sierra Leone); Janko Van der Werf, *"We Live Like in a War" – An Anthropological Investigation into Criminal Gangs in the Rural and Urban Areas of Papua New Guinea*, Melanesian Mission Studies No. 3, Goroka: Melanesian Institute, 2008 (for Papua New Guinea); Henrik Vigh, *Navigating Terrains of War – Youth and Soldiering in Guinea-Bissau*, Oxford: Berghahn Books, 2006 (for Guinea-Bissau).
2. Thokozani Xaba, "Masculinity and Its Malcontents – The Confrontation between 'Struggle Masculinity' and 'Post-Struggle Masculinity' (1990–1997)", in Robert Morrell (ed.), *Changing Men in Southern Africa*, Pietermaritzburg: University of Natal Press, 2001, p. 107.
3. Ibid., p. 114.
4. Vigh, note 1 above, pp. 89–116.
5. Henri Myrttinen, "Histories of Violence, States of Denial: Militias, Martial Arts and Masculinities in Timor-Leste", PhD thesis, University of KwaZulu-Natal, Durban, 2010. Subsequent research has informed Henri Myrttinen, Monika Schlicher and Maria Tschanz (eds), *"Die Freiheit, für die wir kämpfen ...": Osttimor nach der Unabhängigkeit*, Berlin: Regiospectra Verlag, 2011; Henri Myrttinen, "Violence, Masculinities and

Patriarchy in Post-Conflict Timor-Leste", in Michelle Ford and Lenore Lyons (eds), *Men and Masculinities in Southeast Asia*, New York: Routledge, 2012, pp. 103–120.

6. UNDESA, *World Population Prospects: The 2006 Revision and World Urbanization Prospects*, New York: Population Division of the Department of Economic and Social Affairs of the UN Secretariat, 2006.
7. UNDP, *Timor Leste National Human Development Report 2006 – The Path out of Poverty*, Dili: UNDP, 2006.
8. Ricardo Neupert and Silvino Lopes, *The Demographic Component of the Crisis in Timor Leste*, London: London School of Economics, 2006, p. 22.
9. For a study of the gendered division of labour see for example Henri Myrttinen, Domingas Amaral Guterres and Paula Exposto, "Gender Baseline Study for Liquiçá District – RDPL II", Agencia Española de Cooperación Internacional para el Desarrollo, Dili, 2010, pp. 33–56.
10. For a comprehensive overview of the 2006 crisis see UN Commission of Inquiry, "Report of the United Nations Independent Special Commission of Inquiry for Timor Leste", United Nations, Geneva, 2006.
11. CAVR, *Chega! Relatório da Comissão de Acolhimento, Verdade e Reconcilição de Timor Leste*, Dili: CAVR, 2006, p. 44.
12. Geoffrey Robinson, "East Timor 1999: Crimes against Humanity – A Report Commissioned by the United Nations Office of the High Commissioner for Human Rights (OHCHR)", UCLA, Los Angeles, 2003, p. 1.
13. Serious Crimes Unit, "Brief in Support of the Application for the Issuance of an Arrest Warrant for Wiranto – Case No. #5/2003, *Deputy General Prosecutor vs. Wiranto and Others*", Serious Crimes Unit, Dili, 2003, pp. 1–2.
14. See also Saleh Abdullah and Henri Myrttinen, "'Now They Have Guns, Now They Feel Powerful' – Gender, Small Arms and Violence in Timor-Leste", in Vanessa Farr, Henri Myrttinen and Albrecht Schnabel (eds), *Sexed Pistols: The Gendered Impacts of Small Arms and Light Weapons*, Tokyo: United Nations University Press, 2009, pp. 177–208; Edward Rees, *Under Pressure – Three Decades of Defence Force Development in Timor-Leste 1975–2004*, Geneva: DCAF, 2004, p. 47.
15. These are, for the most part, archived online by the East Timor Action Network, https://lists.riseup.net/www/arc/east-timor.
16. Author's interviews with relevant national and international agencies and NGOs, including UNMIT (UN Integrated Mission in Timor-Leste), UNIFEM (UN Development Fund for Women), UNFPA (UN Fund for Population Activities) and Forum Komunikasi Untuk Perempuan Loro Sae (Fokupers).
17. In addition to a preference for imported military fatigues from various nations, designer shades, bandanas and an abundance of military-style gear, Major Reinado sported the "xXx" logo of Vin Diesel's action movie as a tattoo on his neck.
18. Interview with a RAG leader, Dili, 19 April 2007.
19. See also Maj Nygaard-Christensen, "The Rebel and the Diplomat: Revolutionary Spirits, Sacred Legitimation, and Democracy in Timor-Leste", in Nils Bubandt and Martin Van Beek (eds), *Varieties of Secularism in Asia: Anthropological Explorations of Religion, Politics and the Spiritual*, London: Routledge, 2011, pp. 209–229.
20. For the most comprehensive overview of gangs to date see James Scambary, Hipolito Da Gama and João Barreto, "A Survey of Gangs and Youth Groups in Dili, Timor-Leste", AusAid, Canberra, 2006, www.internal-displacement.org/8025708F004CE90B/%28httpDocuments%29/A77AFC5752038E82C1257241003E2987/$file/Report_Youth_Gangs_in_Dili.pdf.
21. See for example Jose Kai Lekke Sousa-Santos, "The Last Resistance Generation: The Reintegration of Freedom Fighters to Civilians in Timor-Leste", in Damian Grenfell, Mayra Walsh, Januario Soares, Sofie Anselmie, Annie Sloman, Victoria Stead and Anna

Trembath (eds), *Nation-Building across the Urban and Rural in Timor-Leste*, Melbourne: RMIT, 2010, pp. 67–71.

22. The concept of "real independence" came up repeatedly in interviews but often remained rather vague. It was based on a notion that the current post-conflict settlement had not fulfilled pre-independence hopes of prosperity and social equality, foreigners (e.g. the UN mission) continued to play a central role and some figures who had opposed independence during the Indonesian occupation had now risen to positions of power. See also Henri Myrttinen, "Nach dem bewaffneten Kampf: Die Veteranen, Clandestinos und der Ruf nach Anerkennung", in Myrttinen, Schlicher and Tschanz, note 5 above, pp. 155–168.
23. Janina Pawelz, "Teenrage Years: Youth Gangs as Victims, Threats and Autonomous Actors in Post-Conflict Timor-Leste", MA thesis, University of Hamburg, 2011, pp. 56–58; Scambary, Da Gama and Barreto, note 20 above, p. 6.
24. These are, however, often detached from their original political meaning, i.e. sporting a Che Guevara t-shirt does not automatically imply a left-wing political stance. Looking at the use of imported icons in Sierra Leone, Hoffman (note 1 above, p. 67) links the identification of young men with these icons with "the potential of male youth to seize power when the existing order denies them recognized forms of authority", connecting them to "extraordinary powers that one might harness through imitation" (ibid.: 249).
25. Geoffrey Gunn and Reyko Huang, *New Nation: United Nations Peacebuilding in East Timor*, Macao: Tipografia Hung Heng, 2006, pp. 126–127; Scambary, Da Gama and Barreto, note 20 above, p. 4.
26. On RAGs and veterans' organizations an invaluable source was James Scambary, "Disaffected Groups and Social Movements in East Timor", 2007, unpublished, quoted courtesy of the author.
27. Mainly this broke down into the vague categories of easterners (*loro sa'e*) versus westerners (*loro monu*). For a critique see for example Vanessa Prüller, "The 2006 Crisis in East Timor – An Ethnic Conflict?", MA thesis, University of Passau, 2008, pp. 70–85.
28. For lineages see also Douglas Kammen, "Fragments of Utopia: Popular Yearnings in East Timor", *Journal of Southeast Asian Studies* 40(2), 2009, pp. 400–401, 404; Scambary, note 26 above, pp. 15–17; Scambary, Da Gama and Barreto, note 20 above, pp. 2–16.
29. Sousa-Santos, note 21 above, pp. 67–71.
30. Steffen Jensen, *Gangs, Politics & Dignity in Cape Town*, Johannesburg: Wits University Press, 2008, pp. 168–192.
31. Natalie Grove, Kiera Zen, Eurosia Bucar, Luis Moniz Cardoso Pereira, Geovana Fernandes and Noemia Amaral, *Like Stepping Stones in the River: Youth Perspectives on the Crisis in Timor-Leste*, Dili: Plan Timor-Leste, 2007, pp. 7–8.
32. Myrttinen (2010), note 5 above, pp. 130–155.
33. Jani de Silva, *Globalisation, Terror and the Shaming of the Nation: Constructing Local Masculinities in a Sri Lankan Village*, Victoria: Trafford Publishing, 2005, p. 28.
34. Myrttinen (2010), note 5 above, pp. 149–150.
35. Sinclair Dinnen, "Violence and Governance in Melanesia – An Introduction", in Sinclair Dinnen and Allison Ley (eds), *Reflections on Violence in Melanesia*, Canberra: Hawkins Press, 2000, p. 12.
36. See also James Scambary, "Anatomy of a Conflict: The 2006–2007 Communal Violence in East Timor", *Conflict, Security & Development* 9(2), 2009, pp. 265–288.
37. On young male expectations see also Ruth Streicher, "The Construction of Masculinities and Violence: 'Youth Gangs' in Dili, East Timor", MA thesis, Freie Universität, Berlin, 2008, p. 28; Ann Wigglesworth, "Young People in Rural Development", in Damien Kingsbury and Michael Leach (eds), *East Timor: Beyond Independence*, Victoria: Monash University, 2007, p. 57.

38. See for example UNTAET, "Gender Equality Programme", Fact Sheet 11, UN Transitional Administration in East Timor, Dili, 2002, p. 3, www.un.org/en/peacekeeping/missions/past/etimor/fact/fs11.pdf.
39. Return to Rai Ketak, "Communication Breakdown", 29 September 2006, WordPress blog, http://raiketak.wordpress.com/2006/09/.
40. Author's interviews with UNPOL officers, Dili, 20 and 21 June 2007; James Scambary, *Groups, Gangs, and Armed Violence in Timor-Leste*, Dili: TLAVA, 2009, p. 1; Bu Wilson, "Smoke and Mirrors – The Development of the East Timorese Police, 1999–2009", PhD thesis, Australian National University, Canberra, 2010, p. 150.
41. At times the Indonesian equivalents (*orang besar* for members of the socio-economic or political elite and *orang kecil* or *rakyat kecil* for ordinary people) are used as well.
42. Author's interview, Dili, 20 November 2007.
43. Sinclair Dinnen and Edwina Thompson, "State, Society and the Gender of Gun Culture in Papua New Guinea", in Vanessa Farr, Henri Myrttinen and Albrecht Schnabel (eds), *Sexed Pistols: The Gendered Impacts of Small Arms and Light Weapons*, Tokyo: United Nations University Press, 2009, pp. 155–156.
44. See also Henri Myrttinen, "Striking Poses – Notes on the Performances of Violent Masculinities in Conflict Situations", *Nordic Journal for Masculinity Studies* 3(2), 2008, pp. 132–149.
45. On *firaku*/Iraq see also Scambary, note 26 above, pp. 39–40; Prüller, note 27 above, p. 38.
46. Upon evading capture by Australian troops, Reinado claimed he was guided by the spirit of Dom Bonaventura, enabling him to become invisible.
47. Scambary, Da Gama and Barreto, note 20 above, p. 16.
48. Australian Broadcasting Corporation, "Youth Workers Blame Drugs for Dili Gang Violence", ABC News, 30 October 2006.
49. Steel arrows or flechettes shot with slingshots, allegedly occasionally dipped into battery acid for additional effect.
50. UN Commission of Inquiry, note 10 above.
51. Reasons may include a fear of confiscation of the weapons by security forces and a fear of escalating inter-group violence by the use of firearms. See also Abdullah and Myrttinen, note 14 above, pp. 184–185.
52. On similarities to militia violence in 1999 see for example Geoff Robinson, "The Fruitless Search for a Smoking Gun – Tracing the Origins of Violence in East Timor", in Freek Colombijn and Thomas Lindblad (eds), *Roots of Violence in Indonesia*, Singapore: Institute of Southeast Asian Studies, 2002, pp. 243–276.
53. David Brown and Ian Wilson, "Ethnicized Violence in Indonesia: The Betawi Brotherhood Forum in Jakarta", Working Paper No. 145, Asia Research Centre, Murdoch University, Perth, 2007, pp. 18–21; Yuhki Tajima, *Mobilizing for Violence: The Escalation and Limitation of Identity Conflicts – The Case of Lampung, Indonesia*, Jakarta: World Bank, 2004, p. 62; Ian Wilson, "The Biggest Cock: Territoriality, Invulnerability and Honour amongst Jakarta's Gangsters", in Michelle Ford and Lenore Lyons (eds), *Men and Masculinities in Southeast Asia*, New York: Routledge, 2012, pp. 121–138.
54. Interviews with Filipino and Samoan UNPOL officers, Dili, 17 November 2008.
55. Author's interview with World Bank consultant, Dili, 2 August 2012; International Crisis Group, "Timor-Leste: No Time for Complacency", Asia Briefing No. 87, ICG, Dili and Brussels, 2009, pp. 1–3, www.crisisgroup.org/~/media/Files/asia/south-east-asia/timor-leste/b87_timor_leste___no_time_for_complacency.pdf.

Part III

Protecting and engaging children and youth in post-conflict environments

5

Protection and participation of children in post-conflict peacebuilding: International law and evolving practice

Vesselin Popovski

A *child* is *not* a *vase to be filled*, but a *fire* to be lit.

Francois Rabelais

The suffering of children[1] during armed conflict has been gradually recognized in international humanitarian law (IHL), international criminal law (ICL) and human rights law (HRL), resulting in the development of specific measures for child protection.[2] Children suffer from armed conflicts directly, being forcefully recruited as soldiers or becoming collateral victims of combat. They also suffer indirectly, as their childhood and family life are destroyed as a consequence of violent conflict. They are the most vulnerable part of the population not only in times of war, but also in post-conflict periods. Under trauma from war, children can become easy and frequent victims of organized crime,[3] smuggling small arms,[4] human trafficking,[5] labour exploitation, post-conflict violence and terrorist acts.

In the transitional period between war and peace – the post-conflict peacebuilding stage – children require additional legal and practical protection measures; these have already been addressed and codified in IHL. However, children are still largely regarded as passive victims. What has been less recognized and addressed, and what this chapter advocates, is the need for empowerment in addition to protection, and to make children in post-conflict situations an equal participatory force in the reconstruction of the societies in which they live. Such a perception of the child

Escaping victimhood: Children, youth and post-conflict peacebuilding, Schnabel and Tabyshalieva (eds), United Nations University Press, 2013, ISBN 978-92-808-1211-4

as an empowered participant in peacebuilding rather than as a vulnerable object of assistance has been gaining initial ground and needs to be further developed. Children are direct subjects of their rights, and, in the same way as adults, are identifiable and participatory individuals on their own, in addition to being members of their family and of the broader society.

This chapter advocates a simultaneous recognition of the needs to advance the protection of children's rights and to promote their participation in peacebuilding. These two processes should be parallel and inseparable. Only a balance of the two will allow channelling resources into long-term empowerment of children, in addition to short-term immediate protection measures. The development of international law signals the adoption of the perception that children are not merely passive recipients of assistance, but also active participants in the process of recovery and peacebuilding. The evolution of IHL addressed most issues of protection of civilians, and children in particular. The evolution of ICL facilitated the unique and unprecedented option of victims' representation as a separate party in trials, introduced by the 1998 Rome Statute for the International Criminal Court (ICC) and materialized in the practice of this court. The first sentence issued by the ICC – against the Congolese warlord Thomas Lubanga Dyilo – was based on crimes mostly against child victims forcefully recruited into the armed forces in the Democratic Republic of the Congo (DRC).

The evolution of child-relevant HRL brought about the Convention of the Rights of the Child (CRC) and led to the establishment of children's participation as one of the main principles of child rights, along with the principle of non-discrimination and the principle of the best interests of the child. This chapter presents the evolution of IHL, ICL and HRL, and discusses the opportunities and shortcomings of child protection and participation in peacebuilding. Addressing children not primarily as victims, but rather as participants in post-conflict reconstruction, supports the main argument of this book: the best way to escape from child victimhood caused by war is through the active engagement of children in peacebuilding. The chapter concludes that the process of peacebuilding is inherently a long-term exercise, necessarily involves children as society's future generation, and therefore should offer a significant participatory role for children.

International law related to children

Three branches of international law – IHL, ICL and HRL – historically originated in different periods of time at different international conferences and were codified through different treaties. Yet they share one major objective, in that they aim to protect vulnerable people from violations and abuses committed against them. Children – as one such specific vulnerable group – form a part in each of the three legal frameworks.

IHL is regarded as applicable in armed conflict, whereas ICL and HRL are applicable at all times. Although international lawyers prefer to steer clear of the classical distinction between armed conflict and peace, in practice this is a complex matter. The situation in post-conflict zones may remain turbulent and fragile; it can relapse into violence, bringing back the applicability of IHL. Also, many conflicts are not a struggle between uniformed armies defending territorial borders, declaring wars, applying rules and etiquette, respecting ceasefires and peace agreements. Violence frequently and spontaneously erupts without declaration between ill-trained rebels and weak governments which not only ignore the norms of war but may even deliberately target women and children as a means to humiliate the enemy. Instead of receiving special protection as a vulnerable group, children may often become a specific target, exactly because of their vulnerability.[6] Notoriously, this can be done not only by rebels but also by governments or government-supported militia. Children may continue to be abused even after the military hostilities de-escalate: they may remain exploited and sexually abused by warlords, and become vulnerable to various criminal activities in peacetime, such as human and drug trafficking, prostitution, terrorism and organized crime.

The changing nature of armed conflict and the increasing deliberate targeting of civilians demand interconnectedness between IHL, ICL and HRL, so that no child at any time remains unprotected from any abuse. IHL has gradually addressed children as a separate vulnerable group during and after armed conflict and developed child-specific protection measures. ICL has more recently also developed gender awareness and special protection for child victims and witnesses, and adopted other child rights approaches in the practice of the international criminal tribunals. One example is the gradual consideration of crimes where victims are predominantly children as being committed in "aggravating circumstances", thus requiring harsher sentences. HRL has also gradually built up child-related principles and approaches, and evolved over the years. The adoption and fast ratification of the CRC and its optional protocols have been a remarkable achievement. Various UN organs – the General Assembly, the Security Council, the Secretary-General, the special representative for children in armed conflict, the UN Children's Fund (UNICEF) and others – have advanced a stronger child-oriented agenda, adopted resolutions and enforced measures to address children's needs in post-conflict situations; these included the reunification of families, re-establishment of children's educational and family lives, demobilization and integration of child soldiers, and child participation in peacebuilding activities.

All these child-related developments must be seen as one holistic exercise, to which all branches of international law contribute while ensuring that no gaps are left behind. IHL is crucial in ensuring safety and protection of children during and in the immediate aftermath of armed hostilities. ICL is important in delivering justice during the transition from conflict to peace. HRL is essential for sustaining children's rights in the long-term process of building economic and political stability. Children, therefore, are both central objects and central subjects in all elements and at all stages of peacebuilding – security sector reform, preserving justice and rule of law, economic reconstruction, strengthening democratic institutions and ensuring gender equality and youth participation.

The interconnectedness between the attention to children in IHL, ICL and HRL can be illustrated by the parallel progress in all branches of law in condemning and banning the recruitment of child soldiers. This notorious practice has been gradually condemned and prohibited in IHL (Article 77, Additional Protocol I to the Geneva Conventions). It has also been addressed in ICL, and declared a specific category of war crime in the Rome Statute for the ICC (Article 8). Symbolically, the first sentence of the ICC against Thomas Lubanga Dyilo (March 2012) was exactly for a crime against children, who, as young as 11, had been taken to military camps, beaten, drugged, abused and forced to take part in the brutal fighting in the DRC in 2002–2003.[7] The recruitment of child soldiers was condemned and prohibited in HRL (CRC, Article 38), in documents of the International Labour Organization and other organizations. Based on these developments, the practice of using child soldiers has also been addressed, condemned and combated through UN Security Council resolutions and the UN Secretary-General's reports.

Protection and participation of children: IHL perspectives

The 1949 Fourth Geneva Convention applies only to a specifically defined category of "protected persons" and to populations in occupied territories. Therefore, its child-related provisions (Articles 24, 50, 51, 68) fall short of covering all indirect, and even some direct, effects of military hostilities on children. The two additional protocols (AP I and AP II, 1977) to the Geneva Conventions attempt to address this shortcoming, and Article 77 (AP I) establishes special respect for and protection against any form of indecent assault against children. It requests all parties to provide children with the care and aid they may need because of their age or for any other reason. This principle of special care for children is extended to apply in non-international armed conflicts in Article 4 (AP II). In addition, AP I and AP II developed a prohibition of the participation of children in armed hostilities in any capacity. Moreover, if children are recruited and take part in hostilities, they are recognized as combatants and accordingly, in the event of capture, are entitled to prisoner-of-war status under the Third Geneva Convention (1949).

All these developments in IHL are still short of a comprehensive child rights approach. It may be argued that whatever child-related progress is made in IHL, there will always be shortcomings, as this is a *lex specialis*, carrying the burdensome task of having to address issues of both military necessity and humanitarian aspirations. These shortages are inherent in IHL, as its origins are rooted not only in humanitarian concerns but also in facilitating military combat. To illustrate this point, evacuating children from the battlefield is a consideration based not simply on the fact that they are the most vulnerable part of the population and may suffer excessively, but also on the fact that armies will fight easier if the military terrain is cleared beforehand of all civilians, including children. Some child-related texts in IHL even create the impression that the concern was more about family reunification, about parents losing their children in time of war and evacuation, rather than the specifically concrete suffering of children as immature and vulnerable people. As a special law applicable in time of war, IHL has for instance developed more concerns and codified provisions on prisoners of war than on children.

Children are, no doubt, part of the civilian population in armed conflict. Although IHL regards them as such, this is insufficient if one does not also take into account that children experience additional and deeper trauma. To illustrate further, a major principle in the child rights doctrine – the non-discrimination against children – may even contradict protection measures in IHL that extend to certain categories of protected people but not others. The return of prisoners of war, captured and in the hands of the enemy, in some circumstances might be prioritized over the return of evacuated civilians, including children.

Additional complexity and challenge come from the fact that in recent conflicts more anti-child methods of warfare have been reported, such as deliberate starvation, forceful deportation, separation of adults from children, sexual violence against women and children, and recruitment of child soldiers. In September 2004 Chechen terrorists deliberately seized a school in Beslan, Ingushetia, Russian Federation, and kept as hostages hundreds of children and their parents attending the opening day of the school. Tragic bloodshed followed, when the Russian security forces attacked the school to liberate the hostages. As a result over 300 lives were lost, half of these children. Beslan remains a tragic symbol of both deliberate targeting of children and total failure to protect children. Also, numbers of child casualties have been very high during military hostilities, such as between Israel and Hezbollah in south Lebanon in August 2006; between Israel and Hamas in Gaza in January 2009 and November 2012; and during the civil war in Syria in 2011–2013. These examples may even lead to the suspicion that children have been specifically targeted, exactly because of their vulnerability.

Children have been dying more often in recent armed conflicts not only because they are increasingly becoming part of excessive "collateral damage", but also because they are deliberately targeted as a vulnerable group. Yet even without going as far as making such a dire pronouncement, one may confidently conclude that Beslan, south Lebanon, Gaza and Syria demonstrate a dangerous slippery slope towards lack, and even abandonment, of child protection measures, which signals the necessity to interconnect IHL with ICL and HRL. Although IHL has gradually codified on paper concerns with the suffering of children in armed conflict and respective measures to address this suffering, it has fallen short of offering a comprehensive implementation machinery of children's protection and participation.

Protection and participation of children: ICL perspectives

ICL, more recently than IHL, also made significant progress towards advancing the rights of children, particularly their participation in international criminal proceedings. It recognized that while child victims need justice no less than adults, children may experience great trauma in the process of giving testimony and participating in criminal proceedings and thus require special measures of protection, anonymity, non-disclosure and counselling. The evolution of the idea of victims' participation has been remarkable; the Rome Statute for the ICC provided for the first time in history the opportunity for victims of crimes, including child victims, to participate directly as a party in the court. This opportunity became a benchmark, a radical shift in ICL from regarding children simply as victims and survivors to regarding them as full participants in the process of post-conflict justice.

A book entitled *Individual Criminal Accountability and the Rights of Children*, edited by Karin Arts and the present author, addresses the evolution of acknowledging children's rights in ICL by drawing on contributions by the chief prosecutors of three tribunals – the ICC, the International Criminal Tribunal for the former Yugoslavia (ICTY) and the Special Court of Sierra Leone (SCSL) – as well as by distinguished scholars and legal experts.[8] The book analyses the gap and advocates the insertion of a child rights approach in the practice of international criminal tribunals and the enhancement of child victims' protection in domestic and international criminal courts. With regard to children who perpetrated war crimes, the book advocates non-prosecution and engagement of ex-child soldiers in positive participatory and integrative exercises during post-conflict demobilization and peacebuilding. In his contribution to the book, David Crane, former chief prosecutor of the SCSL, strongly argues against the prosecution of child soldiers, basing his argument not only on legal and moral grounds but also on discussions with local communities in Sierra Leone, which opposed such prosecutions.[9]

Saudamini Siegrist from UNICEF claims in her contribution to the book that post-conflict accountability does not necessarily involve criminal responsibility and holding children accountable – and therefore does not necessarily require criminal proceedings.[10] Other accountability mechanisms are preferable, including truth commissions or traditional reconciliation forums such as *gacaca* (Rwanda). Non-judicial and less retributive mechanisms are much more child-friendly and better engage ex-child soldiers in peacebuilding instead of isolating them in prison. Accordingly, UNICEF and some non-governmental organizations (NGOs) have developed numerous participatory programmes to integrate ex-child soldiers into society.[11]

The evolution of the child rights approach in ICL also addresses the question of whether judges regard crimes against children and youth as "aggravating circumstances" and, vice versa, crimes committed by children and youth as "mitigating circumstances". In one early case in the ICTY the judges applied mitigating circumstances, reducing the sentence of Dražen Erdemović, a young Bosnian Serb who participated in the killings of 70 Bosnian Muslims in Srebrenica in August 1995. Erdemović did not hide, testified to a TV reporter what happened, entered a guilty plea, explained the duress under which he shot 70 people and gave instrumental evidence to help indict major war criminals including Radovan Karadjić and Ratko Mladić. His initial 10-year sentence was reduced to five years, and he was later granted early release and left his cell in a Norwegian prison on 13 August 1999, exactly four years after the massacre in Srebrenica. In an interesting comparison between the first two ICTY trials, another defendant, Dusko Tadić, a prison guard in Omarska, was not found guilty of any murder but showed no regret to the victims of torture he facilitated. He received 20 years, a much harsher sentence than Erdemović, who had killed 70 people.

In his contribution to *Individual Criminal Accountability and the Rights of Children*, David Tolbert, ICTY deputy prosecutor, demonstrates how the ICTY can apply aggravating circumstances when victims of crimes are children.[12] In the case *Prosecutor v. Kunarać, Kovać and Vuković* three defendants were prosecuted for rape, torture and enslavement of women and girls in detention centres in Foća, Bosnia and Herzegovina.[13] The prosecutor repeatedly emphasized the age of the victims, some below 15, as an aggravating factor, demanding heavy sentences. The judges also stressed the victims' young ages: "We considered in aggravation the fact that the offences had been committed against particularly vulnerable and defenceless women and girls."[14] Sentencing Kovać, Judge Mumba similarly emphasized: "Particularly appalling and deplorable is your treatment of 12-year-old A.B., a helpless little child for whom you showed absolutely no compassion whatsoever, but whom you abused sexually in the same way as the other girls. You finally sold her like an object, in the knowledge that this would almost certainly mean further sexual assaults by other men."[15] The ICTY judgments in *Kunarać* can be seen as landmark child-oriented developments in ICL – David Tolbert says the case is a "significant step in the direction of further protecting children, and provides a strong precedent on which the ICC and other courts and tribunals can build".[16] The judges in *Kunarać* referred to norms and instruments of both IHL and HRL, and confirmed their discretion to regard victims at 19 and 20 years of age as being close to the conventional protected age of 18, thus also awarding them a special-care status where necessary. The International Criminal Tribunal for Rwanda (ICTR) also applied aggravated sentencing for crimes when there were many children among the victims.[17]

In addition to aggravated sentencing for crimes against children, the international criminal tribunals also focused on developing special measures to protect child victims and witnesses. The rules and procedures of the ICTY and ICTR allow child witnesses to be accompanied by a parent, guardian, relative or friend for the duration of their engagement in the court. The victims and witnesses sections of these tribunals are equipped to provide child victims with special care, counselling and privacy protection through the use of pseudonyms, voice distortion, closed sessions without media and closed-circuit TV, so that defendants may not see the witnesses. Essentially, specific measures were developed for victims and witnesses of sexual assault and gender crimes.

The practice of the SCSL is a further step in the evolution of child-related ICL. In *Prosecutor v. Norman* the SCSL paved the way, ruling that the recruitment of children can already be defined as prohibited in customary international law, establishing direct individual criminal responsibility for the recruiters.[18] The importance of *Norman* is that the SCSL has significantly advanced the measures for protection of child victims and witnesses.

For the first time in history the ICC made the victims, including children, direct participants in criminal proceedings. The ICC rules and proceedings establish that in every case involving child victims the ICC appoints a legal representative and fully covers the costs through the court's budget or a national legal aid system. Statistics show, however, that despite protection measures, children are still generally reluctant to testify and exercise their right to participate in ICC proceedings. The first ICC trial, *Lubanga Dyilo*,[19] was also the first at which child victims directly participated as a party in an international criminal tribunal, exposing the gravity of crimes against children – specifically their enlistment, conscription and use in combat. Lubanga first appeared before the ICC pre-trial chamber in November 2006 to hear the charges. Four victims participated and were allowed to present their concerns. On 29 January 2007 the pre-trial chamber confirmed the charges, finding sufficient substantial ground to establish Lubanga's criminal responsibility as a co-perpetrator in enlisting child soldiers. On 26 January 2009 the ICC opened the hearings on merit, and eight legal representatives representing 93 victims, mostly children, participated in the trial proceedings as a separate party alongside the prosecution, the defence and the registry. This was a truly revolutionary moment, as never before in the history of criminal law had children participated directly in the process of such as trial – in all previous cases child victims were solely represented by the prosecution.

Child victims' participation in *Lubanga* was not simply symbolically important. It also strengthened the prosecution's case, which had not been very solid. At one point the judges even ordered the defendant's release, arguing that he could not be held in preventive custody on a speculative basis. However, this order was not implemented with immediate effect; the prosecution could appeal the decision and grant suspensive effect to keep Lubanga in detention until the appeals chamber decided on 8 October 2010 to reverse the trial chamber's decision to stay proceedings. The trial resumed, but was put on hold for six weeks in early 2011 due to various challenges brought by the defence, in particular regarding the disclosure of the identity of witnesses and participating victims. There were not only concerns with the prosecutorial strategy, but also with the investigation.[20] On 23 February 2011 the trial chamber rejected another defence application for a stay of proceedings and on 25–26 August 2011 the prosecution and the defence could finally present their closing arguments, followed by the legal representatives of the victims. "A total of 123 victims, mostly children, participated in *Lubanga*."[21] They could not only express views on various matters, but also cross-examine witnesses on specific issues. On 14 March 2012 Lubanga was found guilty of enlisting and conscripting children under the age of 15 and using them to participate in hostilities in the DRC – a well-established war crime under the ICC Statute.

On 13 June 2012 the trial chamber heard aggravating and mitigating factors to determine the sentence. The prosecution requested an aggravated 30-year sentence, as the crimes were committed against children; but simultaneously it stressed that that it "would not appeal against a 20 years sentence, should this also include a genuine apology and commitment by Lubanga to offer good will co-operation to the ICC to prevent future crimes and promote peace".[22] On 10 July 2012 the ICC sentenced Lubanga to 14 years' imprisonment. The verdict was met with mixed feelings. On the one hand, this was the first completed ICC case, deserving ovations. Michael Bochenek from Amnesty International called it a "historic moment that puts the whole world on notice that anyone who recruits children faces trial and imprisonment".[23] On the other hand, the decision to limit the criminal offence to recruitment of child soldiers excluded other crimes – sexual violence in particular – from consideration. This was very disappointing for many child victims and made one of the judges, Odio Benito, express a dissenting opinion and recommend the ICC to sharpen its attention and seek successful remedies for victims of sexual violence and other gender-based crimes.

A further shortcoming in *Lubanga* was the fact that, as the prosecution was limited to a relatively narrow set of crimes, the pool of victims eligible for reparations was also narrowed to just a mere fraction of those who actually suffered at the hands of Lubanga. The prosecution also failed to recover any assets linked to Lubanga to help pay for his crimes. Thus the entire burden fell on the ICC Trust Fund for Victims and state governments. On 7 August 2012 the ICC issued its first-ever decision on the principles of victims' reparations for harm suffered through the crimes committed by Lubanga: "The judges set out the basis for the award of reparations as well as the process – the Trust Fund will collect reparations proposals from victims, which then will be approved by the Trial Chamber."[24]

The ICC's second verdict – against the former Congolese militia leader Mathieu Ngudjolo Chui – came on 18 December 2012. The participation of victims in this case was further enlarged: 366 victims, including children, were allowed to take part. Sexual violence and gender-based crimes, slavery, rape and cruel or inhuman treatment, including of children, were among the charges. However, the verdict was a disappointment: Ngudjolo was found not guilty after he denied ordering the crimes, claiming that he learned of them days later. The ICC unanimously acquitted him of seven counts of war crimes and three of crimes against humanity, including enlisting child soldiers to carry out killings. It was argued that the prosecutor had not proved beyond reasonable doubt that Ngudjolo was the commander of the attack on Bogoro, DRC, and therefore could not be individually responsible for the crimes committed. The ICC found that some key witness testimony had moreover been contradictory and not credible.[25] In its summary the trial chamber stressed that the ruling did not mean no crimes were committed in Bogoro, nor did it question that people there had suffered; rather, given the standard of proof, the evidence presented to support Ngudjolo's guilt had not allowed the chamber to form a conviction beyond reasonable doubt. Presiding Judge Bruno Cotte ordered Ngudjolo's immediate release and rejected the attempts of the prosecutor to have him detained pending an appeal.

The first ICC cases demonstrate that child victims, even if allowed direct participation in proceedings, might not see satisfactory remedies. Accordingly, the prosecution needs to develop its strategies and be consistent and persuasive. Otherwise victims affected by atrocities may gradually lose their trust and faith in the ICC.

Protection and participation of children in HRL

The child-oriented approach in ICL, and prior to that in IHL, as this chapter has so far presented, has been developed more in theory than in practice. IHL and ICL have mainly responded to crimes that occurred in times of armed conflict. However, more often abuses against children take place in peacetime. Human trafficking, sexual exploitation, drug trafficking and forced labour supported by transnational criminal networks are international crimes that often involve children, yet might be even harder to address than well-recognized international wrongs such as crimes against humanity and war crimes, dealt with by the ICC. Given the lack of international criminal accountability mechanisms, it is primarily HRL and national legal systems that deal with such abuses against children. While HRL also contains a prohibition of recruitment of child soldiers and addresses juvenile justice issues, there has not been much attention to the position of child victims and witnesses in court; thus children's protection and participation, developed in ICL, are also essential in HRL and the implementation of the CRC. As children are crucial witnesses, especially in cases relating to child soldiers, the ICC has developed special measures for their protection and participation and is elaborating on further policies for working with child victims and witnesses. The UN Economic and Social Commission (ECOSOC) has also profiled the role of child witnesses by adopting, in 2005, "Guidelines on Justice in Matters Involving Child Victims and Witnesses of Crime",[26] presenting some good practices, assisting the review of domestic laws and procedures, and guiding those working with child victims and witnesses at national, regional and international levels. Some domestic law, the *Roper v. Simmons* case at the US Supreme Court[27] and decisions from the Inter-American Commission on Human Rights provide further credible legal arguments that existing customary international law extends legal protection against both child recruitment and the death penalty for minors. The practice of the European Court of Human Rights in Strasbourg is another positive example of a child-oriented approach, applicable to both the prosecution of children affected by armed conflict and the defence of children under investigation and prosecution.[28] These developments further signify the importance of a holistic approach, a synergy between IHL, ICL and HRL and also a synergy between international law, regional human rights law and domestic law related to children.

HRL's major achievement in this process is the adoption of the CRC in 1989, the speed at which it came into force (within only one year) and the adoption in 2000 of its two optional protocols: the first addressing children in armed conflict and the second addressing the sale of children, child prostitution and child pornography. The CRC is the initial and most appropriate framework to address issues of child protection and participation, as it spans various chapters in international law and customs in realizing children's rights and establishing principles for their protection and participation. It unites IHL, HRL and juvenile law into one document and is widely seen as the most comprehensive and strong summary of the rights and needs of children worldwide. The fast ratification of the CRC clearly indicates the universal values and global reach of this cause. Even more important is the practical progress that many governmental bodies and NGOs have made in incorporating the CRC into their mission statements and developing child rights approaches to their work.

The CRC defines children as human beings below the age of 18 and grants them all human rights and fundamental freedoms. It establishes as its central purpose the survival and development of children, and determines three major principles: the best interests of the child; non-discrimination by age; and children's participation in all relevant aspects of life. The CRC is particularly useful in creating a framework within which any form of concrete child-oriented activity can take place; the most fundamental components of this framework are the general objectives and principles that the convention prescribes for all actions affecting children and youth.

For a long time children have been considered immature and vulnerable persons – easily humiliated, threatened, beaten, raped. However horrific these abuses might be, they are not the only victimizing experiences: children also suffer from isolation and denial of participation in decision-making and rebuilding life after conflicts. Being respected as equal to adults and having freedom of expression and opportunities to influence and make decisions are powerful antidotes to violence against children. Walt Disney, an influential child rights' advocate and a famous child entertainer, once said that "our greatest natural resource is the minds of our children".[29] Children can no longer be perceived as passive recipients of care and protection, or accidental beneficiaries of policy decisions. Serious attention must be paid to their voice and opinion, and to their participation in all issues related to their welfare and development. Ending violence against children and ensuring their voices are heard and taken seriously are two sides of the same coin, both depending upon perceiving and respecting children as equal persons and holders of fundamental human rights. A child who experienced violence would be a double victim if s/he is not allowed to be heard, nor taken seriously in the process of reconciliation and rebuilding. The participation of children recognizes the inherent dignity and the equal and inalienable rights of all members of the human family.

Children's right to be heard and to be taken seriously, therefore, has developed as a crucial and visionary provision of the CRC. Article 12 states:

> 1. States Parties shall assure to the child who is capable of forming his or her own views the right to express those views freely in all matters affecting the child, the views of the child being given due weight in accordance with the age and maturity of the child.
>
> 2. For this purpose, the child shall in particular be provided the opportunity to be heard in any judicial and administrative proceedings affecting the child, either directly, or through a representative or an appropriate body, in a manner consistent with the procedural rules of national law.[30]

HRL and children's participation in peacebuilding

The main objective and the three main principles of the CRC are of crucial significance for the participation of children in peacebuilding. Survival during turmoil and development during peace are the two objectives and main drivers of the codification and implementation of the child-oriented approach in HRL. The three main principles developed in the CRC – the best interests of the child, non-discrimination and participation – are applicable in the post-conflict period and should be streamlined in all peacebuilding actions. Whether undertaken by governments, international agencies, social welfare institutions, law courts or administrative bodies, the consideration of the "best interests of the child" should guide any decision-making in peacebuilding, and at any time when children are involved.

Peacebuilding is an activity that engages the whole population; it is a long-term process, oriented to create sustainable livelihoods, economic prospects, intercultural tolerance, welfare, political stability and respect for human rights. It integrates a sustainable approach to peace and thus effectively takes into account the next generation – children – when making any decisions. Peacebuilding is necessarily long term, and will not be sustainable – or even possible – without putting children and youth first. If peacekeeping is building bridges between conflicting parties and their armies, peacebuilding is building bridges between entire communities. As children are the future of these communities, they have to participate actively in the process for peace to be sustainable in the long term. As such, peacebuilding can only be an intergenerational undertaking, engaging children naturally, always and everywhere.

The second CRC principle – non-discrimination – is also central and needs stronger consideration and emphasis. Sadly, many peacebuilding programmes still do not address, and may even discriminate against, children in post-conflict rebuilding. There have been many donations and programmes on disarmament and demobilization; while ex-child soldiers may have been part of these, more attention has to be given to child non-soldiers. Furthermore, programmes on ex-child soldiers have mostly benefited boys and only very minimally girl soldiers. Even if up to 40 per cent of child soldiers are estimated to be female, girl soldiers remain largely invisible – as one usually imagines a boy with a weapon when thinking about child soldiers, much of the information collected concentrates on boys' experiences with the armed forces. Elliott Skinner was among the first to state that girl fighters have become increasingly common, and to defeat the misconception that girls do not take part in combat.[31] The conflict in Sierra Leone, for instance, was one of the worst for its use of child soldiers, with approximately half of the rebel fighters (Revolutionary United Front – RUF) being children, many having joined simply to feed and clothe themselves.[32] However, as Isobel McConnan and Sarah Uppard emphasized, there has been gender discrimination in child soldiers' rehabilitation processes.[33] A report by the National Committee for Disarmament, Demobilisation and Reintegration (DDR) of the government of Sierra Leone in May 2002 showed that of almost 70,000 ex-combatants who had been through formal DDR, close to 7,000 were under the age of 18. Although the figures for child ex-combatants were not broken down into girls and boys, the report does state that of all its beneficiaries 92 per cent were male and 8 per cent female.[34] A study by Dyan Mazurana and Susan McKay reveals that most international initiatives and DDR programmes refer only to boys and rarely include girls, such as in the case of

Sierra Leone, where of 1,213 children released from the RUF only 15 were girls.[35] Girl soldiers, most of whom had been sexually assaulted, can be stigmatized forever by their communities and feel ashamed. They may prefer to hide instead of coming out in the open and accessing DDR programmes and benefits. This stigma makes it very difficult even to return home after civil wars, as their families may view them as unruly and promiscuous. When DDR programmes are linked to the requirement to hand in a weapon, this may further exclude girls. Improper attitudes to girl soldiers negatively affect not only demobilization but also long-term reintegration, such as through marriage denials or refusals of reproductive health assistance.

Codification and strengthening of IHL, ICL and HRL gradually addressed the problem of child soldier recruitment, but this needs to be complemented with implementation measures that provide children, their families and communities with viable alternatives to military recruitment. There are already some good practices of successful educational programmes and other rehabilitation and reintegration efforts that engage children in peacebuilding. One lesson from recent experiences is that children should not be overburdened with highly demanding participatory tasks. Playing remains a large and important part of their life through which they can learn to protect themselves and other children, and to express themselves and participate freely. Save the Children Sweden offers an instructive experience. The NGO organized children's clubs in Sierra Leone, which could serve as models on how to help and engage children and practitioners in a post-conflict environment, give children confidence and knowledge of their rights, and empower them to become equal members of society. In her account of these experiences, Charly Cox draws on numerous discussions with children and offers a remarkable overview of how they themselves think about their role in peacebuilding.[36]

While engaging children produces positive results, excluding them may be counterproductive. One needs to be cautious: not all educational initiatives may represent best practices. If educational programmes are primarily targeted at adults, they might ignore children's needs, discriminate against them and become problematic. Kenneth Bush and Diana Saltarelli, for example, question whether educational programmes in post-conflict situations are all inevitably a force for good, showing how education can be manipulated by nationalism to divide rather than unite, particularly in situations of continued tension or violence. They advocate the need for peacebuilding education to transform the very foundations of intolerance.[37]

These experiences signify how crucial the third CRC principle (child participation) is. In fact the mere concept of, and attention to, peacebuilding has been developed as a necessarily long-term process, thus demanding participation by children and youth. Exactly the recognition of peacebuilding's long-term relevance would see children as not only its main beneficiaries but also its main participants. Children are tomorrow's adults, and are those who will sustain and develop peace, security and well-being in 10, 20 or 30 years from now. Sustainable peace and sustainable development are intergenerational and, as main objectives of peacebuilding, are aimed at a society's future, in which today's children play a crucial part. Therefore, the solid participation of children in reconstruction processes will ensure durability, effectiveness and long-term success.

Peacebuilding is a cross-generational exercise, but in the past the focus has been on state building and adult ownership. One important lesson to acknowledge is that peacebuilding should be more about children – how they study, their access to knowledge and innovation, and how they participate and engage together in building a sustainable future for their countries and for the world. The implementation of the CRC's participation requirements remains a major challenge for many actors, even those who claim to represent a child-rights-based mandate. It requires fundamental changes in attitudes towards children, within the spirit and the letter of the CRC.

In summary, the combined objectives and principles of the child-rights-based approach – best interests of the child, participation and non-discrimination – construct a formidable challenge, but also an opportunity for peacebuilding actors. Further research into methods of engaging children in participation in peacebuilding, including collection of best and worst practices, is required.

Conclusion

This chapter presents the shortcomings and opportunities in child protection and participation in peacebuilding and demonstrates how child-related international law – IHL, ICL and HRL – has been developed and how the three branches can mutually complement each other. It argues that children need to be empowered as full participants in the peacebuilding process and should not just be seen as the most vulnerable victims in need of special measures of protection. As an important investment in the eventual need to heal the wounds of war, post-conflict peacebuilding activities should incorporate broader child rights and principles developed in HRL. If IHL applies during armed conflict and ICL applies mostly in the immediate aftermath of conflict, child-relevant HRL applies at all times; therefore its main principles – best interests of the child, non-discrimination and participation – are essential in the midst of war. Peacebuilding does not need to wait until peacekeeping finishes – the two processes run in parallel. If IHL is mostly concerned with the protection of civilians (including children) in armed conflict, if ICL is mostly concerned with punishing international crimes (including those against children), HRL should be the overarching umbrella that leaves no gaps in child protection and participation.

There are opportunities, situations and scope to make international law applicable to all circumstances concerning children. However, there are also differences between the three bodies of law with respect to *opinio juris*, procedures, targets, monitoring and enforcement capacities. It is necessary to adopt a cumulative application of IHL, ICL and HRL when children are concerned, given that they continue to be abused during both wartime and peacebuilding. Children are the most vulnerable, but simultaneously they are also among the main beneficiaries and participants in peacebuilding. Therefore any actions should be inclusive and take into account their best interests. Protection and participation of children should be based not only on mutual recognition, but also on mutual reinforcement of the norms and procedures of IHL, ICL and HRL.

A fruitful accumulation of child-related provisions and approaches can be instrumental in drawing attention to the situation of children in and after armed conflicts and ending notorious criminal practices against them. IHL has become more child-oriented with the 1977 additional protocols to the Geneva Conventions and the recent developments in ICL. The first trials at the ICC demonstrated how important it is to give voice and legal representation to victims, including children. This chapter describes how the road to child rights approaches has gradually been paved, although much still remains to be done. The first ICC trials allowed child victims' direct representation in the legal proceedings, but gaps in the investigation and shortcomings in the prosecutorial strategies – such as the exclusion of sexual violence from the scope of charges in *Lubanga* – still leave a lot to be desired.

The chapter also demonstrates how HRL has evolved from the landmark CRC, although the fast codification of the rights of the child has not been supplemented by similarly efficient implementation efforts. A major gap remains the lack of proper attention to girl soldiers, as gender insensitivity has in fact magnified the victimization of girl soldiers, who suffer from both age and gender discrimination. The chapter presents some good practices in active bottom-up inclusion of children in educational and other reintegration programmes, such as the creation of children's clubs in post-conflict zones, where playing has been accompanied with protection. It appeals for learning lessons from these best practices and avoiding the repetition of bad practices, mistakes and ignorance.

The chapter also delivers a short, sharp message in line with this book's major argument: for peacebuilding to succeed, it has to focus heavily on children. A particularly crucial problem of peacebuilding concerns the fact that it tends to be approached and practised not as an intergenerational but as a short-term process. All too often, international attention to post-conflict countries fades away once human atrocities are no longer front-page stories. Logically, to ensure durability and sustainability of peacebuilding, efforts have to take into account the safety and well-being of the next generation, our children. Nobody can build lasting peace without the voice of children and serious attention to what they say, think, dream and do.

Notes

1. The CRC defines "children" as persons up to the age of 18 years.
2. I have addressed some developments in child protection in IHL and HRL in Vesselin Popovski, "Legal Protection of Children in International Humanitarian Law and Human Rights Law", in Roberta Arnold and Loelle Quenivet (eds), *International Humanitarian Law and Human Rights Law: Towards a New Merger in International Law*, Leiden: Martinus Nijhoff Publishers, 2008, pp. 383–402.
3. For literature on organized crime and children see *Bibliography on the Effects of Organized Crime on Women & Children*, Vancouver, BC: University of British Columbia, International Centre for Criminal Law Reform and Criminal Justice Policy, Faculty of Law, April 1995.
4. Vanessa Farr, Henri Myrttinen and Albrecht Schnabel (eds), *Sexed Pistols: The Gendered Impacts of Small Arms and Light Weapons*, Tokyo: United Nations University Press, 2009.
5. Sally Cameron and Edward Newman (eds), *Trafficking in Humans: Social, Cultural and Political Dimensions*, Tokyo: United Nations University Press, 2008.
6. On 1 September 2004 Chechen guerrillas occupied a school in Beslan, Ingushetia, taking hundreds of hostages – children and their parents attending the first-day opening ceremony at the school. Russian forces opened fire and attacked the school; as a result over 300 were killed, half of them children.
7. *The Prosecutor v. Thomas Lubanga Dyilo*, ICC-01/04-01/06, www.icc-cpi.int/en_menus/icc/situations%20and%20cases/situations/situation%20icc%200104/related%20cases/icc%200104%200106/Pages/democratic%20republic%20of%20the%20congo.aspx. For further analysis see www.coalitionfortheicc.org/?mod=drctimelinelubanga.
8. Karin Arts and Vesselin Popovski (eds), *Individual Criminal Accountability and the Rights of Children*, The Hague: Hague Academic Press, 2006.
9. David Crane, "Strike Terror No More: Prosecuting the Use of Children in Times of Conflict – The West African Extreme", in Arts and Popovski, ibid., pp. 119–132.
10. Saudamini Siegrist, "Child Participation in International Criminal Accountability Mechanisms", in Arts and Popovski, note 8 above, pp. 53–65.
11. UNICEF's Innocenti Research Center has conducted extensive research on the link between transitional justice and children in post-conflict peacebuilding countries like Sierra Leone. It has also brought together useful research on children in armed conflict. A list of projects and publications can be found at www.childreninarmedconflict.org/home.html.

12. David Tolbert, "Children and International Criminal Law: The Practice of ICTY", in Arts and Popovski, note 8 above, pp. 147–154.
13. ICTY, *The Prosecutor v. Kunarać, Kovać and Vuković*. Case information sheet at www.icty.org/x/cases/kunarac/cis/en/cis_kunarac_al_en.pdf. For the full text of the case see www.un.org/icty/foca/trialc2/judgement/index.htm.
14. Ibid.
15. Ibid.
16. Tolbert, note 12 above, p. 153.
17. *The Prosecutor v. Akayesu*, Case No. ICTR-96-4-T.
18. *The Prosecutor v. Norman*, Case No. SCSL-2003-08-PT. For commentary by Justice Geoffrey Robertson, SCSL president, see *Criminal Law Forum* 15, 2004, pp. 247–272.
19. Coalition for the International Criminal Court, "Lubanga Case", www.iccnow.org/?mod=drctimelinelubanga.
20. Susana SáCouto and Katherine A. Cleary, "The Importance of Effective Investigation of Sexual Violence and Gender-Based Crimes at the International Criminal Court", *American University Journal of Gender, Social Policy & the Law* 17(2), 2009, pp. 337–360.
21. Coalition for the International Criminal Court, note 19 above.
22. Ibid.
23. See Amnesty International, "First Sentence: Lubanga Dyilo Sentenced to 14 Years at the ICC", Amnesty International, 10 July 2012, www.amnesty.org/en/news/first-sentence-lubanga-dyilo-sentenced-14-years-icc-2012-07-10.
24. Coalition for the International Criminal Court, note 19 above.
25. See Coalition for the International Criminal Court, "Alleged Congolese Militia Leader Found Not Guilty in Second ICC Trial", Coalition for the International Criminal Court, 18 December 2012, http://iccnow.org/documents/CICC_PR_Ngudjolo_Dec2012.pdf.
26. ECOSOC Resolution 2005/20, "Guidelines on Justice in Matters Involving Child Victims and Witnesses of Crime", 22 July 2005, www.un.org/en/pseataskforce/docs/guidelines_on_justice_in_matters_involving_child_victims_and.pdf.
27. Jennifer Eswari Borra, "*Roper v. Simmons*, 125 S.Ct. 1183 (2005)", *Journal of Gender, Social Policy & the Law* 13(3), 2005, pp. 707–715.
28. Nuala Mole, "Litigating Children's Rights Affected by Armed Conflict Before the European Court for Human Rights", in Arts and Popovski, note 8 above, pp. 167–182.
29. Quoted by *Little Oxford Dictionary of Quotations*, Oxford: Oxford University Press, 1994, p. 62.
30. United Nations, "Convention on the Rights of the Child, Adopted and Opened for Signature, Ratification and Accession by General Assembly Resolution 44/25 of 20 November 1989, Entry into Force 2 September 1990, in Accordance with Article 49", UN Office of the High Commissioner for Human Rights, Geneva, www.ohchr.org/en/professionalinterest/pages/crc.aspx.
31. Elliott P. Skinner, "Child Soldiers in Africa: A Disaster for Future Families", *International Journal on World Peace* 16(2), 1999, pp. 7–22.
32. Myriam Denov, *Child Soldiers: Sierra Leone's Revolutionary United Front*, Cambridge: Cambridge University Press, 2010.
33. Isobel McConnan and Sarah Uppard, *Children, Not Soldiers: Guidelines for Working with Child Soldiers and Children Associated with Fighting Forces*, London: Save the Children UK, 2001.
34. Government of Sierra Leone and World Bank, "Sierra Leone Disarmament and Demobilisation Program Assessment Report", World Bank, Washington, DC, July 2002. See also the analysis by Thokozani Thusi and Sarah Meek, "Disarmament and Demobilisation",

in Mark Malan, Sarah Meek, Thokozani Thusi, Jeremy Ginifer and Patrick Coker, "Sierra Leone: Building the Road to Recovery", Monograph 80, Institute for Security Studies, Pretoria, 1 March 2003, pp. 23–38, www.issafrica.org/pubs/monographs/No80/Content.html.

35. Dyan Mazurana and Susan McKay, "Child Soldiers: What About the Girls?", *Bulletin of the Atomic Scientists* 57(5), 2001, pp. 30–35.
36. Charly Cox, "Playing and Protecting: Learning from Children's Clubs in Sierra Leone", Save the Children Sweden, Regional Office for West Africa, Dakar, 2009, http://resourcecentre.savethechildren.se/sites/default/files/documents/1271.pdf.
37. Kenneth D. Bush and Diana Saltarelli, "The Two Faces of Education in Ethnic Conflict: Towards a Peacebuilding Education for Children", UNICEF Innocenti Research Centre, Florence, 2000, www.unicef-irc.org/publications/pdf/insight4.pdf.

6

Children and security sector governance

David Nosworthy

Conflict impacts disproportionately on young people, robbing them of the secure environment that is the most conducive to developing the fullest of their potential. Whether targeted directly or indirectly as part of the civilian population, children are killed and maimed during conflict and endure multiple forms of exploitation, including sexual violence and underage recruitment into armed forces or groups. As child soldiers they experience at first hand some of the worst atrocities of war, forced to witness and even participate in horrendous acts of violence, at times committed against their own families and communities. Affected as victims, witnesses or even perpetrators of violence, their inherent resilience enables most to deal with and overcome the adversity they experience. However, many may be left suffering the effects of long-term physical or mental trauma.

The destruction of, and disruption to, health and education facilities and other vital infrastructure further negatively impact their chances for a healthy development. The general deprivation associated with conflict exposes children to hunger, disease and displacement. According to UNICEF, "In the last decade, more than 2 million children have died as a direct result of armed conflict, and more than three times that number have been permanently disabled or seriously injured. An estimated 20 million children have been forced to flee their homes, and more than 1 million have been orphaned or separated from their families."[1]

It should be noted that since the early 1990s there has been an overall reduction in the number of situations classified as major armed conflicts.[2]

Escaping victimhood: Children, youth and post-conflict peacebuilding, Schnabel and Tabyshalieva (eds), United Nations University Press, 2013, ISBN 978-92-808-1211-4

However, while ending open conflict is obviously to be commended, ensuring effective closure and meaningful reconciliation is quite another challenge. It is often children who bear the brunt of ongoing feelings of resentment, discrimination and fear. In addition, they are likely to live with ongoing political uncertainty and weak investment in health, education, job creation and other basic services and infrastructure.[3] Notwithstanding the very real local threat of open conflict to education facilities, the 2012 Human Security Report interestingly presents an analysis in which the reason why "educational outcomes are, on average, lower in conflict-affected countries than nonconflict countries is because they were already lower before the war started".[4] Pointing to the "long-term average trend towards better educational outcomes in developing countries in peacetime", the report states that "few of today's wars are deadly or destructive enough to reverse this long-term trend".[5] Based on conjecture, it goes on to suggest that a more significant link can possibly be found between negative educational outcomes and state fragility, putting forward as a policy priority the need to support "effective, legitimate, resilient, and sustainable institutions of effective governance".[6]

This chapter considers the imperative of re-establishing justice and security during conflict transformation, a process in which children and youth – two groups especially affected by armed conflict – are rarely considered. Re-establishing rule of law and respect for human rights requires that all stakeholders, including young people, be engaged in assessing and defining security priorities. Central to this is the acknowledgement that children have an important contribution to make to both the recovery and peacebuilding processes and long-term social change.

Re-establishing security and stability requires the effective and accountable delivery of public goods, including social and security services, to the population as a whole. Viewing security as a public good means that security provision should be approached in much the same way as democratic institutions deliver other public services, guided by principles of good governance, including transparency, accountability and civilian participation. Delivering effective security to the population requires multiple actors working together at multiple levels. At the state level this calls for a cross-government approach, and also an acknowledgement that both state and non-state actors will need to be engaged. Taking security beyond the traditional notion of state security requires policy approaches that respond to the security concerns of communities and individuals, providing opportunity to contribute and engage with the process, and governance mechanisms capable of managing very different and at times apparently conflicting objectives. Including all stakeholders requires that young people are involved in assessing and defining priorities in a context of rule of law and respect for human rights.

In developing an argument for the inclusion of children and youth in the process of conflict transformation, this chapter explores the security governance aspects of post-conflict peacebuilding. Governance can be understood formally as "the structures and processes which enable a set of public and private actors to coordinate their interdependent needs and interests through the making and implementation of binding policy decisions in the absence of a central political authority".[7]

The notion of "security governance" is thus concerned with the mechanisms and structures through which security is provided. At the state level, security governance refers to the organization and management of the security sector, understood here to comprise all the formal and informal bodies (ranging from armed forces, police and intelligence agencies to those institutions that formulate, implement and oversee security policy) whose main responsibilities are protection of the state and its constituent communities.[8]

Armed conflict provides a cocktail of factors that can negatively affect young people, among them insecurity, uncertainty over the future, limited or no access to services including education, availability of small arms and general breakdown in rule of law. Such factors are likely to be manipulated and used by peace spoilers intent on derailing stabilization efforts, whether for political or economic ends, by pushing young people into violence, crime or radicalization.

The phenomenon of child soldiering has become the public face of the problem of children affected by armed conflict, given the vivid image of children bearing arms. There are nonetheless many other dimensions to the problem, including, for example, refugee and internally displaced children, separated and unaccompanied children, and gender-based violence.

Such experiences may mean that affected children will have been socialized towards violence as the only method of conflict resolution, including in personal relationships. Post-conflict reforms will be vital in breaking the cycle of violence. Children will require special protection and assistance and robust rehabilitation, supported by adequately resourced community-based reintegration programmes. Pursuit of restorative and educational approaches to justice is central to addressing recidivism. Re-establishing rule of law and respect for human rights will be central to re-establishing confidence and trust in the system.

Armed conflict and children's security

The impact of armed conflict on children began to receive global attention at the end of the Cold War with the outbreak of conflict across several regions, particularly in Africa, where the end of superpower rivalry resulted in the violent expression of many long-standing grievances. In 1994 the United Nations initiated a study into this impact (the Machel study).[9] Its report, published in 1996, was significant in highlighting a recurring theme at the centre of the protection of children, namely the peace and security agenda, and the important role of the international community in supporting post-conflict peacebuilding and reconstruction. Recognizing the impact of armed conflict on children, it is necessary to understand better the association between their experiences and the broader situation in order to harness more constructively the resource that young people represent for the peacebuilding process. As the Machel study noted, "In a world of diversity and disparity, children are a unifying force capable of bringing people to common ethical grounds. Children's needs and aspirations cut across all ideologies and cultures."[10]

Developing a better understanding of how security affects the lives of young people is essential for better informing policy-makers. One particularly important aspect in this regard is the recognition of children's evolving capacities. As developing individuals, children should not be simply categorized as an inert and static vulnerable group, but should be recognized as important members of society who tomorrow will be making decisions that will influence the prospects for sustainable peace or renewed conflict.

There is, however, a tendency for children, and in particular youth, to be demonized by society – a phenomenon that can be observed around the globe. Just one of the challenges in the post-conflict environment will be how communities handle the reinsertion of former child combatants, and how they respond to a new reality of social interaction. In these circumstances it is important not to address children and youth as a security problem awaiting a security solution, but rather focus on encouraging them to develop as individual and active members of society with a role to play in developing a secure environment.

Children may be politically invisible, but they still have the right to have their security needs addressed. By using a human rights framework to define and analyse the roles and responsibilities of relevant actors, it is possible to inform the process of security sector reform in such a way as to develop and strengthen child protection systems.

Considering children as victims undervalues their potential to be active agents with a contribution to make to society, particularly as agents of peace. Casting them as offenders or perpetrators misses the point that many of these children and youth do themselves come from backgrounds associated with abuse and neglect, making them vulnerable to negative coping strategies such as drugs, violence or crime. Negative circumstances or surroundings, whether associated with family, school or other experiences, are more likely to lead to negative social and security outcomes. It is, however, also important to remember that not all children under such circumstances resort to crime or violent action, even in the face of the most extreme adversity, but a small number do – a minority who can have a devastatingly negative impact on the lives of other people around them.

Children and youth represent a significant resource for communities, and these same communities have the greatest vested interest in promoting and ensuring the security and protection of children. In particular, children and youth can be, and indeed are, active agents in their own security and there is therefore a need for them to be recognized as partners, and for efforts to be made to ensure and promote their active participation in security matters.

Gender plays a significant role in defining the insecurities that girls and boys experience. Gender-based violence needs to be assessed and understood within the wider context of the causes of violence, including individual risk factors and the influence of family and peers, as well as political, institutional, economic and cultural factors.[11]

Gender is a social construct that, while varying across cultural groups, too often thwarts the potential of girls. Discrimination robs girls of the power to make decisions, leaves them with limited opportunities in education and work, and even deprives them of legal protection. While gender equality means girls and boys having equal opportunities to access resources such as education and health, in cultures where girls are deprived of information this can have devastating consequences on their ability to protect themselves. Gender-based analysis is required to identify the issues and challenges that girls and boys face, including unequal power relations, differential access to resources and different needs and interests.

Child rights and security governance

Better recognition of and therefore increased focus on the specific security issues affecting children can best be achieved through strengthening, rather than altering, the existing security governance framework, in particular through reinforcing the human rights perspective of security.

The security sector has a legal obligation to protect and promote the rights of children. Perhaps nowhere is this need more pressing than in conflict and post-conflict environments, where lack of traditional support and protective structures undermines the ability of communities and families to protect their children. Simultaneously, however, the local authorities and security structures that are ostensibly responsible for providing the necessary security cover are unable or unwilling to do so at a time when they themselves are desperately in need of reform.

International human rights law addresses the protection of individuals from violations by governments of their fundamental rights and freedoms. The state is responsible for guaranteeing these human rights for each and every person, and is required to make provision for their realization, in particular in relation to respecting the rights of individuals, i.e. ensuring that "wrongs" are not committed against them, and protecting individuals from violations of their rights by others.

The UN Convention on the Rights of the Child (CRC) is a comprehensive code of rights for children, offering them the highest standards of protection and assistance under any international instrument. By adopting the CRC national governments have committed themselves to protecting and ensuring child rights, and agreed to hold themselves accountable to this commitment before the international community.

The CRC's definition of a "child" as every human being below the age of 18 years is a legal construct that does not depend on the roles and responsibilities children may have in certain societies. Whatever their circumstances, children are still entitled to the special protection that the CRC offers until they reach the age of maturity. Even where maturity is achieved before 18 years, children are able to claim the benefits of maturity while still enjoying the protection that the CRC offers to them.

In the context of armed conflict, children are protected under a range of instruments in both international human rights law and international humanitarian law. International humanitarian law is applicable in not only conflicts between two or more states (international armed conflicts), but also internal conflicts (non-international armed conflicts). It obliges all parties to a conflict, including armed non-state actors, to respect certain minimum humanitarian rules with regard to persons who are not, or are no longer, taking part in hostilities.

In relation to the recruitment or use of children in armed conflict, international law protects children by banning any recruitment and direct involvement in hostilities for those under 15 years in any form of armed force or group, in any type of armed conflict, international or non-international (CRC Article 38 and 1977 additional protocols to the four Geneva Conventions). In other words, under no circumstances should government armed forces, informal armed bodies such as militias, civil defence or local defence forces, or opposing armed groups have persons below the age of 15 recruited or among their fighters.

There is a growing international consensus that forced or compulsory recruitment of children – girls and boys under the age of 18 – and their use in hostilities by armed forces and armed groups are illegal and one of the worst forms of child labour. This consensus is expressed in a comprehensive set of international legal instruments, such as one optional protocol to the CRC and ILO Convention 182 Concerning the Prohibition and Immediate Action for the Elimination of the Worst Forms of Child Labour (1999), and is reinforced by a series of UN Security Council resolutions.

Security governance in the peacebuilding context

While security governance in post-war contexts can be considered as a single, integrated complex, with a range of interconnected issue areas and actors, for both practical and analytical purposes it is possible to distinguish three overarching "themes" within this broader set of issues.[12] The impact of and implications for children and youth need to be considered in each of these dimensions of the peacebuilding process, namely disarmament, demobilization and reintegration (DDR), rule of law and transitional justice, and security sector reform and governance.

The post-conflict peacebuilding context provides one of the most important theatres for reform because of not only the urgent need to put in place new structures but also the imperative of avoiding a slide back towards conflict. Just as in the political and socio-economic dimensions of post-conflict peacebuilding, security requires due attention to governance, particularly good governance in the security sector.[13] The centrality of security sector reform to the post-conflict peacebuilding process is now widely recognized and acknowledged, but what is less well understood is the importance of getting it right for children and youth, and the potentially negative ramifications of not doing so.

Restoring normality to young lives requires that actions aimed at addressing the legacies of conflict, including issues of human rights violations and transitional justice mechanisms, involve young people directly. This includes their active participation, in order to understand better how they have been affected and how to design and implement appropriate programmes to assist them in dealing with the consequences and impact of conflict. By adopting a framework based on good security governance, children become legitimate recipients of security provision.

Disarmament, demobilization and reintegration

When talking about children and DDR, a distinction needs to be drawn between the very different approach that is required to redress a rights violation in the case of children and the regular DDR programmes for adults, which form part of the formal peacemaking process. According to the UN's Integrated Disarmament, Demobilization and Reintegration Standards, child DDR requires that the demobilization (or "release") and reintegration of children, especially girls, be actively carried out at all times, even during a conflict, and that actions to prevent child recruitment should be continuous. Child-specific reintegration shall allow a child to access education, a livelihood, life skills and a meaningful role in society. The socio-economic and psychosocial aspects of reintegration for children are central to global DDR programming and budgeting. Successful reintegration requires long-term funding of child protection agencies and programmes to ensure continuous support for education and training for children, and essential follow-up/monitoring once they return to civilian life.[14]

Rule of law and transitional justice

The rapid reform of national justice mechanisms will be vital to ensuring that accountability is brought to bear for war crimes and human rights violations. Releasing former combatants who have committed war crimes and/or sexual violence against women and children back into their community for "reintegration" seriously affects community perceptions of safety and security. It also risks undermining the legitimacy of the justice system. Specifically related to children, justice reform must include having an appropriate juvenile justice system in place and functioning properly. The goal of an effective juvenile justice system will be the re-education, rehabilitation and reintegration of young offenders into society.

Security sector reform and governance

An unreformed security sector represents a direct threat to rule of law, respect for human rights, sustainable peace and social development. Taking a holistic approach to reform requires attention to the traditional institutions responsible for security provision, namely defence, intelligence, police, justice and prisons, but also the civilian management and oversight bodies which exercise control over the sector and, above all, the key stakeholders in the whole process, namely civil society. In terms of security providers, the police and juvenile justice system in particular are likely to be the first point of contact with the security sector for children, whether as victims, witnesses or offenders. Police reform projects should emphasize police-community relations and involve engagement with young people, the promotion and protection of human rights, mediation and conflict resolution. Community-based policing represents an organizational strategy allowing the police and community to work together to solve problems of crime, disorder and safety.

Understanding the context for reform

Understanding the security, political and socio-economic framing conditions of a given situation (such as the duration, level of violence, factionalism and ethnic or religious dimensions of the conflict) is essential to identifying opportunities and constraints for post-conflict peacebuilding. Experience of continuous violence during childhood will make the younger generation more susceptible to peace spoilers and more inclined to resort to violence. Weak governance often results in a lack of trust in authority, with the population turning to other actors able to guarantee their protection, such as non-state armed factions. Youth will have a significant impact on the shape and nature of the post-conflict environment, and overlooking their needs and concerns is done at great risk.[15]

Strategies to empower civil society and gain trust from citizens should integrate children's views and rights in order to be effective. The well-being of children and youth in many ways reflects the aspirations of society and will directly affect the lives and prospects of their families and communities.

A range of external actors will have an important role to play in promoting reform by providing the resources and expertise to encourage and support both the security and the development goals of post-conflict peacebuilding processes. Key external actors may include peacekeeping forces, transitional administrations, donor governments, relief and development agencies (UN and intergovernmental organizations), plus international non-governmental organizations (NGOs) and private enterprises.

In addition, regional institutions could have a vital role to play. The issues encountered by children during conflict, such as violence, displacement, disease and exploitation, are often felt across frontiers and will need regional approaches to resolve them. In West Africa, for example, a regional youth service scheme aimed at older children operates a structured programme equipping young people with a variety of skills that will be useful upon their return to their various communities. The programme provides an opportunity for young people to engage in community and other development work and, as such, move away from the lure of armed groups. The Economic Community of West African States (ECOWAS) has developed a regional youth policy to provide a comprehensive implementation framework for dealing with cross-cutting issues ranging from child recruitment to child trafficking and labour.[16] In recognizing their mutual interdependence the approach promotes national processes that are strengthened by regional ones, and vice versa.

However, processes that are driven by an exclusively external agenda and fail to embrace the primacy of local ownership will find it hard to install durable peace and stability. The need to define the division of responsibilities clearly and establish mechanisms to build trust between local institutions and international actors in peacebuilding contexts is of utmost importance. The absence of a credible and transparent approach to the transfer of security functions to local authorities, for example, will create unfulfilled expectations on the part of local actors and can threaten the peacebuilding process.

Addressing the legacies of conflict must form an integral part of the security debate from the outset of peace negotiations, covering issues like the needs to disarm, demobilize and reintegrate large numbers of former combatants, including child soldiers; curb and remove remnants of war such as small arms and light weapons, landmines and unexploded ordnance; carry out sweeping reforms in the security sector to establish effective security forces and governance mechanisms; disband non-statutory armed forces, or integrate them into new statutory ones; establish rule of law, including under transitional administrations; redress past crimes and atrocities with some urgency; and promote reconciliation. The multi-dimensional nature of peacebuilding, however, makes a linear sequencing of activities impossible.

Armed non-state actors (ANSAs) play a central role in contemporary armed conflicts in which egregious violations against children are perpetuated. Engaging ANSAs specifically on the issue of child soldiers should be considered as part of a broader engagement to bring attention to human rights standards and international humanitarian law in general. Engaging ANSAs is necessary to promoting understanding of and respect for child rights, and should be used as an entry point to encourage the development of child protection initiatives such as ensuring that children are allowed secure access to education and health facilities.

Engaging all stakeholders in security governance

Duty bearers are the actors, including security sector actors, collectively responsible for the realization of human rights, and held accountable if those rights go unrealized. When a right has been violated or insufficiently protected, not only has someone perpetrated a rights violation, but someone or some institution has failed to perform a duty of protection.

A broad definition of a country's security community goes beyond the traditional concept of considering only armed forces and their oversight bodies, to include a much more diverse range of actors.

- *Bodies authorized to use force:* armed forces; police; paramilitary forces; gendarmeries; intelligence services (both military and civilian agencies); secret services; coastguards; border guards; customs authorities; reserve or local security units (national and presidential guards, militias, etc.).

- *Civil management and oversight bodies:* the president/prime minister; national security advisory bodies; legislature and legislative select committees; ministries of defence, internal affairs and foreign affairs; customary and traditional authorities; financial management bodies (finance ministries, budget offices, financial audit and planning units); statutory civil society organizations (CSOs) such as civilian review boards and public complaints commissions.
- *Judicial and public security bodies:* judiciary; justice ministries; defence attorneys; prisons; criminal investigation and prosecution services; human rights commissions and ombudsmen; correctional services; customary and traditional justice systems.
- *Non-state security forces:* liberation armies; guerrilla armies; traditional militias; political party militias; private security companies; civil defence forces.
- *Non-statutory civil society bodies:* professional organizations, including trade unions; research/policy analysis organizations; advocacy organizations; the media; religious organizations; NGOs; the concerned public.

The last group, "non-statutory civil society bodies", have a key role to play in safeguarding children's security and safety.[17] If children and youth are the holders of rights and have a legal entitlement to their rights being secured, then it is essential that those responsible for delivering on these rights are identified and made accountable for and responsive to any failings. This directly implicates a whole range of institutions and structures, including in particular the state's formal security apparatus, and extends far beyond to include the judiciary, law enforcement agencies, oversight bodies, non-statutory security forces and, particularly important to the protection of children, civil society groups.

Civil society

Unfortunately, states do not always live up to their obligations to children, and one of the specific challenges is that children do not have a political voice by which to express discontent and demand accountability. In effect, it falls to CSOs to provide this key oversight function by monitoring children's situation and ensuring that state institutions live up to their responsibilities to provide appropriately and effectively for child protection.

Child protection goes beyond social and welfare services, health or education, and extends to a range of security and administrative actors which have a direct responsibility to protect and promote respect for child rights. CSOs have a vital role to play in providing the important link between children and the relevant state bodies, acting as interlocutors to represent the security concerns of children, and as intermediaries because of the key role they often play in service delivery. CSOs are very often responsible for establishing or running the independent structures that provide contact points for young people seeking assistance, support or advice, whether in the form of telephone helplines, youth clubs or other targeted programmes on behalf of children and youth. They also have a major role to play in monitoring, reporting and insisting on the accountability of key duty bearers.

The specific engagement of CSOs in the security policy domain contributes to accountability and the maintenance of good governance when they act as government watchdogs and an index of public satisfaction with security sector activity. Actions such as monitoring government performance, policy, compliance with laws and upholding of human rights all contribute to this process. In addition, advocacy by civil society groups representing the interests of local communities and groups of like-minded individuals helps to give voice to often marginalized actors and opens up the policy process to a wider set of perspectives.

At the local level, CSOs are closest to and most acutely aware of the security realities of children. They are also in a position to establish proactive mechanisms for enabling children and young people to express themselves in terms of their concerns and aspirations. CSOs have a responsibility to accord due weight to the opinions of children by representing them to the relevant authorities in a neutral and unbiased way. At the local level, CSOs can also be largely responsible for facilitating contact and dialogue with local government structures and law enforcement agencies.

At the national level, CSOs can provide vital testimony, information and analysis to parliament and other democratic institutions about the way in which national security policies and activities are affecting children and society as a whole. CSOs concerned with freedom of speech, human rights, policing or access to justice issues tend to be in the forefront of discussions on security sector issues, and all should have a vested interest in promoting respect for child rights.

Establishing local ownership is an acknowledged priority of security sector reform and implicitly involves civil society, both in representing the views of local communities to policy-makers so that reforms respond to local conditions and needs, and in monitoring the implementation of those reforms.

The effectiveness of disarmament, demobilization and, in particular, reintegration programmes is dependent on the involvement of local authorities and communities. CSOs can provide detailed information on conditions, attitudes and needed skills in local communities for use in the planning and implementation of DDR processes. They can also monitor and evaluate these programmes and provide feedback for further improvement of future DDR processes. CSOs can help ensure that appropriate training is provided to the right people at the right time. Working with local media, CSOs can raise awareness within local communities about programmes to reintegrate former combatants into community life. They are also the best placed to provide the essential follow-up that DDR programmes require, but which is often lacking.

Engaging children in post-conflict peacebuilding

Children can actively help to create peace through repairing social relationships and directly contributing to a culture of peace and rebuilding of social structures. Their contributions play a role in enhancing security, in reconciliation, in the search for truth and justice, and in rebuilding the education system, the economy and people's livelihoods.[18]

Establishing young people's participation is not only essential to fulfilling the obligations the security sector has to provide for the security of all, but is an imperative if the hard-won peace is to be durable. Children and youth have their own perspectives on their experiences of security and insecurity, and engaging with them will not only allow a better understanding of the issues required for designing and delivering appropriate services, but also provide valuable and realistic insights into potential or evolving security threats.

Listening to the perspectives of young people who have experienced conflict is the first step in promoting their role and importance in the post-conflict peacebuilding process. Children's perspectives may highlight new security challenges, thus helping to guide security sector reforms and approaches. Children's participation is frequently dependent on family and community attitudes relative to their involvement in social activities. Children will benefit from encouragement and practical support from their parents, teachers, community elders and NGOs, as well as figures in public authority, including security sector actors.[19]

At the local level, adults (from local NGOs, local government, schools or the community) may facilitate children's groups and networks to meet and develop peace initiatives. NGOs may provide children with practical resources (for example a basic fund for materials and transport), relevant information (child-friendly versions of relevant government policies or legislation) and skills training (on child rights, life skills, conflict resolution). Adult CSOs can cooperate in identifying and providing the arrangements and conditions needed to support children and young people to speak with decision-makers at various levels. They can find ways to build and strengthen children's and young people's groups at local, subnational and national levels so that regular or permanent cross-generational dialogue forums can be established between government and groups of young people's representatives and, in turn, can create national ongoing intergenerational dialogue.

Examples of children's participation are many and varied, including among others action in support of the right to education for out-of-school children and the development of a code of conduct for teachers and students (Nepal); preventing violence in school through the establishment of school councils (Zambia); action around child protection issues including reporting on violations of their rights (Angola); action against violence and sexual abuse (Cambodia) and against corporal punishment and early marriage (Nepal); and support and care for children affected by HIV/AIDS (Zimbabwe).[20] In many different contexts creative participatory tools, such as risk mapping to understand where girls and boys feel safe and unsafe, and body mapping to explore experiences of conflict, can also be used to help children's perspectives to be shared and acted upon.[21]

Juvenile justice

Where disaffected children and youth are exposed to destabilizing factors such as social exclusion, restricted access to education, long-term unemployment, poverty or political strife, this can lead them into conflict with the law. Urbanization is often associated with an increase in juvenile delinquency, a symptom of social exclusion. For many families life becomes about survival, and as such their children are expected either to contribute to the household (if the family link is maintained) or to take care of themselves (if the family link has been broken). More than half of the world's population now live in cities, with the majority of economic migrants having moved away from rural areas because their livelihoods were no longer secure in environments where traditional forms of community solidarity had broken down. Precarious livelihoods, manifested in a psychology of survival, can blur the perception that juveniles have of the line between legality and illegality.

Juvenile justice is not "compassionate" justice because it concerns children. Being a child does not preclude one's entitlement to benefit from the rule of law and the safeguards it provides: a child has the right of defence, the right to the presumption of innocence, the right of appeal, etc. The juvenile justice system also needs to recognize its responsibilities, not just towards the child offender, but also to the child witness and child victim.

In the case of underage recruitment, it is clear that the actual recruitment itself – more often than not under duress – is a form of exploitation and an abuse of power which requires that the child be treated first and foremost as a victim before being considered as a criminal, regardless of the acts committed in combat.

Efforts to combat juvenile delinquency, however, are often reflected by authorities introducing repressive legislation and a hardening of attitudes among law enforcement and judicial officers. Resulting actions may include reduction in the age of criminal responsibility; increase in the length of custodial sentences for minors (who are sometimes detained with adults – prison being acknowledged as "the school of crime"); dramatic "round-up" actions or crackdown operations; the criminalization of vagrancy and begging; and the creation of educational detention centres (presented as alternatives to prison, but where detention conditions are often equivalent to those of prison).

Where the judicial system is administered in an arbitrary or lax manner, juveniles can find themselves remanded in custody for simple status crimes for lengthy periods of time without speedy trial, decision-making or sentence. They might even be forgotten about altogether. The administration of juvenile justice can become all the more problematic as states faced with internal strife impose exceptional legal regimes (as is the case for Palestinian children in Israel), or a sort of "military law" which waives the requirement to handle juveniles according to the standard criminal code.

Debates over juvenile justice have forever focused on the choice between "retributive" or "restorative" justice (repression or education). The very concept of human security alludes to a restorative-based approach. Good governance with a view to securing democratic progress implies that the state, which is at once the source and the guarantor of human rights, must strive to inform public opinion on child rights and deal with children in line with international norms and standards, including using deprivation of liberty only as a measure of last resort. Any decision or punitive measure that compounds a child's exclusion from the community is unlikely to produce a positive outcome.

Diversion away from formal judicial proceedings is encouraged for all but the most serious offences, in particular when dealing with first-time offenders. Alternatives aim to avoid institutionalization of children, and may include care, guidance and supervision orders, counselling, probation, foster care, education or vocational training, restitution and compensation of victims. However, it is important not to overlook the fact that these alternative solutions also need to provide legal safeguards and protect the rights of the children involved.

Alternatives are at once a means of conflict resolution, restoring social harmony, repairing the harm suffered, improving public safety and promoting respect for child rights. Alternatives may occur pre-trial (diversion by means of out-of-court settlement), pre-sentencing (legal proceedings are suspended while an alternative is sought, and if this is successful the judge dismisses the case) or post-trial (either the convicted youth is not sentenced, or is sentenced but the sentence is not applied while alternatives are sought).

The applicable alternatives must be appropriate for the age and maturity of the juvenile, and match the seriousness of the offences committed. Diversion aims to break the vicious circle of stigmatization, violence, humiliation and the breakdown of social bonds. Contrary to popular opinion, a large majority of first-time offenders who benefit from these alternatives do not reoffend.[22] All the procedures suppose that the actors involved are trained in these practices and the two parties are in agreement (recognition of the deed by the juvenile and the victim's consent).

Good administration of the juvenile justice system requires competency and appropriate specialization on the part of police, judiciary, educational and welfare staff at every stage of proceedings, training in the rules regarding child rights and the implementation of basic rules concerning their protection against any arbitrary exercise of power and violence. Experience shows that the training of public actors in juvenile justice must be multidisciplinary: juvenile justice can only progress if the professionals involved know their respective legal responsibilities, limitations and possibilities.

Holding public office does not allow police or judicial officers to act – or not to act – with total impunity and illegality, or in ways that are an abuse of their power and position. Good governance presupposes that public actors can be monitored, held accountable and, if necessary, sanctioned.[23]

Oversight and monitoring mechanisms

Having secured the commitment of the security establishment to particular standards in the treatment of young people, it is then necessary to have robust mechanisms in place to oversee and monitor their application. As a key duty bearer, not only does the security sector have an important responsibility to protect and promote the rights of children, and ensure that they are not violated by other individuals or groups, but it also has an obligation to ensure that its own actions do not violate those same rights.

Oversight by definition comprises supervision, inspection, responsibility and control, and has six main, interdependent pillars.[24] *Internal* control includes supervision, review and monitoring among the security services and justice providers. *Executive* control comprises government ministries and advisory bodies and their investigative and decision-making procedures. *Legislative* oversight ensures control over budgeting procedures, investigations, law making and enacting as well as visiting and inspecting state-owned facilities, including juvenile prisons and orphanages. The *judiciary* includes civilian and criminal courts, military courts and legal procedures, adjudicating cases brought against security services and individuals, protecting human rights and upholding the rule of law.

Independent bodies such as human rights institutions or ombudsmen investigate complaints from the public, raise awareness of human rights violations and ensure compliance with policy and the rule of law. Truth and reconciliation commissions have become an important means of addressing human rights violations which have had devastating effects on countries, societies and peoples emerging from armed conflict.

Civil society may provide expertise and analysis of security and justice policy as well as investigate and monitor violations against child rights. NGOs have a crucial role in both drawing attention to problems regarding children and promoting and participating in the drafting of standards of international law respecting children.[25] They provide an informal oversight role at the domestic level, and are usually extremely active in advocacy both locally and internationally. Civil society groups can contribute to accountability and good governance of the security sector by observing and monitoring the activities of central authorities and public institutions responsible for providing security, and holding these actors to account.[26]

The ability of oversight agencies to monitor governmental institutions and initiate investigations on their own, without advocates necessarily pressing for such investigation, is also a critical practice for ensuring protection of rights and reforming governmental agencies and actions, particularly in regard to the rights of vulnerable populations.[27]

From an international perspective there are also several entities that perform an oversight function, including for example the UN treaty bodies that monitor adherence to agreed human rights standards within conventions or treaties. International courts such as the International Court of Justice and International Criminal Court can play a significant role in ensuring the security of children through their adjudication. While the jurisdiction of the former is limited, in that only a state party may appear before it, it has the mandate to deal with a number of specific multilateral treaties that relate directly to children, such as the protocol to prevent, suppress and punish the trafficking in persons, especially women and children; the convention on consent to marriage, minimum age for marriage and registration of marriages; and the convention against discrimination in education.

International criminal tribunals and special courts, forming a group of so-called hybrid courts, have been developed based in the country where the atrocities were committed, and apply a combination of domestic and international law. One of the often-cited advantages of this type of approach is the opportunity it provides for rebuilding the capacity of a domestic justice system that may have been significantly weakened by preceding events.

The UN Security Council also plays an important role in the issue of children. Since 1999 the Security Council has debated children and armed conflict on an annual basis and adopted a number of resolutions, including Resolution 1612 (2005), which established a monitoring and reporting mechanism focused on six grave violations committed against children in times of conflict. Collectively, these resolutions have sought to ensure that the concerns of conflict-affected children are reflected in the responses of critical actors during armed conflict, throughout peace processes and in post-conflict contexts. All these resolutions also call for a systematic response by a broad constituency of actors before, during and after conflict.

Recommendations

If peace is to be lasting, the security needs of both the state and its population must be addressed equally and in parallel with the political and socio-economic aspects of reconstruction.

A key premise of this chapter is that security governance considerations provide the necessary framework to assist the sector in developing a better understanding of the nature of insecurities experienced by children and youth, and of adequate methods to respond to these insecurities. Within this analysis is the acknowledgement that children and youth, their families and their communities are all security providers in their own right, and the importance of their engagement needs to be at the heart of security policy development.

The widespread adoption of notions of societal security and human security means communities and individuals respectively are entitled to be the focus of security provision, in contrast to the traditional state-centred perspective. “Human security” is concerned with a wide range of threats to individuals, from anti-personnel landmines, small arms and light weapons to recruitment of children and their use in armed conflict, and other violations of human rights and international humanitarian law.

Acknowledging that the effective delivery of security to children and young people requires multiple actors working together at multiple levels, a range of recommendations are put forward below, specifically targeting CSOs, security institutions and democratic political institutions. The international community is included because of its specific moral obligation to protect and promote human rights and democratic governance, and also its significant role in transition and peacebuilding processes.

Civil society organizations

- Work with national and local authorities to develop strategies aimed at tackling social exclusion and, in particular, support disadvantaged children and youth.
- Establish outreach mechanisms with communities, families and schools to provide avenues for children to express themselves on issues affecting them, including security.
- Establish mechanisms for dialogue with local law enforcement agencies on child protection concerns, including complaints mechanisms.

Security institutions

- Ensure that all activities are guided by human rights principles.
- Work to create trust, mutual confidence and understanding between communities and the security sector, particularly through engaging CSOs.
- Promote the principle of duty of care in clear and transparent operating procedures for all security institutions.

Democratic political institutions

- Place special emphasis on listening to and addressing the concerns of children – the fact that children are politically invisible places a special moral obligation on democratic institutions to act on their behalf.
- Develop a national development plan that places children and young people centre stage, identifying strategies to harness their positive contribution to society.
- Establish formal and informal coordination bodies at the national and local levels, including government officials, law enforcement agencies and representatives of local NGOs.

International community

- Orient assistance programmes to promote youth as active participants in peacebuilding and the democratic oversight of the security sector.
- Stress the importance of engaging civil society in consultative processes, to create local and national ownership of security matters, and in seeking ways to affect change.
- Reiterate the central role of human rights in security provision and respect for rule of law, and ensure that the promotion and protection of human rights are an integral part of all assistance programmes.

Conclusion

The interaction between children and security calls for a broader rights-based approach to security governance that clearly responds to the security needs of children and youth in both policy and practice. Human rights constitute the framework for guiding the actions of the security sector, as well as the bar against which to judge successes and failures. When it comes to security provision, statutory security bodies have primary responsibility for implementing the state's obligations under international law. As a set of performance standards, human rights provide goals and targets by which to plan and evaluate actions. The guiding framework to be adopted is that of good security governance, by which children become legitimate recipients of security provision – where previously they have been invisible.

Acknowledgement

This chapter builds on an earlier version of the text published as David Nosworthy, "Placing Children and Youth on the Security Governance Agenda", in David Nosworthy (ed.), *Seen, But Not Heard: Placing Children and Youth on the Security Governance Agenda*, Münster: LIT, 2009, pp. 3–31.

Notes

1. UNICEF, "UNICEF's Role in Emergencies", 26 May 2012, www.unicef.org/emerg/index_33296.html.
2. Renata Dwan and Micaela Gustavsson, "Major Armed Conflicts", in *SIPRI Yearbook 2004: Armaments, Disarmament and International Security*, Oxford: Oxford University Press, 2004, pp. 95–131.

3. Save the Children Norway, "Global Evaluation: Children Affected by Armed Conflict, Displacement and Disaster", Save the Children, Oslo, April 2005.
4. Human Security Report Project, "Human Security Report 2012: Sexual Violence, Education, and War: Beyond the Mainstream Narrative", Human Security Press, Vancouver, BC, 2012, p. 109, hsrgroup.org/docs/Publications/HSR2012/2012HumanSecurityReport-FullText-LowRes.pdf.
5. Ibid., p. 111.
6. Ibid., p. 110.
7. Elke Krahmann, "Conceptualizing Security Governance", *Cooperation and Conflict* 38(1), 2003, p. 11, http://dcafsp.tripod.com/readings/Security%20Governance.pdf.
8. Alan Bryden, Timothy Donais and Heiner Hänggi, "Shaping a Security Governance Agenda in Post-Conflict Peacebuilding", Policy Paper No. 11, DCAF, Geneva, 2005.
9. United Nations, "Impact of Armed Conflict on Children", report of Graça Machel, expert of UN Secretary-General, UN Doc. A/51/306, New York, August 1996.
10. Ibid.
11. UN General Assembly, "Fact Sheet on Violence against Children in the Caribbean", report of independent expert for UN Study on Violence against Children, UN Doc. A/61/299, New York, October 2006.
12. Ibid.
13. Nicole Ball, "The Challenge of Rebuilding War-Torn Societies", in Chester Crocker, Fen O. Hampson and Pamela Aall (eds), *Turbulent Peace: The Challenges of Managing International Conflict*, Washington, DC: US Institute of Peace Press, 2001, pp. 723–725.
14. UN Inter-agency Working Group on DDR, "Integrated Disarmament, Demobilization and Reintegration Standards (IDDRS)", Module 5.30: Children and DDR, United Nations, New York, 2006.
15. Etienne G. Krug, Linda L. Dahlberg, James A. Mercy, Anthony B. Zwi and Rafael Lozano (eds), *World Report on Violence and Health*, Geneva: World Health Organization, 2002.
16. Funmi Olonisakin, "Children Affected by Armed Conflict: Engaging a New Constituency of Actors", in David Nosworthy (ed.), *Seen, But Not Heard: Placing Children and Youth on the Security Governance Agenda*, Münster: LIT, 2009, pp. 219–238.
17. Nicole Ball, "Reforming Security Sector Governance", in Robert Picciotto and Rachel Weaving (eds), *Security and Development: Investing in Peace and Prosperity*, London and New York: Routledge, 2006, pp. 313–331.
18. Maggie Brown, *Global Evaluation: Children Affected by Armed Conflict, Displacement or Disaster*, Oslo: Save the Children Norway, 2005.
19. Claire O'Kane, Clare Feinstein and Annette Giertsen, "Children and Young People in Post-Conflict Peacebuilding", in David Nosworthy (ed.), *Seen, But Not Heard: Placing Children and Youth on the Security Governance Agenda*, Münster: LIT, 2009, pp. 259–284; Chapter 2 in this volume.
20. O'Kane, Feinstein and Giertsen, ibid.
21. Save the Children Norway, "Thematic Evaluation on Children's Participation in Armed Conflict, Post Conflict and Peace Building", Save the Children, Oslo, 2007, www.reddbarna.no/chp.
22. According to the Center on Juvenile and Criminal Justice, "Many programs target first time offenders but CJCJ recognizes that 70% of first time offenders never offend again, and therefore considers it more effective to concentrate funding and rehabilitation services on repeat offenders, who generally have more complicated needs and are consequently more difficult to serve." House of Hope, "Detention Diversion Advocacy Program (DDAP)", *News and Articles*, 13 January 2009, https://www.ammado.com/nonprofit/102466/articles/5324. According to Muntingh, "A very small percentage of participants re-offended, 6.7% in the first 12 months after participating in a diversion

programme and a further 9.8% were recorded in the second survey." Lukas M. Muntingh, "The Effectiveness of Diversion Programmes – A Longitudinal Evaluation of Cases", South African National Institute for Crime Prevention and the Reintegration of Offenders, Cape Town, May 2001.

23. Bernard Boëton, "The Juvenile Justice System, a Key to Human Security Policy Reform", in David Nosworthy (ed.), *Seen, But Not Heard: Placing Children and Youth on the Security Governance Agenda*, Münster: LIT, 2009, pp. 127–143.
24. Organisation for Economic Co-operation and Development/Development Assistance Committee (OECD/DAC), *Handbook on Security System Reform: Supporting Security and Justice*, Paris: OECD, 2007, p. 112.
25. Claire Breen, "The Role of NGOs in the Formulation of Compliance with the Optional Protocol to the Convention of the Rights of the Child in Involvement of Children in Armed Conflict", *Human Rights Quarterly* 25(2), 2003, p. 53.
26. UNDP and DCAF, *Public Oversight of the Security Sector: A Handbook for Civil Society Organizations*, New York: UNDP, 2008.
27. Stephen Owen, "Current Ombudsman Issues: An International Perspective", in Patrick Emmanuel (ed.), *The Ombudsman: Caribbean and International Perspectives*, Cave Hill: University of the West Indies, 1993, pp. 102–107.

7

The resilience of children and youth during conflict and its contribution to post-conflict stability: The case of northern Uganda and "night commuting"

Azar Eskandarpour

Introduction

According to Colletta and Cullen, intra-state conflicts often weaken the social fabric of communities, as "they divide the population by undermining interpersonal and communal group trust, destroying the norms and values that underlie cooperation and collective action for the common good".[1] These conflicts can therefore impede communal and state abilities to recover after hostilities cease, as they erode the social cohesion communities possess during times of peace.

If the population are resilient during conflict, however, they have the ability to maintain social cohesion, contributing positively to the odds of stable peace and security after hostilities. The greater the degree of social capital, social trust and agency, the more "likely it is that a society will be cohesive and thus possess the inclusive mechanisms necessary for mediating or managing conflicts before they turn violent".[2] Thus resilience strategies that foster social capital, trust and agency are likely to be more cohesive and help to promote post-conflict recovery. It is for this reason that resilience should be viewed by local and international actors as integral to successful peacebuilding.

"Night commuting", a resilience phenomenon developed and maintained by children and youth during the war in northern Uganda, demonstrates this peacebuilding potential.[3] Night commuting refers to the short-term, short-distance, repetitive overnight displacement of children from IDP (internally displaced person) camps and villages to nearby

Escaping victimhood: Children, youth and post-conflict peacebuilding, Schnabel and Tabyshalieva (eds), United Nations University Press, 2013, ISBN 978-92-808-1211-4

towns. It was an institutionalized strategy which was used by up to 40,000 children and youth civilians in the northern districts of Pader, Gulu and Kitgum to avoid the threat of violence during conflict.[4] This phenomenon was largely successful in providing relative safety to children and youth, not only by decreasing the main risk of violence, i.e. rebel abduction, but also by promoting well-being through the mitigation of other risks and difficulties such as sexual violence and subsistence and socialization needs. In other words, night commuting as a resilience strategy developed, maintained and strengthened networks and relationships necessary for cooperation and collective action, thus enhancing the social cohesion needed for successful reconciliation in the post-conflict period.

In the past there has been little focus on coping strategies used by children and youth *not* actively participating in conflicts as combatants, although much research has been done on child and youth combatants. Thus this chapter instead addresses non-combatant young people and their non-violent response to the adversities of conflict. This is important, since often, and especially in conflicts involving child combatants, children and youth are key actors in successful peacebuilding efforts and post-conflict stability. This chapter argues, using the case of northern Uganda, that resilience in conflict is not only a mechanism by which to provide protection from violence, but also a key contributing factor to maintaining and strengthening social capital, social trust and agency, demonstrating the capacity of children and youth to contribute to social cohesion within their community and, as a result, to today's peacebuilding efforts.

The first section defines terms and concepts used, and explains the relevance of this analysis. The second section provides a brief background to the conflict, and a description of the Lord's Resistance Army (LRA) and its use of forcefully recruited children. Section three tracks the progress of resilience in the community and demonstrates the evolution of night commuting from a crisis-driven strategy to a social institution of resilience, serving not only to protect but also other purposes promoting well-being. The final section analyses the way in which night commuting contributed to social cohesion and peacebuilding within Uganda.

Defining terms, concepts and relevance

Resilience, violence and peacebuilding

When we say that children and youth in northern Uganda demonstrated great resilience to violence, what do we mean by violence and resilience? Violence is defined as "the intentional use of physical force or power, threatened or actual, against another person, or against a group or community, which either results in or has a high likelihood of resulting in injury, death, psychological harm, maldevelopment or deprivation".[5] For the purposes of this chapter, resilience refers to a "dynamic process encompassing positive adaptation within the context of significant adversity, where adversity is represented here as the acute risk of violence and maladaptation within a chronic conflict situation".[6]

Implicit within the notion of resilience are "two critical conditions: (1) exposure to significant threat or severe adversity; and (2) the achievement of positive adaptation despite major assaults on the developmental process".[7] Resilience not only has a great impact on the capacity of local populations to cope positively during violence, but, as this chapter argues, also has great potential for peacebuilding. As found in the Ugandan context, through their resilience children and youth maintained and developed relationships which contributed significantly to social cohesion in their communities. This was a crucial contribution to post-conflict peace and stability, and young people should be considered as key stakeholders and actors in peacebuilding efforts.

The war in Uganda was a protracted armed conflict which lasted 21 years. At first sight it might appear to be conceptually discordant to look at resilience under chronic conditions such as these. Indeed, resilience appears to imply a point of "acute" shock. My application of the concept proposes to reconcile this by looking at night commuting as a resilience strategy emerging at a moment of significant adversity, or "acute violence", within the condition of the chronic and protracted war. As a consequence, to measure and explain resilience we need to envision a point at which violence reaches a threshold of "acuteness", and then analyse the effect this has on the civilian population and whether resilience can be observed. Normally, an acute condition is one where a single large exposure to violence is involved.[8] In the northern Uganda context this point occured in 2002 after Operation Iron Fist, a failed government campaign against LRA bases. As a result, the LRA exponentially increased its violence against and abductions of children and youth in the northern region of Acholi.[9] It was at this point that the agency of the young developed into night commuting and formed a social institution promoting well-being and leadership.

According to James Neill, resilience can hibernate, remain alive during times of difficulty and then re-emerge when circumstances are more favourable and events become overwhelming.[10] It can also foster and maintain the local resources and social capital necessary for post-conflict recovery. Thus resilience is seen in this case as more than a tool for children and youth to combat victimhood during conflict; it is also a measure which can have great positive and long-term impacts on peacebuilding.

For purposes of this chapter, peacebuilding refers to the process of resolving conflict and bringing about reconciliation. Because this type of process demands sustainability and local, community-level ownership, "peacebuilding cannot happen solely through political change".[11] To secure long-term peace and stability, in addition to signing agreements, social and psychological change at the grassroots level is required, on both sides of a conflict.[12]

In fact, the importance of resilience as a topic of research lies in its policy relevance for development and humanitarian assistance. Recognizing and building resilience of at-risk populations have become increasingly popular targets of community intervention, youth work, social work and personal development programmes.[13] Efforts to enhance resilience through intervention programmes have been increasingly seen as proactive, preventive, potentially cost-saving and positive approaches to minimizing psychological dysfunction. They should also be seen as contributing factors to post-conflict peace and stability. By identifying resilience in the conflict in northern Uganda, and how it developed and contributed to social cohesion, this chapter aims to facilitate a deeper understanding of the importance of such strategies and their real potential for contributing to peacebuilding. The role of children and youth in peacebuilding efforts is critical and must be taken into account if post-conflict stability is to be sustainable.

Because the phenomenon of night commuting is rarely studied, there is limited literature on analytical issues regarding its development and impact. This chapter is based on preliminary research and relevant literature available to date, but much more research is needed. More specifically, greater attention needs to be paid to the concept of resilience, factors that promote it, its contribution to boosting social cohesion and its positive potential for peacebuilding.

Northern Uganda

Contextual background

The precipitating conditions that enabled and fuelled the conflict in northern Uganda between the LRA and the Uganda People's Defence Force (UPDF) have a long history rooted in colonialism. During the period of colonial administration in Uganda (1894–1962), the British laid the foundation of religious, economic and ethnic divisions in the country.[14] Although these had worked to the colonial administration's advantage, they were to prove fatal in the post-independence period. In the colonial era the country's southern tribes were favoured by the British colonial administrators at the expense of northern tribes, in the sense that they were given substantial political power and influence in the colony. They had more access to education and soon controlled the colonial administrative and civil service.[15] As these southerners became increasingly Christianized and Westernized, their economic and political power became entrenched.[16] The favourable environmental conditions in the south allowed these tribes to play a central role in the country's emerging modern economy. "Conversely, the harsh northern environment, the nomadic lifestyle of some, the long distances from colonial capitals, made the north less amenable to colonial needs and investments."[17] Overall, at independence the north was much less developed compared to the south. Because the anti-colonial movement was originated by southerners, the British divided the population by employing mostly southerners in the civil service and recruiting primarily northerners (especially the Acholi) into the armed forces.[18] These northern-based armed forces were used to counter and combat the mostly southern-based anti-colonial movement. This north-south divide is thus deeply rooted in competition for power in both the government and the military. Although these conditions were largely set during colonial rule, they were then manipulated and left unresolved by post-independence governments.[19]

Since achieving independence from Britain in 1962, "Uganda has suffered almost uninterrupted violence. Armed rebellions, mostly split along ethnic lines, have wrecked the population."[20] The current president, Yoweri Yakuta Museveni, seized power from the Acholi government of Tito Okello (president from 29 July 1985 to 26 January 1986) as the head of a guerrilla army in a violent coup. Museveni has since claimed victory in several presidential elections, including the 2011 elections, which marked his fourth win. In these victories, however, opposition leaders have accused Museveni of fraud and intimidation.[21] Museveni, a Christian member of the Banyankole tribe (from western Uganda), was blamed by the Acholi for atrocities his forces committed when he came to power and for denying the region what they say is their share of development funds.[22] In 1986, when Museveni first took power, Okello's Acholi soldiers retreated to northern Uganda and southern Sudan.[23] In the same year an Acholi mystic, Alice Auma "Lakwena", led a rebel army of some 5,000 Acholis to within 50 miles of the capital before being defeated by government army troops and forced into exile.[24] A year later, in 1987, Joseph Kony formed what would become the Lord's Resistance Army and pledged to overthrow Museveni.[25]

After two decades of brutal conflict, a formal cessation of hostilities agreement was signed on 26 August 2006. A final peace agreement was reached in late 2008, but Joseph Kony, wanted by the International Criminal Court (ICC), has refused to sign the deal unless the ICC drops its indictments.[26] Although Kony avoided signing this latest peace agreement, the absence of war within Uganda in the last few years has enabled a resettlement process in which IDPs have left the camps and begun to return to their ancestral villages.[27] In 2007 the government launched a three-year peace, recovery and development plan, and in turn humanitarian assistance to LRA-affected regions decreased significantly. However, the fragility of the recovery process has become increasingly evident, as continued high levels of vulnerability, particularly in terms of food insecurity, have led to renewed instability.[28]

The Lord's Resistance Army and its tactics

Throughout the years of conflict the Ugandan government was unable to maintain security in the region and crush the LRA insurgency. The government stationed over 30,000 soldiers across northern Uganda to defeat the LRA, which was believed to have only 3,000–4,000 soldiers;[29] despite this, the extent of the LRA's violence against civilians throughout the conflict remained extremely high.[30]

Kony stands at the apex of the LRA structure, politically, militarily and spiritually. He is central to its organization, actions and purpose. During the conflict he sought to rule all Uganda and also called for the creation of a new state in northern Uganda.[31] According to the *Economist*, "A self-declared spirit medium, Joseph Kony claims to be possessed by the Holy Spirit, and to have been called by God to replace the Ugandan constitution . . . A former altar boy, he preaches a blend of Catholicism, traditional spirit worship and the occult."[32] During the conflict the LRA rebels roamed northern Uganda's Acholi countryside in small units, surfacing to torch villages, kill people and kidnap children before returning to the forest. "The LRA's terror tactics and the bloody clashes between the rebels and the army caused 1.7 million people, or about 90 percent of northern Uganda's population, to flee their homes and become internally displaced."[33]

The LRA maintained its numbers through abductions targeting the Acholi child/youth civilian population. As the LRA could not attract enough adult fighters into its ranks, it filled them primarily by abducting children. According to the *Economist*, "As many as 90% of the LRA's fighters are abducted children."[34] Human Rights Watch indicates that "Between 1987 and 2006 at least 20,000 Ugandan children were abducted."[35] Forced recruitment of children became a central feature of the conflict and a principle form of violence waged against civilian populations. Abductions became such a prominent factor in northern Ugandan society that fear of violence developed into a social routine for children and youth. Using personal agency evident through local resilience strategies, children adapted to protect themselves better against violence and victimhood.

One of the most clearly visible strategies demonstrating this agency was "night commuting": parents faced with the continued insecurity of child abductions sent their children to sleep in town while they stayed at home.[36] Around dusk, children began to walk from up to 10 kilometres away into the towns of Gulu, Kitgum and Pader to seek shelter, and then returned home the next day at dawn.[37] This phenomenon started during an acute moment of violence within the war. In 2002, during the course of Operation Iron Fist, a UPDF offensive against LRA strongholds, the level of violence and abduction of children rose dramatically.[38] This sharp increase in the intensity of violence instigated adaptive behaviour, exemplified by night commuting. "At the height of the conflict some 40,000 'night commuters' [slept] under verandas, in schools, hospital courtyards and bus parking lots."[39] They were mostly children and adolescents, but also included women who fled their villages or IDP camps each night for town centres in search of safety from gender-based violence.

Night commuting

The historical evolution of resilience

To understand the practice of night commuting and how it developed to create agency and well-being and contribute to post-conflict stability, the first task is to track its evolution throughout the conflict. This analysis shows that night commuting adapted to the shifts in the nature of the conflict and developed from a spontaneous, crisis-driven strategy into a social institution providing strong protection against victimhood.

Phase 1: Rural-to-rural commuting

The first displacement of children began in northern Uganda as a reaction to the atrocities and abductions committed by the LRA in the period following the military confrontation of Operation North in 1991. Operation North combined government efforts to defeat the LRA through the National Resistance Army (NRA) and efforts to cut the LRA's possible support base among the local population. The government created "Arrow Groups", local militia of Acholi men who were armed with bows and arrows to confront the LRA. This was an unsuccessful campaign. Despite having fought side by side with the NRA during the military operation, the Acholi did not enjoy the protection of the government in the aftermath and the local population were left to fight for themselves.[40] Northerners were accused for the failure of the operation in combating the LRA and of conspiring with the rebel group. The north was cut off from the south and declared a no-go area. Political leaders in the north "were arrested and beaten badly", and military leaders "convinced Museveni" that the Acholi "were sabotaging" military operations in the north.[41] Local Acholi sources reported that "Operation North destroyed the rapport" which some commanders "had tried to build between the army and the population between 1988 and 1991".[42]

Lunde notes that "Unable to withstand the LRA, many civilians chose to escape to the bush at night, as a strategy to avoid attacks from the LRA who preferred to attack in the dead of night."[43] Based on her research in 2006 in northern Uganda, she further observes: "During this period of commuting both adults and children were hiding in the bush, some regularly, others when rumours were spreading about rebels in the area."[44] As she describes:

> some people built semi-permanent structures in the rural areas surrounding their villages, while others found new hiding places every night in an attempt to trick the rebels. Parents left their children naked or dressed them in dark clothes and told them to hide in the bush surrounding their villages, as they knew they would be unable to prevent the rebels from abducting them if they were raiding the village.[45]

Hiding in the bush as a spontaneous strategy for protection is not an unusual response to extreme insecurity and is seen in many conflicts around the world. When defenceless civilians find themselves faced with the threat of violence at their doorstep and without any chance of defending themselves, the most natural reaction is to flee. Lunde reports an officer at the Probation and Welfare Office in Gulu commenting: "the commuting to the bush lessened in scope because the bush turned out not to provide the protection that people were searching for. The LRA frequently moves around in the rough country and are accustomed to the terrain."[46] Lunde explains that the main factor which ended commuting to the bush was "the government's decision to move the population into 'protected villages' as a part of their military strategy against the LRA".[47]

Phase 2: Displacement into "protected villages"

The strategy of forced displacement was implemented to protect the civilian population from rebel attacks, cut the rebels from their resource base and isolate them from potential supporters in the local communities.[48] President Museveni officially announced the creation of the camps on 27 September 1996, and "one week later the army started forcibly moving people and clearing the villages in Gulu district with the help of military means. Artillery and mortar bombs were fired into the villages to scare people away from their homes and into the newly established IDP-camps."[49] Lunde explains that in 2002 "there was a new campaign forcibly moving 300,000 people within two days. The village residents were told that after a deadline set at 48 hours anyone found outside the 'protected villages' would be perceived as a rebel or rebel collaborator and treated accordingly."[50] These threats were soon acted upon, with military action by the government.

The IDP camps were supposed to be a temporary arrangement, but by 2005 the population in camps and other displaced settlements had increased, reaching approximately 1.7 million and constituting practically the whole Acholi population in the region. Instead of bringing the conflict to an end, the displacement became a permanent humanitarian disaster for the Acholi people. Contrary to the original intentions, the camps replaced the villages as resource bases for the rebels, and while in camps people still experienced abductions, killings and attacks by the LRA.[51]

Phase 3: In-camp commuting

As a response to the risk of LRA abductions while in IDP camps, a new commuting pattern was established. Children started migrating from the outskirts to the centre of the displacement camps as a strategy to avoid abduction: some were sent by their parents, while others decided on their own. According to Lunde:

> In some camps fenced-in shelters have been erected for the children to spend the nights in. The paradox of the protected shelters within the "protected villages" is a strong symbol of the UPDF's inability to bring security to the population in the camps. The UPDF soldiers deployed to protect the camps were until recently stationed at the camp centre, making the IDPs feel like living shields between the UPDF and the LRA. Some camps only had military protection during daytime even though the LRA are known for attacking at night or in the early morning.[52]

Phase 4: Rural-to-urban "night commuting"

As Lunde explains:

> Some children are reported to have been night commuting regularly to Gulu town since 1996, but rural/urban commuting as an institutionalised coping strategy did not come into being until the security situation for the population in Acholiland gravely deteriorated in the aftermath of the "Operation Iron Fist", launched by the UPDF in March 2002 ... after an agreement between the Government of Uganda and the Government of Sudan, allowing the UPDF to pursue the LRA into their bases on the Sudanese side of the border.[53]

The operation was a failure, however: "Rather than 'wiping out' the rebels in their camps in Sudan, the UPDF was outflanked as the LRA escaped back into Uganda and right into the arms of the local population."[54] The LRA began to:

> relocate in smaller groups and dramatically increase their attacks on civilians in the Acholi region on the Ugandan side of the border ... Lootings, killings and abductions sharply increased and gravely affected the humanitarian situation in the region ... The steep increase in violence and abductions was what forced tens of thousands of children and also a number of adults to flee to town areas to seek shelter.[55]

One can see the direct relationship between the level of violence/abductions and night commuting at various points in the conflict. According to Lunde:

> Data collected from the Probation and Welfare Office ... in Gulu shows that the number of commuters at the shelters in Gulu dropped from 21,000 in November 2004 to 7,000 the following month when there was a ceasefire between the UPDF and the LRA and negotiations were in progress. The peace talks broke down on December 31, and fighting resumed the day after. In January there was again a steep increase in the number of commuters.[56]

The towns known to have received night commuters, Gulu, Kitgum and Pader, are within the three main Acholi districts of the north. Gulu has a population of 154,300, Kitgum town population is about 59,700 and Pader is a district with a population of 13,500.[57] Since the UPDF had a greater presence in the towns than in camps and dispersed villages, the LRA did not attack these areas. Thus these urban contexts provided a type of safe zone for children and youth escaping abduction.

Night commuting as an institutionalized resiliency practice

As the commuters' extreme vulnerability and the government's inability to protect them became known to the outside world through media reports and local actors, international organizations intervened to assist these young people. On the ground, "Blankets were distributed, and the first night commuter centres established for the sole purpose of caring for the commuters came into being. Initiatives for establishing more suitable places for the children to spend their nights came both from the local and the international community."[58] Although the international community institutionalized the phenomenon, it was not its cause or its inventor. After 2002, "With the establishment of the specialised night commuter centres, the commuting became shaped within a structural framework and developed into a social institution."[59] The children had a fixed and safer place to spend the night, "with adult supervision and rules and regulations to obey". By 2006 a large number of night commuter centres existed in Acholiland: "Gulu and Kitgum have 19 centres each while some additional shelters were found in camps and rural areas."[60]

It is evident that this phenomenon developed from a crisis-driven individual action into an institutionalized social practice with both informal norms and explicit rules and regulations. Barnes defines social practices as "socially recognized forms of activity, done on the basis of what members learn from others, and capable of being done well or badly, correctly or incorrectly".[61] Thus a social practice is something more than just a routine pattern of behaviour, and "has a performance aspect [which] is the main characteristic that distinguishes it from mere habitual behavior".[62]

As Lunde demonstrates through her field research, "With the establishment of special night commuter centres, the commuting became shaped within a structural framework and became a social institution in the Acholi society."[63] A social institution can be defined as "a social-material structure of social interaction, often complemented with written rules, a physical building or a specialized staff".[64] Social institutions can also be defined in terms of the purposes they serve in society, as "the relatively permanent structural configurations centred around the tasks of meeting the important material and nonmaterial requirements of a society".[65]

Successful tool against non-victimhood: Providing protection, subsistence and socialization

Although often cited as only addressing LRA abduction, children and their households also used night commuting to tackle other risk factors. In addition to mitigating risks of abduction, Lunde shows that this strategy was used for other protection (against sexual and domestic violence), subsistence (access to work and centre resources) and socialization needs (interaction with other children).[66]

Protection from domestic and sexual violence

The fear of abduction was the main reason for commuting. This is apparent with the rise and fall of commuting which followed the pattern and intensity of the conflict. Night commuting was "a barometer of the intensity of the conflict. When rumours start to spread of rebels in the area, the number of children coming to sleep in the shelters immediately multiplies."[67] However, the LRA was only one of the threats facing the children of the north; other risks came from violence and sexual abuse perpetrated at home and by UPDF soldiers.

In over 20 years of conflict, drunkenness, general desperation and feelings of hopelessness resulted in a high level of domestic violence and sexual abuse.[68] Lunde states: "Domestic violence and abuse is an increasing problem among the displaced population and is, according to Michael Copland, UNICEF's Child Protection Officer in Gulu, one of the reasons why children seek protection in the shelters."[69] In a Save the Children survey, 27 per cent of commuters reported experiencing abuse in their own household and 40 per cent did not live with either of their parents.[70] Lunde explains that "The child exposed to violence at home may act as an agent on its own behalf and decide to spend the nights at one of the centres rather than risking abuse at home, while the decision might be made by other persons close to the child."[71]

In addition, UPDF soldiers have been accused of sexual violence against civilians within the IDP camps. Rapes perpetrated by the UPDF, particularly mobile units, are assumed to have been widespread within camps.[72] Most women and girls, out of fear of stigmatization and retribution, would not come forward to accuse their rapists.[73] Survivors of rape first had to contact the police, who were not present in most camps, or the local leadership, often perceived to be in league with the UPDF.[74] In many cases UPDF soldiers accused of rape had impunity, and the risk of rape remained prevalent for women in camps.[75] This caused some women and girls to continue participating in night commuting even when the conflict was in a lull.

Social mobility and subsistence

A minority of children also used night commuting as a strategy to make themselves relevant to non-governmental organizations (NGOs) and foreigners. "The fact that some youths came to the centres hoping for a job or to enter 'manhood' shows that commuting can be a strategy for social mobility for some."[76] By leaving home, these youths gained independence beyond their parents and used networking within the centres to find positions with hierarchical standing. In addition, the phenomenon served other subsistence needs, such as "relieving the pressure on physical space in the household".[77] Crowding was a push factor in the Acholi community, making children go to centres; the extreme population density in IDP camps made this very likely.[78] In a survey conducted at Médecins Sans Frontière's night commuter centre in Lacor hospital in November 2005, "32 percent of the children came from households with one hut available and an additional 30 percent from two hut households".[79]

Socialization

Some children slept at the same centre for years; these children bonded with each other as commuting became a social practice of everyday life.

"Particularly for children with weak connections to their families, the centre represented a social alternative that potentially fulfilled some of their needs of social belonging."[80] Alyce, a 12-year-old girl staying at one of the Gulu commuter centres, expressed her belonging by being integrated into life at the centre, and enjoying being captain in the room where she and her sisters slept.[81] Other children listened to her and came to her with their problems. When asked what she thought about sleeping at the centre, she responded, "I find sleeping here is good, and also I am used to these children sleeping here, so that I can't even leave here."[82] Lunde affirms that "For the regular commuters their interaction with the other commuters and the volunteers at the centre is an important part of their social life."[83] There is reason to expect that the maintenance of social relations, social bonds and an alternative environment where children felt safe, confident and at home promoted well-being, shielding them from some of the negative effects of the conflict. This resilience increases the potential for positive contributions of children and youth to their post-conflict communities.

In some situations, armed violence can generate a positive collective community response, thereby reducing the impact and costs of violence on the community.[84] Night commuting not only decreased the impact and costs of violence and the threat of abduction, but also reduced other vulnerabilities such as sexual and domestic abuse or lack of subsistence and socialization. All of this contributed to advanced coping mechanisms and well-being.

The relative success of this phenomenon lies in its multifactor intervention at both interpersonal and collective levels.[85] In other words, the night commuting addressed multiple risk factors in the same strategy, and these interventions are more effective in reducing risk and lowering levels of actual violence.[86] Night commuting as a phenomenon was a successful resilience strategy, and its agency enabled tens of thousands of children to contribute positively towards reducing the potential damage of the conflict. Moreover, their experience in resilience to violence also demonstrates their capacities and potential to contribute actively to post-conflict recovery and peacebuilding.

Night commuting and its contribution to post-conflict peacebuilding

The children of northern Uganda can be considered as having avoided victimhood, enhancing their ability to negotiate with their environments in a peaceful and positive manner by building upon and strengthening social capital, social trust and self-efficacy. Night commuting demonstrates that resilience can be both a mechanism for children and youth protection and provide them and the community at large with resources invaluable to post-conflict peace and stability.

Through night commuting, social capital and social trust were maintained and strengthened, promoting agency of the children and youth of the region. This demonstrates their great capacity to take part in decision-making, problem-solving and teamwork. The formation of a social institution such as night commuting enhanced the psychological and physical well-being of the largest segment of the population affected by the conflict. Today, we can assume that the impact of this is evident in the engagement seen by these same young people in the peacebuilding efforts in northern Uganda.

Maintaining and building social cohesion though social capital, social trust and agency

While resilience contributed to providing security and decreasing the risks of violence during the conflict in northern Uganda, why does it also play a vital role in post-conflict rehabilitation and peacebuilding? The resilience strategy observed was strongly based in and supported the formation of social cohesion through strengthening social capital, social trust and self-efficacy. These three elements, which are key factors for the building of cohesive communities, allow for the maintenance of inclusive mechanisms necessary for mediating or managing conflicts.

Social capital

The existence of social capital represents a positive resource on which children and youth in northern Uganda drew for their resilience. Based on relationships and connections between actors located at different levels, night commuters possessed and fostered densely interlaced social capital, which promoted their well-being during the conflict and ultimately increased their capacity to contribute positively to the peace and stability of their community.

The central idea of social capital is that networks and associated norms of reciprocity have value. A person's family, friends and associates constitute an important asset, one that can be called on in a crisis.[87] The endowment of community social capital, defined as trust, norms and networks facilitating cooperation and collective action, is thus a prime aspect in determining the success or failure of management of collective action.[88] According to Robert Putnam, social capital "refers to the collective value of all and the inclinations that arise from these networks to do things for each other".[89] It is in this way that social capital contributes to post-conflict peace and security: those communities endowed with a diverse stock of social networks and civic associations are in a stronger position to confront poverty and vulnerability, take advantage of new opportunities and resolve disputes.

Therefore, while in most cases social capital is eroded and broken down during intra-state conflicts, through their resilience children in northern Uganda showed their capacity to rebuild it. Night commuting promoted and fostered links, bonds and networks, creating a sense of community and extended family for many children. New friendships were formed at the shelters or in sleeping areas; children showed solidarity by beating on drums to welcome those who arrived at the night shelters; and connections were made with humanitarian institutions and NGOs as well as with Ugandan politicians and leaders. These connections and links were maintained and strengthened during the conflict, positively affecting the social organization of children and youth. Now in possession of stronger networks and links, young people have contributed to the general social cohesion of their community, building a protective barrier against the re-emergence of violence. As stated by Colletta and Cullen, "peacebuilding involves the fundamental revitalization of positive social capital and the strengthening of social cohesion".[90] The more social capital within a society, "the more likely a society will be cohesive and thus possess the inclusive mechanisms necessary for mediating/managing conflicts before they turn violent".[91] In this way, night commuting significantly contributed to Uganda's peacebuilding agenda.

Social trust

A further important element connected to social cohesion and capital is social trust. As Woolcock argues, "social trust is not part of the definition of social capital but it is certainly a close consequence, and therefore could be easily thought of as a proxy".[92] Among night commuters there is evidence that social trust was very high indeed and the bonding and linking networks enabled a high level of trust in peer support, mobilization and community education. These are important transferable skills and tools that support peacebuilding efforts such as peace education, community engagement and conflict mediation.

This commuting phenomenon has made a positive contribution to strengthening social trust. Through community education one can observe the assistance that community members provided to one another to evade violence. According to Blattman, "children and youth initiated training programs in escape strategies or counter-indoctrination education; these increased the likelihood that younger abductees would run away if abducted or reduce their value to the rebel group".[93] Anecdotal evidence suggests that by 2002 "informal community networks had begun to conduct such education for exactly that purpose".[94] Also, former abductees and night commuters often explained that they taught their friends and siblings how to commute, what not to believe if abducted and how to escape.[95]

Another example which demonstrates the capacity of resilience, and night commuting specifically, to contribute to social trust and post-conflict stability is its promotion of peer support and mobilization. Some children and youth created networks and partnerships to organize their efforts and assist their peers, work with local leaders, influence change within their community and promote their own protection.[96] This shows the development and emergence of civil society organizations created by children and youth for the benefit and assistance of other young people. Creating solidarity helps overcome social stigma, exclusion and challenges with resource mobilization, information exchange and knowledge acquisition. Night commuters utilized both pre-existing and newly developed relationships of trust to mobilize and address the problems of protection and future violence.

Self-efficacy and agency

A final way in which night commuting contributes to peacebuilding is through the strengthening of self-efficacy and agency within the child and youth population. Acknowledging agency is integral to understanding violent acts and the choice made in committing or resisting those acts.[97]

The human agency demonstrated by young people can be explained by its foundation in self-efficacy. According to Benight and Bandura, self-efficacy "affect[s] whether individuals think in self-enhancing or self-debilitating ways; how well they motivate themselves and persevere in the face of difficulties; the quality of their emotional life and vulnerability to stress and depression; [and their] resilience to adversity".[98] Those with a strong sense of efficacy can, through ingenuity and perseverance, figure out ways of exercising some measure of control in environments containing limited opportunities and many constraints.[99] Moreover, "Those who have a high sense of coping efficacy adopt strategies and courses of action designed to change hazardous environments into more benign ones".[100]

Through night commuting, it is evident that the children of northern Uganda gained a strong sense of self-efficacy. This is demonstrated through their involvement in commuting and their comparatively healthy psychological state, both as commuters and as individuals who had previously been abducted.[101] A UNICEF study of the state of these youth has shown that the majority show remarkable resilience; two-thirds report low to medium amounts of emotional distress, and over 90 per cent reported fairly high levels of positive social functioning and low levels of aggression.[102] Family connectedness was also reported as being quite high.[103] Through this healthy psychological and social state, we see that the affected population faced risk in a self-enhancing manner, putting them at better odds to contribute to their community after the conflict.

Children, youth and engagement in peacebuilding

As mentioned, peacebuilding and the ability to engage in non-violent everyday conflict management require the strengthening of social cohesion within conflict-affected communities. Ideally, "This restoration of resources such as social capital, social trust and self-efficacy (agency) will support bonds, build bridges, and link vertical and horizontal relations, thus strengthening the overall cohesiveness of society."[104] Such an understanding could enhance the abilities of international actors and policy-makers to carry out peacebuilding more effectively through reconciliation, reconstruction and development. Where possible the international community should take into consideration existing local strategies, like night commuting, to facilitate peacebuilding efforts. In other words, youth leadership, networks and bonds already put in place should be considered, to use these resources better when designing programming. Today in Uganda, children and youth (both formerly abducted and night commuters) are asserting themselves as active agents in the peacebuilding process. Many are endorsing this role, and concrete illustrations are evident in different areas, including civil society activities, democratic decision-making, sport and media production, conflict transformation and reconciliation programmes, psychosocial recovery and economic recovery.

In addition to participating in existing institutions, an increasing number of young people are forming youth groups to provide social services and support to communities, such as on HIV/AIDS awareness and recreational and income-generating activities.[105] Some of these organizations take an approach which puts young people at the forefront as advocates for reconciliation and non-violent conflict resolution. For instance, in Gulu alone, "there are more than 200 youth groups registered with the Gulu District NGO Forum".[106] Indeed, the primary benefit of group membership, according to the young people, is the relationships the groups foster, thus building social capital within the post-conflict environment. The Women's Refugee Commission spoke with members of youth groups who explained that the group had become their family, which is particularly significant for the many youth who have lost parents and relatives due to the conflict.[107] Fellow members give each other advice, support and encouragement.

Today, youth participating in programmes aimed at reintegration appear to be adjusting well while actively addressing community problems. Despite the countless post-conflict challenges which remain, such as a lack of economic opportunities, sexual abuse and exploitation, health threats including HIV/AIDS, food insecurity and stigmatization, young people continue to be a source of resilience in their communities, working to restore social cohesion and development.[108] As Uganda moves forward and faces the challenges of rebuilding, these young people will continue to play a key role in contributing to this recovery, due to their strong social capital, social trust and self-efficacy resources. Much of this was fostered by resilience in the conflict. UNICEF claims that "With adequate support and access to necessary resources, they can become agents for change and provide a foundation for rebuilding lives and communities, contributing to a more just and peaceful society."[109] Night commuting promoted social cohesion by providing children and youth with surrogate families and community links, physical protection and emotional and economic support that are part of a peacebuilding continuum.[110] Thus the efforts of these young people, working on peacebuilding through civil society groups and organizations, should be upheld and promoted. The children and youth participating in these organizations possess a long track record in successfully building social capital and social trust while remaining engaged through strong commitment to their community.

Concluding remarks

This northern Uganda case study provides an example of resilience waged by a community of children and youth facing violence in an acute period of a protracted conflict situation. Through a historical exploration, an evolutionary process of resilience has been discovered, showing the dynamism of adaptation in the population. The lack of human security in northern Uganda created a vast humanitarian crisis, and it is beyond doubt that the children were among those most affected by the violence. The combination of the LRA's tactics, the violence perpetrated by UPDF soldiers and the lack of government security to counter these threats led to the attempt by the affected child/youth population of Acholi to provide for their own security. Their vulnerability did not exclude ability. In a context of extreme marginalization with very limited options available to the majority of the population, going to night commuter centres represented an alternative, and as such, increased people's capability for action and resilience to violence. From being a spontaneous survival strategy motivated by a context of crisis, night commuting developed into a social institution that children and entire households used to cope with the challenges they met in their daily lives.

Most importantly, the phenomenon harnessed the social capital and social trust within the Acholi population and helped to maintain and strengthen it during the conflict, contributing to a more cohesive community. This strategy provided protection against the damages of the conflict and helped maintain well-being, confidence and agency. The peacebuilding task of bringing the Acholi community together after armed violence will no doubt continue to be assisted by the networks these young people maintained during the conflict. Former night commuters and even combatants abducted by the LRA have taken part in local peacebuilding initiatives and organizations, showing their capacities to participate and meet the challenges of post-conflict reconciliation.[111] This is a lesson to be learned about the power and agency of children and youth in conflict contexts and their potential in peacebuilding efforts. Today, we witness how youth within the region are able and willing to contribute and engage with others to promote reconciliation, peace and security. With the widespread victimization of children and youth in the conflict in northern Uganda, as either child combatants or night commuters, it is easy to assume that their high level of successful participation in peacebuilding efforts today is related to their coping abilities and their maintenance of basic well-being during the conflict. The experience of night commuting shows that one must think of children as powerful and effective agents of their own development who, even during times of great adversity, consciously act upon and influence the environments in which they live. Ugandan children and youth were able to negotiate and adapt to a landscape marked by violence and limited resources, and maintain and strengthen key resources such as social capital, trust and self-efficacy, which all promoted social cohesion. The more cohesive a society is, the more likely it is that it will possess the inclusive mechanisms necessary to mediate and manage conflicts, cooperate and work collaboratively to solve problems. Thus peacebuilding efforts must recognize that resilience strategies developed during conflict can have an important impact on social cohesion and non-violent mechanisms to manage conflicts. The potential of the young to contribute to social change should be better recognized and given a central role in post-conflict reconciliation, peacebuilding and development.

First, rebuilding social cohesion should be seen as central to successful and sustainable peacebuilding in Uganda. Young people's local resilience initiatives, such as night commuting, should be recognized for their potential to contribute to rebuilding social cohesion. Leadership and participation of children and youth should be supported by local authorities and the government to allow their contributions in the dialogue and political processes towards peacebuilding. Finally, support should be provided and sustained for the development of inclusive child- and youth-led organizations, networks and partnerships while sensitizing adults to the importance of children's participation in peacebuilding activities. In this way, Uganda can assure an inclusive process which takes into account and takes advantage of the resources offered by these children and youth to contribute to rebuilding social cohesion and thus a sustainable peace.

Notes

1. Nat J. Colletta and Michelle L. Cullen, "The Nexus between Violent Conflict, Social Capital, and Social Cohesion: Case Studies from Cambodia and Rwanda", Social Capital Initiative Working Paper No. 23, World Bank, Washington, DC, 2000, p. 1, http://siteresources.worldbank.org/INTSOCIALCAPITAL/Resources/Social-Capital-Initiative-Working-Paper-Series/SCI-WPS-23.pdf.
2. Ibid., p. 13.
3. In this chapter, those under the age of 13 are referred to as "children", and those between the ages of 13 and 18 as "youth".
4. See WCRWC, "No Safe Place to Call Home: Child and Adolescent Night Commuters in Northern Uganda", Women's Commission for Refugee Women and Children, New York, July 2004, http://womensrefugeecommission.org/resources/doc_download/452-ug-nightcom. The resilience strategy of "night commuting", although a self-developed initiative, was still one of forced displacement. In light of the very high likelihood of violence, children were forced to leave their villages/camps to find safety elsewhere.
5. Small Arms Survey, *Small Arms Survey 2008: Risk and Resilience*, Cambridge: Cambridge University Press, 2008, p. 213.
6. Ibid., p. 247.
7. Suniya S. Luthar, Dante Cicchetti and Bronwyn Becker, "The Construct of Resilience: A Critical Evaluation and Guidelines for Future Work", *Child Development* 71(3), 2000, p. 543.
8. See "Basic Hazards – Acute and Chronic Health Effects", Yale University Learning Centre, ChemSafe, http://learn.caim.yale.edu/chemsafe/references/effects.html.
9. Acholi is an ethnic group from districts of northern Uganda, an area commonly referred to as Acholiland.
10. James Neill, "What Is Psychological Resilience?", *Wilderdom*, 16 April 2006, http://wilderdom.com/psychology/resilience/PsychologicalResilience.html.
11. Julia Firestone, "Teaching Peace: An Exploration in Youth Peace Building through Peace Education Programs in Gulu Municipality, Northern Uganda", *ISP Collection*, 1 April 2009, p. 10, http://digitalcollections.sit.edu/isp_collection/679.
12. Ibid.
13. There are many projects in the field of resilience promotion. Examples include projects such as Bounce Back!, an organization which promotes child resilience; the Boreal Forest & Community Resilience Project of the University of Minnesota, which focuses on environmental resilience; and the World Bank's various resilience projects, including in the social protection and climate sectors.
14. For a full history of the colonial era in Uganda see Gardner Thompson, *Governing Uganda: British Colonial Rule and Its Legacy*, Kampala: Fountain Publishers, 2003.
15. Kefa M. Otiso, *Culture and Customs of Uganda*, Westport, CT: Greenwood Publishing, 2006, p. 16.
16. Ibid.
17. Ibid, p. 17.
18. HRW, "The Scars of Death: Children Abducted by the Lord's Resistance Army in Uganda", Human Rights Watch, London, 1997, www.hrw.org/legacy/reports97/uganda/.

19. International Crisis Group, "Northern Uganda: Understanding and Solving the Conflict", Africa Report, International Crisis Group, Nairobi/Brussels, April 2004.
20. Paul Raffaele, "Uganda: The Horror", *Smithsonian*, February 2005.
21. BBC, "Uganda's Museveni Wins Election", BBC News, 25 February 2006, http://news.bbc.co.uk/2/hi/africa/4750040.stm.
22. HRW, note 18 above.
23. Ibid., p. 73.
24. Raffaele, note 20 above. A mystic refers to "a person who seeks by contemplation and self-surrender to obtain unity with or absorption into the Deity or the absolute, or who believes in the spiritual apprehension of truths that are beyond the intellect", Oxford Dictionaries Online, http://oxforddictionaries.com/.
25. Raffaele, note 20 above.
26. Matt Brown, "Ugandan Peace Deal in Danger of Collapse", *The National*, 18 August 2009, www.thenational.ae/news/world/africa/ugandan-peace-deal-in-danger-of-collapse.
27. Einar Braathen and Agnes Ojera, "Northern Uganda: Local Actors Preparing for Peace", Norwegian Institute for Urban and Regional Research, Oslo, 2008, p. 36.
28. Ellen Martin, "Capacity-Building and Partnership in Northern Uganda", *Humanitarian Exchange Magazine* 46, March 2010, www.odihpn.org/humanitarian-exchange-magazine/issue-46/capacity-building-and-partnership-in-northern-uganda.
29. International Crisis Group, note 19 above.
30. Heidi Rose and Irene Sattarzadeh, "Northern Uganda Human Security Update: February 2005", Liu Institute for Global Issues, Vancouver, BC, 17 February 2005, www.ligi.ubc.ca/sites/liu/files/Publications/HSR-Northern_Uganda.pdf.
31. *The Economist*, "Uganda's Rebel Child-Soldiers: The Lord's Army Resists", *The Economist*, 20 April 2002, www.economist.com/node/1087447.
32. Ibid.
33. Raffaele, note 20 above.
34. *The Economist*, "A Catastrophe Ignored", *The Economist*, 22 July 2004, www.economist.com/node/2952450.
35. HRW, "Q&A on Joseph Kony and the Lord's Resistance Army", Human Rights Watch, 21 March 2012, www.hrw.org/news/2012/03/21/qa-joseph-kony-and-lords-resistance-army#4.
36. WCRWC, note 4 above, p. 4.
37. Ibid.
38. Ibid., p. 3.
39. Namrita Talwar, "Fostering Terror: Child Soldier Crisis in Uganda", *UN Chronicle* 41(2), 2004, p. 7.
40. Adam Branch, "Neither Peace Nor Justice: Political Violence and the Peasantry in Northern Uganda, 1986–1998", *African Studies Quarterly* 8(2), 2005, pp. 1–31.
41. P. Matsiko wa Mucoori and Steven Kibuuka, "Why Has Kony Survived UPDF Fire for 22 Years?", *The Independent*, 11 December 2009, www.independent.co.ug/news/news-analysis/587-why-has-kony-survived-updf-fire-for-22-years?format=pdf.
42. Ibid.
43. Henriette Lunde, "Night Commuting in Gulu, Northern Uganda: From Spontaneous Strategy to New Social Institution", MA thesis in peace and conflict studies, Fafo Report 549, Oslo, 2006, p. 34, www.fafo.no/pub/rapp/549/549.pdf.
44. Ibid.
45. Ibid.
46. Ibid., p. 35.
47. Ibid.
48. Morten Bøås and Anne Hatløy, "Northern Uganda Internally Displaced Persons Profiling Study", UNDP, Kampala, September 2005.

49. Lunde, note 43 above, p. 35.
50. Ibid.
51. Lunde, note 43 above, pp. 35–36.
52. Lunde, note 43 above, p. 36.
53. Ibid., p. 37
54. Ibid.
55. Ibid.
56. Ibid., p. 47.
57. Thomas Brinkhoff, "Uganda City Population", 17 June 2012, www.citypopulation.de/Uganda-Cities.html.
58. Lunde, note 43 above, p. 39. Dozens of local and international organizations intervened to improve the conditions of night commuters, including the American Jewish World Service, Women's Commission for Refugee Women and Children, African Medical and Research Foundation, UNICEF, War Child Canada, Gulu Walk, Gulu District NGO Forum, OCHA, Charity for Peace Foundation, Noah's Ark, Rural Focus Uganda, Médecins Sans Frontières, Oxfam and International Rescue Committee.
59. Ibid.
60. Ibid.
61. Barry Barnes, "Practice as Collective Action", in Theodore R. Schatzki, Karin Knorr Cetina and Eike von Savigny (eds), *The Practice Turn in Contemporary Theory*, London: Routledge, 2001, p. 19.
62. Lunde, note 43 above, p. 4.
63. Ibid.
64. D. Østerberg, *Sosiologiens Nøkkelbegreper*, 6th edn, Oslo: Cappelen Akademisk Forlag, 2003, p. 99, cited in Lunde, note 43 above, p. 4.
65. Frances A. Boudreau and W. M. Newman, *Understanding Social Life: An Introduction to Sociology*, Minneapolis/St Paul, MN: West Publishing, 1993, p. 112, cited in Lunde, note 43 above, p. 4.
66. Lunde, note 43 above, p. 1.
67. Ibid., p. 47.
68. "The Security Situation in Northern Uganda: Overview and Recommendations", Liu Institute for Global Issues, Vancouver, BC, 2004, cited in Lunde, note 43 above, p. 52.
69. Lunde, note 43 above, p. 53.
70. Lehnart Falk, Jessica A. Lenz and Patric Okuma, *Sleepless in Gulu: A Study of the Dynamics behind the Child Night Commuting Phenomena in Gulu, Uganda*, Copenhagen: Red Barnet/Save the Children Denmark, 2004, p. 23.
71. Lunde, note 43 above, p. 53.
72. CSOPNU, *Nowhere to Hide: Humanitarian Protection Threats in Northern Uganda*, Kampala: Civil Society Organisations for Peace in Northern Uganda, December 2004, cited in Lunde, note 43 above, p. 23.
73. HRW, "Uprooted and Forgotten: Impunity and Human Rights Abuses in Northern Uganda", Human Rights Watch, London, 20 September 2005, p. 34, www.hrw.org/reports/2005/09/19/uprooted-and-forgotten.
74. Ibid., p. 44.
75. HRW, "Abducted and Abused: Renewed Conflict in Northern Uganda", Human Rights Watch, London, 15 July 2003, p. 3, www.hrw.org/reports/2003/uganda0703/.
76. Lunde, note 43 above, p. 67.
77. Ibid.
78. Ibid., p. 82.
79. Ibid., p. 60.

80. Ibid., p. 78.
81. Ibid., p. 73.
82. Ibid., p. 76.
83. Ibid., p. 83.
84. Small Arms Survey, note 5 above, p. 229.
85. Ibid., p. 267.
86. Robert D. Putnam, *Bowling Alone: The Collapse and Revival of American Community*, New York: Simon & Schuster, 2000, p. 19.
87. Robert D. Putnam, "Social Capital: Measurement and Consequences", *Canadian Journal of Policy Research* 2(1), 2001, pp. 41–51.
88. Ganga Ram Dahal and Krishna Prasad Adhikari, "Bridging, Linking, and Bonding Social Capital in Collective Action: The Case of Kalahan Forest Reserve in the Philippines", International Food Policy Research Institute, Washington, DC, 2008, http://ideas.repec.org/p/fpr/worpps/79.html.
89. Putnam, note 87 above.
90. Colletta and Cullen, note 1 above, p. 32.
91. Ibid., p. 4.
92. Lunde, note 43 above.
93. Christopher Blattman, "The Causes of Child Soldiering: Evidence from Northern Uganda", paper presented at International Studies Association 48th Annual Convention, Chicago, IL, 28 February 2007, www.allacademic.com/meta/p179774_index.html.
94. Ibid., p. 26.
95. Ibid.
96. Lunde, note 43 above.
97. Small Arms Survey, note 5 above, p. 239. To reinsert agency back into the discussion of resilient action, I borrow from social cognitive theory of post-traumatic recovery and transformational action. Social cognitive theory adopts an agentic model of adaptation and change. Within this agentic perspective, resilience to adversity relies more on personal enablement than on environmental protectiveness. To understand better the night commuter's personal capacity for action, I look at self-efficacy in human functioning to explain resilience.
98. Charles C. Benight and Albert Bandura, "Social Cognitive Theory of Posttraumatic Recovery: The Role of Perceived Self-Efficacy", *Behaviour Research and Therapy* 42(10), 2004, p. 1131.
99. Ibid.
100. Ibid., p. 1132.
101. Jeannie Annan, Christopher Blattman and Roger Horton, "The State of Youth and Youth Protection in Northern Uganda: Findings from the Survey for War Affected Youth, a Report for UNICEF Uganda", September 2006, p. 10, http://chrisblattman.com/documents/policy/sway/SWAY.Phase1.FinalReport.pdf.
102. Ibid.
103. Ibid.
104. Colletta and Cullen, note 1 above, p. 1.
105. Jenny Perlman Robinson, "Listening to Youth: The Experiences of Young People in Northern Uganda", Women's Commission for Refugee Women and Children, New York, June 2007, p. 5, www.unhcr.org/refworld/docid/48aa83150.html. Youth organizations engaged with peacebuilding efforts include the Acholi Youth Peace and Reconciliation Initiative, Active Vision Youth Foundation, Advocacy for Peace and Development, ACONGA Youth Alliance and the Youth Social Work Association Uganda.
106. Jenny Perlman Robinson, "Listening to Youth: The Experiences of Young People in Northern Uganda (Summary Report)", Women's Commission for Refugee Women

and Children, New York, September 2007, p. 13, http://womensrefugeecommission.org/resources/doc_download/451-ug-machel-short.

107. Ibid.

108. Ibid., p. 5.

109. UNICEF, "Map of Programmes for Adolescent Participation During Conflict and Post-Conflict Situations", UNICEF, September 2003, p. 3, www.unicef.org/emerg/files/Map_of_Programmes.pdf.

110. Carolyn Nordstrom, *Girls and Warzones: Troubling Questions*, Uppsala: Life & Peace Institute, 1997.

111. Organizations with participants who include former combatants and night commuters can be identified at www.insightonconflict.org/search/?country=uganda&cat_tag=all.

Part IV

Children and youth as peacebuilders

8

Do youth programmes contribute to post-conflict peacebuilding? Some reflections on existing practice

Valeria Izzi and Chetan Kumar

It is always "Youth, youth", when there is nothing else to be said.

Anton Chekhov, *The Seagull*

Introduction

In recent years the peacebuilding and state-building agendas have shown a new interest in youth. Policy documents stress the importance of taking into account the needs and priorities of young people as an essential element of a lasting peace in post-conflict societies.[1] The emphasis at the policy level has been accompanied by a momentous increase in funds and resources for "youth programmes" geared towards conflict prevention and peacebuilding. A glance at the programme portfolio of the UN Peacebuilding Fund (PBF) shows a definite emphasis on providing young people with employment and livelihood opportunities, as a means to harness their energy towards peace and discourage their recruitment for violence.[2]

While this is undoubtedly a welcome development, a critical reflection is needed on the underpinning assumptions of these interventions, as well as their impact. This chapter attempts an analysis of this new trend of youth programming from a peacebuilding perspective. It sets out to unpack the conceptual foundations and analytical assumptions underpinning the "youth and peacebuilding" paradigm. It then highlights some

Escaping victimhood: Children, youth and post-conflict peacebuilding, Schnabel and Tabyshalieva (eds), United Nations University Press, 2013, ISBN 978-92-808-1211-4

common challenges faced by national and international actors in youth programming. Finally, some tentative conclusions and areas for further reflection are offered.

Why youth?

The main rationale given by donors and international organizations for the inclusion of youth in the peacebuilding discourse is that idle and disaffected young people provide fertile ground for recruitment by different types of violence entrepreneurs.[3] In some contexts armed groups can be perceived by young people as protection networks, providing training, employment opportunities, identity and empowerment. In short – the argument goes – if there are too many youths to be absorbed in a productive way in society, their energy can be channelled to destructive ends. Thus the combination of a surging youth population, uncontrolled urbanization and widespread unemployment is seen as presenting a threat to peace and security in many regions of the world.[4]

The "youth-bulge" theory

In drawing a direct causal relationship between high percentages of youth in society and a high risk of instability, this rationale is influenced by the youth-bulge theory, according to which countries undergoing demographic transitions (typically due to rapid decreases in infant mortality rates) are especially vulnerable to civil conflict and other forms of violence. First formulated in the 1960s,[5] the youth-bulge theory has gained increasing currency in recent years, particularly after the terrorist attacks on 11 September 2001, as many scholars and policy-makers have used it to explain the "roots of rage"[6] in the Arab world and the recruitment appeal of terrorist networks.

Despite its popularity in many circles, the youth-bulge theory has been widely criticized for posing a deterministic linkage between demography and violence, thus scapegoating young people and overlooking wider societal factors such as inequality, bad governance and competition for scarce resources.[7] Critics have also remarked that the theory is inherently gender biased, equating "youth" with angry and aggressive young men, who are considered innately prone to violence, and virtually ignoring the role of young women as well as the socially constructed nature of gender relations.[8]

Even in purely demographic terms, the youth-bulge theory is debatable. Certainly, high-income countries tend to be, on average, both "older" and "safer" than low-income ones. However, the causal relationship is not straightforward – high-income countries are not necessarily safer *because* they have a different demographic composition. Rather, other factors can be identified that account for both the lower risk of violence and the lower percentage of young people: high-income countries have more advanced healthcare systems (thus higher life expectancy), more advanced family planning (thus fewer children per woman) and better-functioning security systems (thus less crime).

When it comes to developing countries, demographic indicators are not significantly correlated to the history of violence. For example, there is no statistically significant demographic difference between African countries that have experienced internal violence on a massive scale (e.g. Liberia, Sierra Leone, the Democratic Republic of the Congo) and those that have shown resilience to civil wars (e.g. Botswana, Tanzania, Ghana).[9]

In the view of the most vehement supporters of the youth-bulge theory, African cities, with their ever-rising concentration of young men, are the quintessential example of the dreadful effects of youth bulges. Robert Kaplan famously described West African capitals as filled with "out of school, unemployed, loose molecules in an unstable social fluid that threatened to ignite".[10] Kaplan's views – if not his apocalyptic tones – have been echoed by many scholars and policy-makers. Yet, as Marc Sommers notes, there is hardly any evidence of these catastrophic effects: while varying degrees of urban violence are present in many African cities, the majority are far from being the explosions of societal madness dreaded by the proponents of the youth-bulge hypothesis.[11]

Youth unemployment and violence

A more nuanced argument links violence with youth unemployment, rather than the youth demographic *per se*. In his 2001 report on the prevention of armed conflict, the UN Secretary-General stated that "Young people with limited education and few employment opportunities often provide fertile recruiting ground for parties to a conflict. Their lack of hope for the future can fuel disaffection with society and make them susceptible to the blandishments of those who advocate armed conflict."[12] This was reaffirmed in 2006 in the "Progress Report on the Prevention of Armed Conflict":

> Ever-rising youth unemployment undermines the possibility of progress in countries emerging from conflict, in a broad socio-economic and political sense, and risks destroying the political and social structures in countries that are currently stable ... A society where unemployment is high and where young people feel alienated and excluded from opportunity becomes a fertile breeding ground for politically and criminally violent groups.[13]

The "youth unemployment as a security issue" argument was elaborated in detail by the report "Youth Unemployment and Regional Insecurity in West Africa", produced in 2005 by the UN Office in West Africa. It describes current levels of youth unemployment in West Africa as a "ticking time bomb" for the region and beyond. The report argues:

> Youth unemployment – and its corollary, underemployment – has become a central political-security issue in West Africa, in addition to being a socio-economic one. Its causes lie in both spheres, as do its effects. Youth who are able bodied but unskilled, jobless and alienated, have been ready to take up arms in exchange for small amounts of money – together with the promise of recognition, loot and "wives" – and are more likely to be drawn into the influence of warring factions or criminal gangs to gain this "empowerment". This unemployment fuels conflict and crime, both of which then in turn increase unemployment still further by their effects on economic performance, investor confidence and social, physical and institutional structures.[14]

The potential for youth unemployment to breed instability is seen as particularly strong in countries recently emerging from violent conflict. According to the Secretary-General's 2012 report "Peacebuilding in the Aftermath of Conflict", youth unemployment is key to explaining the recurrence of violent conflict ("90 per cent of conflicts between 2000 and 2009 occurred in countries that had previously experienced civil war"[15]), along with other factors such as "political exclusion, real or perceived discrimination against social groups, severe corruption ... and unequal distribution of natural resource wealth".[16]

The International Labour Organization estimates that at the end of 2010 there were more than 75 million young unemployed people in the world – 4.6 million more than in 2007.[17] The global economic crisis has further exposed the vulnerability of youth in the job market: young people are "the 'first out' and 'last in' during times of economic recession",[18] and are disproportionately represented in the ranks of the long-term unemployed. In a sense, these figures alone contradict the catastrophic view according to which unemployed young people are naturally prone to violence: clearly, the vast majority of unemployed young people have chosen not to resort to violence, or else the world would be a much more violent place that it currently is.

Furthermore, official unemployment statistics have a limited utility for understanding the extent and nature of the youth unemployment problem in post-conflict societies. Speaking of "unemployment" conveys an idea of idleness that does not capture the informality and hustling prevalent in the lives of young people in post-conflict settings. Most young are busy "getting by" in the informal sector, with no guarantees of safety or long-term prospects.[19] For analytical, policy and programming purposes it is necessary to go beyond an employed/unemployed dichotomy and consider forms of exploitative, unsafe or extremely precarious work in which young people engage.

Youth as actors of peace

An emerging counter-discourse contests the depiction of youth as a threat to peace, focusing instead on the "positive, preventive and transformative"[20] roles that young people play in many conflict and post-conflict settings, typically with very limited resources and little visibility. In their analysis of youth-generated peacebuilding in post-conflict settings, Celina Del Felice and Andria Wisler provide a number of examples, including the work of Peacelink in Sierra Leone. Created in 1990 as a non-profit, non-denominational youth-led organization, Peacelink employs visual and performing arts as a vehicle of expression and a means of healing the wounds of war. Music, drama, dance and painting are used to help reconcile communities, build trust among participants and boost the personal self-esteem of young people. While small in scale and low in resources, these initiatives can count on the power of peer-to-peer influence, and are therefore able to reach out to young people in a way that traditional interventions cannot.[21]

In spite of their potential, youth-generated efforts have not been properly documented beyond some anecdotal examples, and their impact has not been studied in any detail. According to Siobhán McEvoy-Levy, this analytical gap is due to the fact that "youth social movements are rarely unambiguously 'peace' oriented, at least as it is defined in the mainstream literature ... Rather than seeking for youth that campaign for peace, one might look to those who are involved in social development, capacity building, and political education for youth members of political groups."[22] In other words, the fact that youth-promoted peace initiatives remain off the radar screen of donors and international agencies may point to the limitations of the radar screen itself.

Translating policies into programmes

The renewed attention on youth at the policy level has resulted in an increase of resources for youth programmes with a peacebuilding rationale – as either stand-alone interventions or "youth components" within mainstream development programmes. These projects seek to enhance youth participation, promote youth leadership or implement specific dialogue and reconciliation activities targeted at the younger strata of society.

Youth programmes feature prominently among the interventions financed by the UN Peacebuilding Fund. Most focus on youth employment and livelihoods. For example, in Sierra Leone the PBF supported a project on youth employment through the creation of small-scale enterprises for unemployed young people.[23] In Guinea-Bissau support for youth training and employment was considered a peace-multiplier measure, aimed at "reducing the possibility of youth being targeted for recruitment by armed factions during civil conflicts and their involvement in clandestine migration, drug trafficking and organized crime".[24]

Youth empowerment is another strong focus of PBF-funded programmes. One example is the Youth Empowerment Services for Peacebuilding and Stability project in Liberia, launched in 2009. The programme moved from the observation that, until then, the majority of international assistance and funding had been directed to former combatants, while "other young people who have an equal stake in the consolidation of peace"[25] had been overlooked. The aim of the programme was building youth's "capacities and enhancing their opportunities to initiate and participate in peacebuilding and development activities".[26] The project also focused on "creating youth friendly spaces [to] harness the creativity and potential of young people as the foundation for social cohesion and change".[27]

Assessing the impact of youth programmes is challenging, in part because evaluations are not systematically carried out. As noted by Marc Sommers:

> [A] significant weakness in the literature is the scarcity of quality evaluation documents. Relatively few program evaluations exist. Evidence of lasting program impact on youth lives is virtually unknown. Most ... of the evaluation documents reviewed are not of high quality, and do not, for example, examine the lives of program graduates after programs have ended. Many also do not critically compare the situation of program participants to their counterparts who did not participate in programs.[28]

Even in the absence of systematic evaluations, however, a number of challenges emerge as crucial for the design and implementation of youth programmes. They are discussed in the following paragraphs.

Defining youth

The United Nations defines youth as the segment of the population aged 15–24.[29] This definition is not binding, however, and it is widely acknowledged that "youth" is more a social construct than a rigid age category.

Youth can be seen as "a sort of transition territory between the more established social categories of childhood and adulthood",[30] generally linked to rites of passage of some kind, with considerable variation across time and space.

A comparative analysis of national youth policies and similar documents around the world shows a progressive "stretching" of the notion of youth, well beyond the official definition of 15–24, with the upper ceiling pushed into the 30s. This can be associated with the fact that social and economic opportunities for making the transition to full adulthood are increasingly scarce, especially in the developing world. As remarked in a UN Development Programme study, "there is increasing evidence from different parts of the world that full adulthood is more and more difficult to achieve, due to social and economic constraints".[31] In other words:

> youth is not serving as a transitional phase to a more established social status, but is an enduring limbo. This is a source of tremendous frustration. Instead of leaving youth behind and entering adulthood by marrying and establishing independent households, an increasing proportion of this "lost generation" ... are unable to attain any social status.[32]

The sharp increase of the age for entry into full adulthood creates a demographic paradox. In many post-conflict countries, where life expectancy is in the 40s or 50s, "stretching" youth means, in practice, significantly reducing adulthood as an analytical category or a demographic group. For programming purposes, using a definition of youth that spans two decades (15–35, as in many African national youth policies) rather than nine years (15–24, as in the UN General Assembly definition) certainly has implications when it comes to identifying criteria for beneficiaries and selecting young people who fit these criteria. Development practitioners often express frustration over the difficulty of reaching young people in their teens and early 20s, as programmes become "monopolized" by older beneficiaries. This may happen, in particular, when international actors interface with official youth organizations, whose leadership is often composed of older youth – *de facto* recreating, on a smaller scale, the same age-based hierarchies that can be found in society at large.

One could say that youth programmes are stuck in a catch-22. What young people really need is support to exit the youth category and become full-fledged members of society. In reality, however, the very proliferation of youth programmes may be contributing to unnaturally stretching the youth category upwards in many developing countries. In societies where resources are scarce and competition for development funds is fierce, the infusion of youth-earmarked resources can lead an increasing portion of the population to define themselves as "youth", with significant, and yet unexplored, societal implications.

Identifying programme beneficiaries within the overall youth category

Very often, programmes declare an objective of reaching the most "vulnerable" or "at-risk" youth. However, this is a difficult judgement call to make in situations where a large portion of the population falls within the youth category, and the overwhelming majority face similar challenges and experience similar levels of vulnerability. Partly as a consequence, criteria for inclusion/exclusion of young people in programmes are often left extremely vague. As noted by Marc Sommers, "profiles of which youth are in and not in a program [are] often either unclear or not mentioned. It is frequently difficult to determine the gender, class, educational accomplishment, war experience, household stability, and ethnicity of youth in these two groups [i.e. beneficiaries versus general youth population]."[33]

There is a general sense that youth programmes tend to benefit disproportionately a certain type of youth (urban-based, relatively educated and already represented in official or semi-official structures like youth organizations and networks), while they have difficulties reaching the most marginalized. Often programmes start from the "easiest to reach" in the pilot phase, with a view to replicating the interventions with other segments of youth later on. For example, the above-cited PBF-funded project on youth training and employment in Guinea-Bissau establishes an initial target of 500 youth, located in the capital city and its surroundings, envisaging that "Such a project can be replicated through follow-up funding to expand the targeted number of youth and focus areas for assistance in youth training and employment-generation."[34] What is often left vague is how this scaling up is supposed to happen, and with which resources. Albeit well meaning, this approach may reinforce a feeling of discrimination and exclusion among certain young people, who are often precisely the "vulnerable, at-risk" youth that the project wants to reach, and who instead feel left out for not being able to speak the language of development organizations. Youth organizations that are located in the capital, near the donors' offices, are almost invariably privileged compared to those located in more remote areas. In the worst cases, vagueness of criteria as to which young people to include can feed into and reinforce existing dynamics of patrimonialism and corruption.

It is also important to consider that different groups of young people may have been affected very differently by the conflict. For example, research conducted by Marc Sommers and Stephanie Schwartz in South Sudan identifies three groups of youth: those who remained in South Sudan during the civil war; those who fled to north Sudan (now Sudan), also known as "the Khartoumers"; and those who fled to the surrounding East African countries, who are referred to as "diaspora youth".[35] Even within these categories there are important variations connected with gender, social status and level of education, among other factors. The differences between the various groups and subgroups in terms of memories of conflict, experiences of post-conflict recovery, vulnerabilities and needs may be as strong as the common factors that define them as "youth".

Fully incorporating a gender perspective

Youth – as a concept and a category – has a crucial gender dimension. According to Mensch, Bruce and Greene, "During adolescence, the world expands for boys and contracts for girls."[36] In many societies, "cultural norms dictate that females are sheltered at the stage of puberty, for reasons such as purity and marriageability, stigma, or family reputation".[37] Programmes focusing generically on "youth" may disregard gender-discriminating traditions, such as access to education, as well as the challenges faced by young women in travelling, particularly in insecure contexts. Indeed, there is evidence that youth programmes tend to attract more young men than young women, partly due to the fact that the latter are burdened with different types of household chores and tend to have less free time. Young women are also less represented in youth organizations, which are often the main partner of international actors in the implementation of youth programmes.

This gender bias is also a consequence of the underlying security rationale of many youth programmes. Male youths are seen as actual or potential generators of violence, to be kept busy in order to maintain social peace, while female youth are still often regarded as passive victims. This view overlooks many dimensions related to the direct or indirect involvement of young women in violence and their role in socializing young men for violence. It also ignores the fact that many young men choose alternative models of non-violent masculinities, often suffering social marginalization because of this choice.

Incorporating gender sensitivity means more than just involving girls at the implementation stage. It means gaining an understanding of gender roles and relations, prevalent forms of masculinities and femininities, and the social censorship of non-prevalent gender roles, and incorporating this enhanced understanding into the design and implementation of youth programmes.

Reconciling youth programmes with overarching development strategies in post-conflict contexts

Considering the sheer size of the youth population in most countries (if nothing else), it is clear that a significant change can only be achieved by a coordinated effort to address youth needs at the strategic level. To date, there has been a clear gap between youth programmes and development strategies. For example, while there is a proliferation of youth employment programmes in West Africa, the problem is not treated in great detail in the poverty reduction strategy papers, which generally limit themselves to indicate youth as a "vulnerable group" particularly hit by unemployment.

In post-conflict contexts, basic infrastructures are generally in disarray, raising transaction costs and limiting access to markets, and the purchasing power of local populations is very limited, while war economies and criminal networks continue to thrive. Governance institutions suffer from low legitimacy, are often plagued by corruption and fall short of their obligation to provide security and basic public services. Human capital is particularly weak, as many young people have missed out on education due to the conflict and many qualified workers have been killed or left the country. Decimated post-war economies are ill equipped to absorb new workers, however skilled or unskilled they may be.[38] In short, limited economic opportunities for young people are linked more to the overall challenges of a post-conflict economy than to the specificity of their age.[39]

The singling out of youth as a target group for programmes can have important catalytic effects for improving the impact and effectiveness of development. However, it also carries the risk of putting youth in a box, isolating them from their context and seeing them as another "sector of intervention", "cross-cutting theme" or programming niche. Youth crisis is often the most visible sign of societal crisis, whose causes are mostly exogenous to youth, having to do instead with the shrinking of economic and social opportunities for the population as a whole. Hence youth challenges are not adequately tackled by programmatic interventions that are *ad hoc* in nature and limited in scope and duration: symptoms are treated, while root causes remain unaddressed.

Conclusions and recommendations

This chapter has attempted a critical analysis of the (relatively new) attention on youth in the context of peacebuilding at the policy and programming levels. While this emphasis on youth is a welcome development, as it addresses an age bias formerly prevalent in the peacebuilding field, there are a number of challenges that deserve closer attention.

Challenges derive from the dilemma of *reconciling a development rationale with a security rationale*. The overall discourse of youth appears today heavily "securitized", and nowhere is this more evident than in the field of employment. Young people are targeted not primarily in view of their particular vulnerability to unemployment, but because unemployed and disaffected young people (read: young men) are seen as a potential threat to security. There is reason to argue that the "securization" of youth employment may have a negative impact in the long run. The fact that many youth employment programmes have been designed with the main rationale of "keeping young people busy" has meant unbalanced attention to the employability[40] of young people, mostly through training programmes, at the expense of the macroeconomic interventions that would be necessary to make the job market work for young people in a sustainable way.

If programmes are based on the assumption that young people "at risk" should be targeted, the message sent to youth is that presenting a threat to society "pays off": being the "dangerous ones" makes them eligible for priority support and help, compared to those who do not pose a risk. It also favours males over females, as the former are considered to be the troublemakers who need to be kept busy and off the streets.

In any context, young people participating in violence are always a minority. As Nicolas Argenti puts it, "the remarkable thing is not why some of Africa's youth have embraced violence, but why so few of them have".[41] There has not been, so far, a systematic reflection on the factors promoting and reinforcing youth resilience. In fact, often analyses proceed backwards – starting from the motivations of young people involved in violence, and going on to generalize from them to youth as a whole. While it is certainly important to understand the motivations of youth who are mobilized (or mobilize themselves) for violence, it is equally important to consider those who – faced with the same challenging conditions and lack of opportunities – choose not to resort to violence. Simply providing opportunities or benefits for some randomly selected young people is very unlikely to result in concrete benefits in terms of enhanced security.

Based on the above considerations, a number of recommendations can be formulated for development practitioners to take into account in the design and implementation of youth programmes.

- *Carefully define the problem that the development programme is seeking to address*. The presence of a large population of young people is not, in itself, a problem, nor should it be presented as such. Vague and undocumented statements pointing to the "disaffection" and "marginalization" of young people are also unhelpful. What are young people disaffected from? Who or what is "marginalizing" them? Unless there is some clarity on these dynamics at the design stage, the chances that the programme can address them during implementation are slim.

- *Avoid using "youth" as a catch-all expression.* Contrary to what is often assumed in interventions, young people do not necessarily consider the fact of being young as their overarching source of identity, and what divides different groups of youth may be stronger than what unites them. To continue with the example above, does the diagnosis of "disaffection" and "marginalization" apply to young people across the board, or to certain categories of young people in particular? Navigating social complexity beyond sheer demographic data is important in assessing whether a youth programme is indeed useful, and what priority it should address.
- *Fully incorporate a gender dimension at the design, implementation, monitoring and evaluation stages* – not merely by trying to get "more girls" on board, but by gaining an understanding of the similarities and differences between the needs and priorities of young men and young women, the different ways in which they negotiate their transition to adulthood and the ways that notions of masculinity and femininity are socially constructed.
- *Once the "problem" is defined, carefully consider whether or not a youth programme is the best way to address it.* In any given setting, the need for a youth programme should be evaluated rather than simply assumed. A youth-specific intervention may or may not be the best way to address the needs and challenges of young people. In some cases it may be better to focus on making issues that affect young people an integral component of overarching development strategies and mainstream development programmes. According to Helen Brocklehurst, Stephanie Schwartz suggests in her analysis of youth in post-conflict reconstruction, interestingly and "counter intuitively", that community-based programmes may be a more useful way to engage young people compared to demographic-based ones.[42] The (understandable) urge to "do something" for young people should not come at the expense of careful reflection on what is best to do and how it is best to operate. The benefits of a youth programme should also be weighed against the possible risk of "doing harm" (e.g. creating expectations or reinforcing tensions among different groups of youth).
- *Once it is decided that a youth programme is indeed the way to go, clearly state the rationale for this programme, and ensure that this rationale is reflected in the objectives and activities.* Often, youth programmes are driven by a security rationale (e.g. prevent unemployed

young men from rioting), but feature traditional development activities (e.g. microfinance, training and support to self-entrepreneurship) and vaguely defined criteria for selection of beneficiaries. A programme stating that "youth unemployment is a risk for security" in a situation where the majority of the population are young and unemployed, and then providing jobs and training for just a few hundred of them, is bound to fail in its own terms.

The dichotomy between "youth as a threat to peace" and "youth as a force for peace" is ultimately unhelpful. The two labels are two sides of the same coin – i.e. the simplification of youth as a homogeneous category to fit the schemes and paradigms of external interveners. In any given situation, as youth make up the majority of the population, there will be some who are actively engaged in violence, some who are actively promoting peace, some who are just trying to get by and some who are disengaged and disillusioned but still not violent.[43] Young people have an agency that is far more complex and nuanced than is allowed by the majority of youth-focused interventions.[44] Richard Fanthorpe and Roy Maconachie note "the importance of distinguishing the realworld efficacy of youth agency in Sierra Leone from that constructed within the political imaginary of international development and human rights".[45]

Providing long-lasting opportunities for young people around the globe is a mission that goes far beyond what can be achieved through discrete youth programmes – however well intentioned, well designed or well funded. It requires development and peacebuilding strategies that fully take into account the specific challenges and difficulties young people face in living their youth and in leaving it behind, completing their transition to full adulthood in freedom and dignity.

Notes

1. This is a sharp departure from the 1990s. For example, youth are not significantly mentioned in the Secretary-General's "Agenda for Peace" or its supplement. See UN Secretary-General, "An Agenda for Peace: Preventive Diplomacy, Peacemaking and Peace-keeping", UN Doc. A/47/277–S/24111, New York, 17 June 1992; UN Secretary-General, "Supplement to an Agenda for Peace: Position Paper of the Secretary-General on the Occasion of the Fiftieth Anniversary of the United Nations", UN Doc. A/50/60–S/1995/1, New York, 3 January 1995.
2. The Peacebuilding Fund was launched in 2006 by the UN Secretary-General to support activities, actions, programmes and organizations that seek to build a lasting peace in countries emerging from conflict. The PBF is managed by the UN Peacebuilding Support Office, www.unpbf.org/.
3. UN Secretary-General, "Prevention of Armed Conflict – Report of the Secretary-General", UN Doc. A/55/95–S/2001/574, New York, 2001.

4. According to the report of the High Level Panel on Threats, Challenges and Change, "While it may not reach the level of war, the combination of a surging youth population, poverty, urbanization and unemployment has resulted in increased gang violence in many cities of the developing world. As one woman poignantly asked during the Panel's consultation with civil society organizations in Africa, 'How have we let what should be our greatest asset, youth, become a threat to our security?'" United Nations, "A More Secure World: Our Shared Responsibility, Report of the High Level Panel on Threats, Challenges and Change", UN Doc. A/59/565, New York, 2 December 2004, para. 45, www.un.org/secureworld/report.pdf.
5. The key elements of the youth-bulge theory can be found in the work of scholars like Herbert Moller in the 1960s. The actual term "youth bulge" was coined by German social scientist Gunnar Heinsohn in the mid-1990s and has gained great popularity in recent years, thanks to the work of American political scientists Gary Fuller and Jack A. Goldstone. For a review see Henrik Urdal, "The Devil in the Demographics: The Effect of Youth Bulges on Domestic Armed Conflict, 1950–2000", Social Development Papers No. 14, World Bank, Washington, DC, 2004. See also Herbert Moller, "Youth as a Force in the Modern World", *Comparative Studies in Society and History* 10(3), 1968, pp. 238–260.
6. See Fareed Zakaria, "The Roots of Rage", *Newsweek* 138(16), 2001, pp. 14–33.
7. Sommers argues that it may be more useful to ask why certain people are so threatened by some young men rather than why those young men seem so threatening. Marc Sommers, "Fearing Africa's Young Men: The Case of Rwanda", Social Development Papers No. 32, World Bank, Washington, DC, 2006. See also Anne Hendrixson, "The 'Youth Bulge': Defining the Next Generation of Young Men as a Threat to the Future", *Different Takes* 19, Winter 2003. (This is a publication of the Population and Development Programme at Hampshire College.)
8. UN Development Programme, "Youth and Violent Conflict: Society and Development in Crisis?", UNDP Bureau for Crisis Prevention and Recovery, New York, 2006, www.fewer-international.org/images/lib/Youth%20and%20Violent%20Conflict%20UNDP-BCPR_160.pdf.
9. Demographic data for this chapter were gathered from the World Bank, http://data.worldbank.org.
10. Robert D. Kaplan, *The Ends of the Earth: From Togo to Turkmenistan, from Iran to Cambodia, a Journey to the Frontiers of Anarchy*, New York: Vintage Books, 1997, p. 16.
11. Marc Sommers, "Urbanization, War, and Africa's Youth at Risk – Towards Understanding and Addressing Future Challenges", Basic Education and Policy Support Activity, USAID, Washington, DC, 2003, www.beps.net/publications/beps-urbanizationwaryouthatrisk-.pdf.
12. UN Secretary-General, note 3 above, para. 124.
13. United Nations, "Progress Report on the Prevention of Armed Conflict, Report of the Secretary-General", UN Doc. A/60/891, New York, 2006, para. 25.
14. UN Office for West Africa, "Youth Unemployment and Regional Insecurity in West Africa", UNOWA Issue Papers, Dakar, 2005, p. 16.
15. United Nations, "Peacebuilding in the Aftermath of Conflict – Report of the Secretary-General", UN Doc. A/67/499–S/2012/746, New York, 2012, para. 3. For statistics on the recurrence of civil war see World Bank, *World Development Report 2011: Conflict, Security and Development*, Washington, DC: World Bank, 2011.
16. United Nations, note 15 above, para. 3.
17. ILO, "Global Employment Trends for Youth: 2011 Update", International Labour Organization, Geneva, 2011.
18. Ibid., p. 1.
19. For an analysis of the phenomenon of hustling in Liberia see Jairo Munive, "The Army of 'Unemployed' Young People", *Young: Nordic Journal of Youth Research* 18(3), 2010,

pp. 321–338. The author defines hustling as "capitalizing on every opportunity to procure a good or a service to supplement income and symbolic capital", and identifies two mechanisms at stake for Liberian youth: "first, hustling serves as a tool of adaptation to material constraints and second, the act of hustling reproduces a self-efficacious, meaningful existence. Thus, hustling is ... both a survival strategy and a means of crafting an identity."

20. Celina Del Felice and Andria Wisler, "The Unexplored Power and Potential of Youth as Peace-Builders", *Peace, Conflict and Development* 11, 2007, p. 4.
21. Ibid. For more information on Peacelink see http://peace-links.org/new/index.html.
22. Siobhán McEvoy-Levy, "Youth as Social and Political Agents: Issues in Post-Settlement Peace Building", Occasional Paper No. 21, Kroc Institute, Notre Dame, IN, 2001, p. 25.
23. Jillian Lewis, "Final Programme Narrative Report", UNDP Sierra Leone, Freetown, 31 December 2010, http://mptf.undp.org/document/document/download/6326.
24. See "PBF/GNB/D-1 Youth Professional Training and Employment", project factsheet, Multi-Partner Trust Fund Office, UN Development Group, http://mptf.undp.org/factsheet/project/00066674.
25. Peacebuilding Fund, "Peace Building Fund Liberia: Mid-Term Review March 2010", March 2010, p. 54, www.betterpeace.org/files/PBF-Liberia-Midterm-Review-March2010.pdf.
26. Ibid.
27. Ibid.
28. Marc Sommers, "Youth and Conflict – A Brief Review of Available Literature", USAID, Washington, DC, 2006, p. 24, www.crin.org/docs/edu_youth_conflict.pdf.
29. UN General Assembly, "The World Programme of Action for Youth in the Year 2000 and Beyond", UN Doc. A/RES/50/81, New York, 1995.
30. UN Development Programme, note 8 above, p. 16.
31. Ibid., p. 23.
32. Charlotte Spinks, "Pentecostal Christianity and Young Africans", in Alex De Waal and Nicolas Argenti (eds), *Young Africa: Realizing the Rights of Children and Youth*, Trenton, NJ: Africa World Press, 2002, p. 193. See also Marc Sommers, *Stuck: Rwandan Youth and the Struggle for Adulthood*, Athens, GA: University of Georgia Press, 2012. Research conducted by Marc Sommers and Stephanie Schwartz in South Sudan identifies the increasing inability of young men to meet rising demands for bride price as a factor with wider repercussions on social cohesion and possibly stability. Marc Sommers and Stephanie Schwartz, *Dowry and Division – Youth and State Building in South Sudan*, Washington, DC: US Institute of Peace, 2011.
33. Sommers, note 28 above, p. 24. See also Marc Sommers, *West Africa's Youth Employment Challenge – The Case of Guinea, Liberia, Sierra Leone and Côte d'Ivoire*, Geneva: UNIDO, 2007.
34. Guinea-Bissau, "Priority Plan for the UN Peacebuilding Fund", June 2008, unpublished, internal government document.
35. Sommers and Schwartz, note 32 above.
36. Barbara S. Mensch, Judith Bruce and Margaret E. Greene, "The Uncharted Passage: Girls' Adolescence in the Developing World", Population Council, New York, 1998, p. 2, www.popcouncil.org/pdfs/passage/passage.pdf.
37. UN Development Programme, note 8 above, p. 30.
38. Christopher Maclay and Alpaslan Ozerdem, "'Use' Them or 'Lose' Them: Engaging Liberia's Disconnected Youth through Socio-Political Integration", *International Peacekeeping* 17(3), 2010, p. 349.
39. See Valeria Izzi, "Just Keeping Them Busy? Youth Employment Projects as a Peacebuilding Tool", *International Development Planning Review* 35(2), 2013, pp. 103–117.

40. See Ronald W. McQuaid and Colin Lindsay, "The Concept of Employability", *Urban Studies* 42(2), 2005, pp. 197–219.
41. Nicolas Argenti, "Youth in Africa: A Major Resource for Change", in Alex De Waal and Nicolas Argenti (eds), *Young Africa: Realizing the Rights of Children and Youth*, Trenton, NJ: Africa World Press, 2002, pp. 123–153.
42. Stephanie Schwartz, *Youth and Post-Conflict Reconstruction: Agents of Change*, Washington, DC: US Institute of Peace, 2009, reviewed in Helen Brocklehurst, "Engaging with Youth, Engaging with War", *Georgetown Journal of International Affairs*, Spring/Fall 2012, http://journal.georgetown.edu/wp-content/uploads/Engaging-with-Youth3.pdf.
43. McEvoy-Levy, note 22 above.
44. Susan Shepler, "Youth Music and Politics in Post-War Sierra Leone", *Journal of Modern African Studies* 48(4), 2010, pp. 627–642. Interestingly, the author analyses pop songs as an avenue to understand Sierra Leonean youth better on their own terms. See also Sylvanus N. Spencer, "The Use of Pop Songs by Sierra Leonean Youths in Enjoying the Space Created for Freedom of Expression after the Civil War", *Africa Today* 59(1), 2012, pp. 71–86.
45. Richard Fanthorpe and Roy Maconachie, "Beyond the 'Crisis of Youth'? Mining, Farming, and Civil Society in Post-War Sierra Leone", *African Affairs* 109(435), 2010, p. 272.

9

"Conflict is a preventable disease": Recovering child soldiers teach the practice of peace

Deborah Davis

Introduction

This chapter discusses the work of a small group of former child soldiers calling themselves Friends of Orphans, who train other former child soldiers to be peacebuilders in their communities. The group operates in northern Uganda, where a rebel militia known as the Lord's Resistance Army (LRA) waged a brutal war of attrition against members of its own ethnic group, the Acholis, for more than 25 years from the late 1980s until a peace agreement was finally signed in early 2009.[1] During that period the LRA, led by the notorious Joseph Kony, abducted an estimated 40,000–60,000 Acholi boys and girls as young as eight years of age, and indoctrinated them into a nihilistic crusade of cultural destruction by forcing them to kill their parents, teachers, neighbours and siblings.[2] Those who resisted were hacked to death as an example to other children.

While an estimated 4,000–5,000 managed to escape and find their way to an IDP (internally displaced person) camp or were rescued by the Uganda People's Defence Force (UPDF), tens of thousands of others were never seen again. Based on the horrifying stories told by the children who came back, most of the missing died from starvation or disease, were shot trying to escape or are still being held as "wives" of the soldiers. Those who made it to a camp were given medical care and trauma counselling for a few weeks by one of the aid agencies in the conflict zone. Some agencies also hired men from the camps to carry out abbreviated versions of the traditional Acholi forgiveness and conciliation rituals,

Escaping victimhood: Children, youth and post-conflict peacebuilding, Schnabel and Tabyshalieva (eds), United Nations University Press, 2013, ISBN 978-92-808-1211-4

since the tribal elders were too demoralized by the disintegration of their communities to perform them.[3] An unknown number of children were recaptured by the LRA, were rejected or killed by the villages to which they returned or were so tormented by the spirits of the people they had killed that they committed suicide. The older brother of Richard (Ricky) Anywar, the founder of Friends of Orphans, was one of the latter.

A note on methodology

The chapter uses an ethnographic approach[4] to examine the peacebuilding methods of Friends of Orphans in the IDP camps in northern Uganda. This approach was chosen for two reasons. First, the author's training as a cultural anthropologist and community development specialist provided useful research tools in the absence of quantitative data, which is a significant research constraint in northern Uganda, as in all conflict-affected societies, due to the disruption of normal data gathering by local governments and the dangers for outside researchers. And second, the ethnographic approach was much better suited to describing Friends of Orphans' highly original system of *micro-peacebuilding*, for which metrics have not yet been developed. It will be left to future researchers to carry out quantitative assessments of the organization's results.

The main research was conducted between August and October 2008, when the Acholis were still being terrorized by the Lord's Resistance Army. This was a period during which stalled peace negotiations, the continuing abduction of children and the emergence of severely damaged children from the bush were all taking place simultaneously. The research consisted of a literature review and extensive interviews. The literature review included studies of traditional Acholi peacebuilding practices;[5] UN documents pertaining to the issue of child soldiers;[6] the International Criminal Court's (ICC) indictment of LRA leader Joseph Kony in 2005 and legal writings pertaining to the indictment;[7] and field reports on the situation in northern Uganda by international agencies.[8]

The interviews were conducted with Friends of Orphans founder Ricky Anywar; with the group's co-founder and programme director, Francis Orem; and with volunteers and relief agency staff who have worked in partnership with Friends of Orphans on trauma counselling, skills training, art, music, athletics and other healing activities. The interviews with Anywar and Orem were held by telephone from Washington, DC: Anywar spoke from his office in Kampala, and Orem from the group's training centre in Pader town council, the municipality closest to the IDP camps in which Friends of Orphans operates. In addition, face-to-face interviews with Ricky Anywar were conducted in New York, where he travelled in

October 2008 to receive an award from an international child protection agency. At that meeting, he provided the author with copies of the group's community training manuals, concept papers, funding proposals, budgets, transcriptions of testimonies of escaped child soldiers and other non-published materials. A further face-to-face interview took place in Washington, DC, in November 2011, when Anywar was in the United States to raise money for a community radio station.

Additional research was carried out in March and April 2012, as this chapter was being prepared for publication, to include references to several important studies that consider the degree of culpability of child soldiers.[9] There is new material on the peace negotiations with the LRA, and Kony's refusal to sign a peace agreement until the ICC dropped the charges against him. New material has also been added on the controversy surrounding the film *Kony 2012*,[10] which many in northern Uganda feel is diverting attention and resources from what is now a much more serious problem – the spread of a fatal neurological illness known as nodding disease. Like the LRA, nodding disease targets children between the ages of five and 15 in conflict-affected areas of northern Uganda.[11] The Ugandan Ministry of Health is currently investigating a possible link between nodding disease and war trauma. Much of this new and supplementary material is not included in the narrative but is elaborated in the endnotes. If read in parallel with the main text, the notes will provide a deeper understanding of the issues.

Child soldiers and restorative justice: Is their survival evidence of their guilt?

The involvement of child soldiers in atrocities has raised questions about whether they should be treated as victims or perpetrators, and the relative merits of retributive versus restorative justice – of punishment versus forgiveness and reintegration into the community. The advocates of retributive justice, including the majority of the international legal community, support the ICC's indictment of Joseph Kony and his associates as war criminals.[12] However, the question of how to handle the abducted children has been more complicated. Their very survival is proof that they carried out atrocities for the months or years they were under the LRA's control – if they had refused to do so, they would have been killed. Moreover, many who returned now have no feelings of connectedness, no inhibitions against violence, and are therefore quite capable of killing again. The Acholi tell many stories of children who have killed after their return. One girl, for example, had an argument with her mother, hacked her to death with a machete, and did not understand why that was wrong.

The unbearable tragedy of the child soldier situation has made the government unwilling to prosecute them for war crimes. Instead, the Amnesty Law, adopted in 2000,[13] provided for those who returned to be given "reinsertion packages" consisting of a tent, seeds, gardening tools and cooking utensils – everything they would need to get their lives going again, except for a way of not becoming permanent outcasts. "Children like that," Ricky Anywar says, "remain in the community and live lonely, miserable lives, steal food to survive and get into fights, and are so weak and malnourished that even the army doesn't want them. They can go on that way for about five years, and then they fall sick and always die because nobody will feed them or take care of them. When you're extreme, people just look at you." The ones who escape this fate often end up in prison for assault, murder, rape or other violent crimes. Former child soldiers now comprise more than 70 per cent of the juvenile prison population in Uganda.[14]

The failure of restorative justice to help child soldiers

Efforts to ease the minds and spirits of these children have largely failed in northern Uganda because they have been unconnected to community healing.

In northern Uganda, as in other agrarian societies, restorative justice practices evolved as a way to prevent grievances over land or water rights, theft of women or livestock and affronts to dignity from escalating into a cycle of murder and revenge killings. The entire community would be involved in the rituals of confession, apology and restitution between the wrongdoer and the victim's clan or family. This form of justice all but disappeared in Africa during the colonial period, and was not revived until South Africa's Truth and Reconciliation Commission – followed by a similar commission in Sierra Leone and by the village-level *gacaca* courts after the genocide in Rwanda – used public confession as a way to heal the deepest kinds of societal wounds, the kind that cannot be healed merely by punishing the perpetrators. The power of this modest, victim-led mechanism of reconciliation and forgiveness to restore social equilibrium in Rwanda, Sierra Leone and South Africa was all the more remarkable, in the view of Western legal scholars, in that it no longer involved families arguing about personal insults or local water rights, but armed groups that had inflicted mass trauma on the population in order to achieve political power.

Restorative justice in these countries was successful for two important reasons. First, the truth-telling process, whether carried out in a national (South Africa and Sierra Leone) or community-level (Rwanda) public forum, was endorsed and financed by the government. And second, the process took place *in addition to – not as a substitute for* – the ICC trials of the major war criminals.

Indigenous justice in northern Uganda, however, has been problematic for several reasons. First, the healing ceremonies are not authentic, not concerned with truth-telling and not rooted in the wisdom of elders; rather, as noted above, they are superficial rituals that are reconstructed by outsiders to help an individual. Second, Joseph Kony's demand for restorative justice *instead* of a criminal trial – his refusal to sign the peace treaty, his continued abductions and killings when the ICC would not drop the charges against him – drained the concept of all meaning.[15]

By 1999, when Friends of Orphans was created, an entire generation of Acholis had grown up in the camps and knew nothing about indigenous justice; and many of the older people in the camps, those who had lost their homes or their children, no longer believed in justice of any kind. Some aid agencies nevertheless attempted to use Acholi justice rituals to facilitate the reintegration of groups of escaped child soldiers after they completed their few weeks of trauma counselling. In recreating these rituals, the agencies took care to use the correct roots for the bitter drink in the *mato oput* (reconciliation after a killing) ceremony, and the correct leaves to cover the egg that is stepped on in the *nyono tonggweno* (cleansing and welcoming back) ceremony, following procedures detailed in studies of Acholi culture.[16] However, these enactments did not come close to capturing the lengthy processes of mediation, confession, apology, explanation and discussion about the sources of the problem, which were facilitated over a period of months by the elders of the affected clans and traditionally preceded the public ceremonies. As a result, they did little to relieve the sense of estrangement between the escaped child soldiers and others in the camps, who continued to fear and despise them. "The entire community," Ricky says, "was at war with itself."

Ricky's story

Ricky Anywar was abducted by the Lord's Resistance Army in 1988, when he was 14 years old. His brother, abducted at the same time, was 17. They were forced to watch as the LRA burned down their house with their family inside. Then they were marched at gunpoint into the bush, where they were held for two-and-a-half years. "There was no talking about escape," Ricky remembers. "If you even looked like you were thinking about it, the abductors would kill you." Ricky and his brother were in different brigades that operated in the same area. "I used to see my brother often, and we would talk in parables. I told him, 'if any of us becomes the first to reach *obeno,* then greet them for me'." *Obeno*, the Acholi word for the cloth used to strap a baby to its mother's back, was the brothers' code word for home. "I once saw him carrying a wounded commander on his back who had been freshly shot on the battlefield. My brother was covered with his blood. He died on my brother's back." Horrified by that experience, soon afterwards his brother escaped. By the time Ricky was able to escape and return to *obeno* three months later, his brother had committed suicide. The neighbours said he had been tormented by the ghosts of the people he had killed. "He thought it was the end of the world, the end of the road," Ricky says. "He lost confidence in life."

With the last of his family dead, Ricky survived in the village by working for food. He was abducted again, escaped again, and found work with a woman who was known to give jobs to escaped child soldiers. Ricky went to work in her small factory, sewing blue jeans. "She asked me what I wanted," Ricky recalls. "I said I wanted an education, so she paid my school fees." It was the early 1990s and the non-governmental organizations (NGOs) had not yet come to northern Uganda, so there were no reception centres to provide food and medical care for escaped child soldiers and no programmes to rehabilitate them. "But my employer talked to me, different people talked to me, and I was more resilient than my brother. Despite all I had gone through, my spirit never went low, because I saw what had happened as completely abnormal." Ricky worked in the woman's factory until he finished high school. Then he left the war zone for Kampala and found a job in the personnel department at the Ministry of Education. At night he took courses at the university in business and development studies. He earned a business degree and opened a small stationery store that brought in enough money for him to live on. "But my heart kept telling me I wanted to help them," Ricky says. "I wanted to go back to Northern Uganda to help the children." He bought an old Toyota pickup truck for $2,000 and began driving out to the IDP camps every weekend, leaving Friday night and arriving on Saturday, a 14-hour journey over 600 kilometres of unpaved and broken roads; then driving back to Kampala on Sunday night in time to open up his stationery store on Monday.

In the war zone, Ricky saw children who had escaped from the LRA wandering the streets with vacant eyes, which to the community meant they were possessed by evil spirits because of the abominations they had committed. Some were missing limbs or had bullet wounds; some were out of their minds with grief or trauma. Ricky drove them 80 kilometres to the nearest hospital. For those who were capable of going to school, he paid the school fees. These children were orphans in a way that Acholi children had never been orphans. Ricky says:

> All children used to be our community children. We didn't have street children. Families would farm together, cook together in big pots, eat together in one big group, and that's how orphans were accommodated. But then the war came and people were moved into IDP camps and could not grow their own food, and the World Food Programme [which supplied food to the camps] would count the number of people in a family. Taking in an extra person would not change the family's food allocation; it just meant less food for the family.

The shortage of food caused near-starvation in the camps. "Some families took them in, but there was very, very little food, all the children had extended stomachs and almost everyone was malnourished."[17]

After two months of travelling back and forth, Ricky set up Friends of Orphans with Francis Orem and two others from the university who had also been child soldiers. In 1999 they opened a reception centre in the heart of the conflict zone, in Pader district, where the aid agencies would not send their staff. "I went to an opinion leader, a retired teacher," Ricky says, "and she gave us land inside the camp on which we built a small building. Then the community started bringing the children to me, and I tried to wash away the tears that had been rolling down their cheeks for a long, long time." He paid for their food out of his savings until he was able to persuade the World Food Programme to contribute food to his project.

The military had imposed a rule that all child soldiers taken in by an aid agency must be turned over for questioning before they could receive assistance of any kind. They were normally released within two or three days, although an unknown number were kept to help the army locate LRA weapons' caches. Others were recruited as government soldiers. Says Orem:

> From the moment we got them back, we began by finding something for these people to feed on, because the majority of them were malnourished. That is the first thing, something to eat, and then secondly you need to dress them because their clothes are all dirty and torn. Each time it is a process, you have received them, you have given them clothes, you have given them food, you have given them maybe something to sleep on, then you begin getting near to them, building relationships, sitting and playing together with them, and then you begin asking them where the parents are, how they entered into the bush, so that you know the child's story before you begin doing the counselling. Because if you rush and ask these questions when they have just come from the bush, they can become very violent.

For its first three years of operation, the Friends of Orphans reception centre provided the same basic services as those run by aid agencies in other parts of northern Uganda – emergency medical care and psychosocial support through both individual and group counselling. "What we did first depended on the level of trauma," Ricky says. The most traumatized children, those who were highly aggressive, terrified of strangers, or sat by themselves and cried, received extensive individual counselling by one of the former child soldiers working with Friends of Orphans. "We started talking to them about their situation and how we could help them, telling them that what happened to them wasn't their fault, that they could make their own future when they are rehabilitated." Some were so tormented by nightmares, hallucinations, suicidal thinking and fear of being reabducted that Ricky took them to the hospital for medication. The psychiatrist who treated them served as an adviser to Friends of Orphans until his death from Ebola haemorrhagic fever in 2005.

The children also attended group counselling sessions aimed at helping them to control their aggression, so they could interact safely with the community and be able to walk away from the many people who rejected or insulted them, instead of attacking and perhaps killing them. Children who did not get this type of counselling could be extremely dangerous. Referring to the incident mentioned above, Ricky told of one girl who escaped from the LRA and returned home without having gone through a reception centre. Her family accepted her, and her mother took her out to dig in their garden. They had angry words, and the girl cut off her mother's head. Then she continued to dig next to her mother's dead body. "She was too traumatized to know what she did," Ricky said. "It was only when one of the elders talked to her that she started crying."

"Just because the guns are silent, it doesn't mean there is peace"

Rejection by the community was a pervasive problem, particularly for older boys and for girls who had suffered sexual violence and returned with children born from that violence. This was not a situation that could be solved by the reception centres, which had a limited mandate and, in any event, lacked the capacity to follow up on the children's progress. The girls with babies, whom Ricky calls "child mothers", were generally accepted by their parents, but regarded with contempt by siblings and community members. Their babies were especially vulnerable to stigmatization, which increased the child mother's distress. Many boys reacted to the rejection by gambling, drinking, stealing or bringing guns into the camps, which served to isolate them further. Some overcame their feelings of uselessness by going back to the LRA or enlisting in the army, for which they needed forged papers and a community leader's recommendation. "We were in a process of recycling these children," Ricky says.

"They were in the centre for two weeks, brought home, killed or re-abducted, or they committed suicide, which created more conflicts in the community. Just because the guns are silent, it doesn't mean there is peace."

Ricky saw that the evil of the LRA had penetrated every aspect of Acholi life – every month, whole families were murdered in land disputes; every day, women were beaten by their husbands or deliberately infected with HIV/AIDS, and children were disciplined by means of burning or starvation. He had a powerful sense that the Acholi people were in the grip of *kirr*, or abomination,[18] which disturbs the spirit world, disrupts the moral order and breeds collective trauma. In the community's unwillingness to care for its children, Ricky recognized a manifestation of that trauma. "It was clear that the entire society was suffering," he says. "The community had been grieving for a long, long time."

Elements of micro-peacebuilding: The continuous creation of peace

In 2002, as other aid agencies began to open reception centres in Pader district, Friends of Orphans turned its attention to the larger problem of how to break through the cycle of violence and despair that had taken hold of the Acholi community. The group had already expanded its programme to include skills training – in brickmaking, iron work, tailoring, cooking, accounting – to help former child soldiers regain their self-respect, earn their own livelihoods and be of some value to the community. Those who received training were expected to create self-sustaining micro-enterprises, which Friends of Orphans supported with small amounts of microfinance. As other reception centres were opened, Friends of Orphans expanded its training programme and began to focus on the larger issue of how to create peace. Ricky's idea was to incorporate what he calls *micro-peacebuilding* into every aspect of life in the camps.

In conceptualizing his approach, Ricky looked to the literature on human rights and conflict resolution. From the human rights literature, Ricky identified two categories of actors in the struggle for dignity and justice – *rights holders* and *duty bearers*. Adapting these ideas to community peacebuilding, he defined rights holders as former child soldiers, child mothers, HIV/AIDS victims, the illiterate, the unemployed and adult defectors from the LRA. They were all struggling to survive, even without knowing that they had the *right to have rights* – to peace, security, respect, education, healthcare and productive activity. The duty bearers were community elders, religious leaders and local elected officials who had an *obligation to respect those rights* and, in every action they took, to help make them a reality for those who did not yet have them. The conflict resolution literature gave Ricky a framework for analysing the components of violence in the camps – its *root causes,* such as poverty, greed, grievance, corruption; *immediate triggers,* such as drunkenness, wife beating, disputes over land or boreholes; *relationship between the parties*, whether intact, broken, cooperative or power based; and *stage of the conflict*, either emerging, escalating, confrontation, stalemate or crisis. Using every instance of conflict in the camps as an opportunity to talk to a traumatized population about their mutual rights and obligations, Ricky began the process of re-empowering those whose rights were habitually being violated, including by illness, as well as those whose natural authority in the community had been lost.[19]

One of his most important acts of empowerment was to train former child soldiers as community peace counsellors. Of the 500 who applied to participate in the initial round of training, Friends of Orphans chose 80 women and 120 men who had done the most to rebuild their lives – by pursuing university studies, building a business, finding a paying job at an NGO – and so had the potential to become opinion leaders. Friends of Orphans trained them in human rights and conflict resolution; then each peace counsellor was given responsibility for developing a peace plan for his or her section of the camp. The counsellors began by talking to the residents about what was wrong in their lives and how they could help them. Some women had been given a cow or goat by Friends of Orphans to support their role as caregivers to young children, and those animals were grazing in other people's gardens. "These were the kinds of things that used to lead to family, community conflict," Ricky says. "So the peace counsellors sat together with their group of families to consider the problem, and they agreed to put aside a separate plot of land only for grazing." Some who had not been given an animal were resentful, so the counsellors led discussions in which the community decided that the offspring would be given to those who did not yet have an animal.

As more peace counsellors were trained, Friends of Orphans began to address issues of culturally embedded violence such as wife beating, which was a point of pride with many men in the camps – "if you don't beat your wife, you're not a man," Ricky observes. The counsellors began holding community sensitization meetings to talk about human rights, the equality of women and men in the eyes of God, the obligation to treat the woman as a partner, the dangers of beating the mother of one's children. "The woman will go away, and feeding the children needs two people," the counsellors said. "Or you can inflict injuries, you can disable or kill them, then you will go to jail and leave the children as orphans, and we have enough orphans already." There are also sensitization meetings on the issue of children's rights, with the peace counsellors explaining that children have a right to be protected and cared for, and not to be beaten, used for labour or turned over by community leaders to the UPDF. The meetings often end with peace counsellors asking for ideas about the way forward, and the community talking about the need to protect one another and report instances of wife or child abuse to the police. These protections are reinforced by a network of peace scouts trained by Friends of Orphans, who act as watchdogs for those who have been abused.

The rights and obligations of people in the camps have also been reinforced in a number of other ways. For three years, Friends of Orphans held a series of children's parliaments,[20] which passed resolutions – no more abductions, beatings or sexual defilement, and equal treatment of orphans – that were broadcast over the radio, with Friends of Orphans paying for airtime. The peace counsellors have organized peace clubs in the schools, where children talk about what it means to live a peaceful life. For the women there have been women's parliaments, which have issued resolutions demanding the right to own property, to choose their own husbands, to inherit land and not have it taken by their husband's family, to refuse sex with infected men and to not be beaten. These resolutions have also been broadcast.[21] With these broadcasts, the peace clubs and peace scouts and the community on the alert, it has become a matter of public knowledge, and shame for the abuser, if someone whose voice has been heard then has his or her rights violated. "Men and their bad cultural practices started fearing to be exposed to the community," Ricky says, "so the level of violence went down."

Ricky Anywar also sees HIV/AIDS as a threat to peace in the camps, since "people who are sick cannot think about peace". He invented an AIDS awareness game[22] for young people; it is played by four teams, each consisting of two girls and two boys. Each team is responsible for the welfare of a fictional teenage girl who, over a period of three years, is faced with a series of situations that put her under pressure to exchange sex for the food or money she needs for her survival or that of a parent or sibling. The objective is to get the girl through the game without her suffering HIV infection, pregnancy or family breakdown. The girls on the team learn to respect themselves enough to resist pressures to have sex, and to think of alternative ways of coping with their situation; while the boys learn to feel protective rather than aggressive towards the girls, and to understand how their behaviour can have life-changing consequences.

Friends of Orphans found that other forms of violence could not be addressed without the involvement of the police, the UPDF or the national parliament. Land theft used to be one of the most dangerous problems. Ricky says:

> Land wranglers were rampant in the area. They would bribe the police to declare them the owners of other people's land, which led to many killings. So we went on the radio, brought community leaders to talk. We said no. We told our MP [member of parliament] that we wanted Parliament to give back the power to resolve land issues to clan and community leaders, since they knew where every family had lived for the last 50 years.

The change was enacted, and the land killings stopped.

Yet there is always the unrelenting problem of child soldiers: how to keep the children away from both the LRA and the UPDF, and how to help them when and if they make it back. For most of the time that Friends of Orphans has been in existence, children in northern Uganda were still being abducted by the LRA and still, with the cooperation of community leaders, being recruited by the UPDF; and this ongoing militarization of the youngest people in the camps – despite the comprehensive peacebuilding activities – was a continuing source of destabilization, grief and despair. The peace counsellors talked to the children about how to behave if they were abducted. "Sometimes when people are abducted they go wild," Ricky said. "We teach them, 'when you are abducted don't abuse people, let it not come from you, always try to be calm and try to escape, if you are told to fight, you do what you have to, but do not have it be your idea to kill'." The children with this training who were abducted and later escaped were considerably less traumatized than those who had not had such training. Friends of Orphans also held community meetings with the UPDF to discuss the army's practice of recruiting child soldiers, and to ask for more protection from LRA attacks. Former child soldiers spoke at these meetings about how their experiences had made them lose hope in life, and they appealed for an end to the recruiting. Although the army continued to deny that it was using child soldiers – and parliament, on the same grounds, refused to pass a law forbidding the practice – the community leaders who had been participating in the recruitment decided to stop playing their part, and the numbers went down. The UPDF did agree to respond more quickly when it received reports that the LRA was approaching the camps. Since the peace scouts and other former child soldiers knew the LRA's travel routes and locations of its weapons' caches, their information has made it possible for the army to capture a number of LRA commanders, recover thousands of weapons and free hundreds of abducted children. With the army's greater attention to LRA activity in the area, the number of abductions also went down – although the LRA is now abducting children in Sudan and Congo (DRC).

With all that Friends of Orphans has done to end the violence in the camps in Pader district over the past 14 years, peace remains elusive at the national level. Anywar believes that lasting peace will come only through an accord between the government and the LRA. As a partner in the Acholi Religious Leaders Peace Initiative, Friends of Orphans, along with other civil society groups, helped to persuade the government to offer amnesty to Joseph Kony, the leader of the LRA. Kony telephoned the BBC saying he was ready to talk in 2004, but the ICC indicted him for war crimes the following year, and Kony announced that he would not sign a peace agreement until the indictment was withdrawn. But since that time more than 50 of the LRA's 1,000 field commanders have come out of the bush, saying they had learned from Friends of Orphans' radio broadcasts that others who had come back had not been punished, but instead had gone through the months of discussions about what went wrong that constituted restorative justice. "Kony also listens to our radio broadcasts," Ricky said. "He has been calling in to the radio programs to give his opinion. He says that people have been suffering for many years and need peace. He says he is ready for peace talks." Does he believe that Kony can change? "Peace is the only solution," Ricky said.

Conclusion and recommendations

As this chapter was being finalized, Ricky Anywar contacted the author to ask for help raising money to continue the work of Friends of Orphans. The group has been operating on a budget of several hundred thousand dollars a year, some of it from the European Commission but most from small NGOs and individuals. The lack of predictable funding is a serious threat to the group's existence. Friends of Orphans has not received support from any of the multidonor DDR (disarmament, demobilization and reintegration) operations in Africa; and when the author referred him to the head of the Kampala office of an international aid agency involved in such programmes, he was unable to get an appointment.

The rehabilitation of child soldiers is a complicated business that cannot be carried out in isolation from the social and political environment that gave rise to the problem. While donor-driven DDR programmes, with their emphasis on regional peace initiatives and the demobilization of adult combatants, have been a significant factor in stabilizing countries burdened by conflict, they have done little to support local initiatives that are dedicated to rebuilding the lives of child soldiers by creating sustainable change in their communities. Such programmes depend first and foremost on the creation of normal, predictable resource transfer systems from national or local governments. They also depend on the ability and willingness of local governments to take account of such programmes in their developing planning. And finally, the sustainability of local peacebuilding initiatives depends on the development of community-level social capital, so that conflict-affected communities can play an active role in their own healing and development.

In the past three years several former child soldiers who created successful enterprises with support from Friends of Orphans have been elected to local councils, where they are advocating for the needs of child soldiers and attempting to generate support for the group's programmes. Their efforts may be paying off; a local government official told Ricky Anywar that he would like to consult with him about developing planning. Yet resources remain scarce for all of northern Uganda, and these development plans will need to be supported by larger donor programmes.

A starting point would be for one of the large multidonor DDR programmes to conduct a needs assessment of all community-based peace initiatives in northern Uganda and identify those that would benefit from untied donor support. Over the longer term, so as not to foster dependence on external sources of aid, donors would do well to work with national and local governments to develop mechanisms to support grassroots peacebuilding initiatives, so that communities torn apart by the abduction and destruction of their children can leave their victimhood behind and become agents of their own development.

Notes

1. For a history of the conflict see Zachary Lomo and Lucy Hovil, "Behind the Violence: The War in Northern Uganda", Monograph 99, Institute for Security Studies, Pretoria, March 2004, www.issafrica.org/uploads/Mono99.pdf.
2. For further details on the LRA's methods of indoctrination and control see ibid.
3. These traditional rituals, based on ancient customs and long-standing family relationships, used to take weeks or months to carry out. The elder would go back and forth between the two families, slowly rebuilding trust and a sense of mutual obligation, and when the public reconciliation ritual finally occurred, the entire community was involved in witnessing it.
4. The ethnographic method has its roots in cultural anthropology. Its purpose is to generate understanding of a culture from an insider's point of view rather than through theories or hypotheses. Ethnographers often play the role of participant-observer, immersing themselves in the culture and recording their observations. The method can also rely on interviews with key informants who are part of the culture but who, through education or travel, have gained an objective understanding of its practices, values and webs of meaning. For a detailed discussion of the principles and methods of ethnographic research see Michael Genzuk, "A Synthesis of Ethnographic Research", Occasional Papers Series, Center for Multilingual, Multicultural Research, Rossier School of Education, University of Southern California, 2003, www-rcf.usc.edu/%7Egenzuk/Ethnographic_Research.pdf. For recent in-depth ethnographic studies of northern Uganda see Sverker Finnström, *Living with Bad Surroundings: War, History, and Everyday Moments in*

Northern Uganda, Durham, NC: Duke University Press, 2008; Kristen E. Cheney, *Pillars of the Nation: Child Citizens and Ugandan National Development*, Chicago, IL: University of Chicago Press, 2007.

5. For a detailed description of traditional Acholi peacebuilding practices see Erin Baynes, "The Cooling of Hearts: Community Truth-Telling in Acholi-land", special report, Justice and Reconciliation Project, Gulu District NGO Forum, Liu Institute for Global Issues, University of British Columbia, Vancouver, BC, July 2007. Also see William Meeker, "Traditional Cleaning and Reconciliation Rituals of the Acholi", research paper submitted to American University School of International Service, September 2007 (contact: meeker.will@gmail.com). The author is grateful to William Meeker for generously allowing her to use this and other material.
6. For UN reports on child soldiers see Office of the Special Representative of the Secretary-General for Children and Armed Conflict, www.un.org/children/conflict/english/index.html. For the UN position on child soldiers in Uganda see "Report of the Secretary-General on the Situation of Children and Armed Conflict Affected by the Lord's Resistance Army", 25 May 2012, www.watchlist.org/wordpress/wp-content/uploads/SCWG-Conclusions-LRA-2013.pdf.
7. For discussions of the ICC's indictment of Kony see David Lanz, "The ICC's Intervention in Northern Uganda: Beyond the Simplicity of Peace vs. Justice", Fletcher School of Law and Diplomacy, Medford, MA, May 2007; Adam Branch, "Uganda's Civil War and the Politics of ICC Intervention", *Ethics & International Affairs* 21(2), 2007, pp. 179–198.
8. Justice and Reconciliation Project, "Alice's Story: Cultural and Spiritual Dimensions of Reconciliation in Northern Uganda", Field Notes No. 1, February 2006, Liu Institute for Global Issues, Vancouver, BC, and Gulu District NGO Forum, www.ligi.ubc.ca/sites/liu/files/Publications/22Feb2006_FieldNotes_AlicesStoryJRP.pdf.
9. There is a growing body of legal, medical and policy literature devoted to a nuanced consideration of whether, to what degree and at what age child soldiers can be held responsible for their actions. See, for example, Mark A. Drumbl, *Reimagining Child Soldiers in International Law and Policy*, Oxford: Oxford University Press, 2012; Grace Akello, Annemiek Richters and Ria Reis, "Reintegration of Former Child Soldiers in Northern Uganda: Coming to Terms with Children's Agency and Accountability", *Intervention* 4(3), 2006, pp. 229–243. On the different ages at which children can legally be recruited under various international laws and conventions see Steven Freeland, "Child Soldiers and International Law", presentation, http://150.203.86.5/Cipl/Lectures_Seminars/2007/Freeland%20-%20Powerpoint.pdf.
10. The video *Kony 2012* was produced by Invisible Children Inc., an NGO based in San Diego, California, and, according to Mike Pflanz, was posted to the film-sharing sites YouTube and Vimeo in March 2012 as part of the group's viral social action campaign to turn Joseph Kony into a type of celebrity monster, with the aim of forcing the US government to send military advisers to Africa to help capture him. To keep up the pressure, the group's online store sold Kony Action Kits: for $30 an activist would get a Kony t-shirt (sizes XS to XL), a Kony bracelet, a Kony action guide, Kony stickers, a Kony button and Kony posters. "People will think you're an advocate of awesome with this official Action Kit," the group's website explains. "Since KONY 2012 is a yearlong campaign, you can decorate yourself and the town all year long with this one-stop shop. Everything you'll need to take part in our KONY 2012 campaign is included." There were only two problems: Kony had already fled Uganda and was presumed to be hiding in the Democratic Republic of the Congo; and US military advisers were already working on the Kony issue with African Union troops. Further, the majority of people in northern Uganda feared that "Making Kony 'famous' could make him stronger", as noted by Javie Ssozi, an influential Ugandan blogger cited by Pflanz. Ssozi also felt that

"Arguing for more US troops could make him scared, and make him abduct more children, or go on the offensive." What the Ugandans really wanted was aid to rebuild. See Mike Pflanz, "Joseph Kony 2012: Growing Outrage in Uganda over Film", *Daily Telegraph*, 8 March 2012, www.telegraph.co.uk/news/worldnews/africaandindianocean/uganda/9131469/Joseph-Kony-2012-growing-outrage-in-Uganda-over-film.html.

11. See Gretchen Vogel, "Mystery Disease Haunts Region", *Science* 336(6078), 13 April 2012, pp. 144–146. The US Centers for Disease Control and Prevention and the World Health Organization are investigating several possible causes, including a parasitic infection of the brain and a new form of epilepsy. The Ugandan Ministry of Health is investigating a possible link between nodding disease and war trauma, since the nearly 2,000 children affected by the disease are concentrated in the three districts in northern Uganda where the LRA had been most active, as well as children in the LRA-infested areas of the Democratic Republic of the Congo and South Sudan. On the war trauma theory see www.cinemaforpeace-foundation.com/Projects/trailer-of-the-day/childrens-brain-disease-through-war-trauma.
12. Many national and international experts in the DDR field argue that it was the ICC's determination to prosecute Kony that caused the failure of the peace negotiations between the LRA and the government of Uganda, known as the Juba peace process, which began in 2006, the year after Kony's indictment, and lasted until 2009. Articles about this controversy have been compiled by the Coalition for the International Criminal Court, www.iccnow.org/?mod=newsdetail&news=1843. For more information on the ICC's impact on the Ugandan peace process see John Prendergast and Adam O'Brien, "A Diplomatic Surge for Northern Uganda", Center for American Progress, Washington, DC, 12 December 2007. For an alternative view see Robert Feldman, "A Deal with the Devil: Issues in Offering Joseph Kony Amnesty to Resolve the Conflict in Uganda", *Small Wars and Insurgencies* 18(1), 2007, pp. 134–143. For a more in-depth analysis see US Department of State, "Northern Uganda – Recovery Process – Peace and Reconciliation", United States Virtual Presence Post, US Department of State, Washington, DC, http://northernuganda.usvpp.gov/peacerec2.html.
13. The Amnesty Act of 2000 provides that any Ugandan wishing to abandon rebellion will be granted amnesty without risk of criminal prosecution or punishment in a national court for offences related to the insurgency. DDR initiatives in Uganda between 2000 and 2008 were carried out within the framework of the Amnesty Act and the Amnesty Commission, as a necessary response to the flow of escaping child soldiers. In 2008, after the failure of the Juba peace process, the government of Uganda began to work with donors to develop two formal peace and reconciliation processes in the conflict area. One programme, the Peace, Recovery and Development Plan for Northern Uganda, addresses some of the issues raised during the Juba process about inequitable treatment of the north by promoting economic development in the region. The other, the Emergency Demobilization and Reintegration Project, supports the Amnesty Commission's mandate of demobilizing and reintegrating rebel soldiers who have defected from the LRA. The latter programme, supported by a World Bank-managed Multi-Donor Trust Fund, will be carried out in close collaboration with several implementing partners and networks, including the organizations that currently manage reception centres for escaped child soldiers. The US Agency for International Development and the UN Development Programme are also supporting the work of the Amnesty Commission through the International Organization for Migration. For more information on formal DDR efforts in Uganda see www.mdrp.org; www.unddr.org/country programmes; and www.worldbank.org. For a more general discussion of these issues see Anna Borzello, "The Challenge of DDR in Northern Uganda: The Lord's Resistance Army", *Conflict, Security & Development* 7(3), 2007, pp. 387–415.

14. Akello, Richters and Reis, note 9 above.
15. When the government of Uganda finally acceded to Joseph Kony's demands and formally asked the ICC to drop the charges against him (which the ICC did not do, although its deliberations bought Kony some time), he dishonoured the idea of restorative justice further by fleeing the country.
16. See, for example, Thomas Harlacher, Francis Xavier Okot, Caroline Aloyo Obonyo, Mychelle Balthazard and Ronald Atkinson, "Traditional Ways of Coping in Acholi: Cultural Provisions for Reconciliation and Healing from War", Caritas Gulu Archdiocese, Kampala, 2006, https://docs.google.com/a/caritasgulu.org/viewer?a=v&pid=sites&srcid=Y2FyaXRhc2d1bHUub3JnfHd3d3xneDo3ODI2NGYwNmRjNmVjMWVi.
17. The food crisis in the camps lasted until 2006, when the LRA retreated to Sudan and it became safer for people to leave the camps and work in their vegetable gardens.
18. Justice and Reconciliation Project, "'Abomination': Local Belief Systems and International Justice", Field Notes No. 5, September 2007, Liu Institute for Global Issues, Vancouver, BC, and Gulu District NGO Forum, www.ligi.ubc.ca/sites/liu/files/Publications/JRP/JRPFN5Sept2007.pdf. Research was carried out in IDP camps of northern Uganda.
19. The human rights and conflict resolution literature contains many variations of these ideas, and Ricky did not cite any specific sources. Useful documents include UK Department for International Development, "Conducting Conflict Assessments: Guidance Notes", DFID, London, January 2002; Barry Hart, James N. Doe and Sam G. Doe, *Trauma Healing and Reconciliation Training Manual: A Handbook for Trainers and Trainees*, Monrovia: Sabanoh Printing Press, 1993. On the relationship between health initiatives and post-conflict reconciliation see for example J. Macrae, A. Zwi and H. Birungi, "A Healthy Peace? Rehabilitation and Development of the Health Sector in a PostConflict Situation – The Case of Uganda: Report on a Pilot Study", London School of Hygiene and Tropical Medicine, London, 1995; Act Alliance, "Guide on Community-Based Psychosocial Support: Stages of Mediation", http://psychosocial.actalliance.org; Graeme MacQueen and Joanna SantaBarbara, "Peace Building through Health Initiatives", *British Medical Journal* 321, 29 July 2000, pp. 293–296.
20. Approximately 3,000 children per year participated in the children's parliaments, which met three times a week for two years. Each session consisted of a new group of around 20 children of different ages and backgrounds.
21. Funding for the broadcasts was provided by the NGO WarChild UK. Although there are no further funds for the women's parliaments, their discussions and resolutions are continually rebroadcasted throughout northern Uganda.
22. Created in 2009, the game is available from Friends of Orphans, www.frouganda.org, or the author of this chapter, deborahdavis2@yahoo.com.

Part V

Conclusion

10

Escaping and moving beyond victimhood: Children and youth as peacebuilders

Anara Tabyshalieva and Albrecht Schnabel

In many post-conflict contexts, children and youth are trapped in transition processes as mere subjects who receive and should benefit somehow from peacebuilding activities and broader reforms of society, the state and its institutions and public services. While children and youth are supposed to benefit from many of these rebuilding and transformation programmes, they tend to be given very little opportunity to influence the planning and implementation of these processes. This is the case despite the fact that they are bound to be the main beneficiaries of constructive peacebuilding programmes, and also the victims of botched ones. Rebuilding a society is a major effort that should be based on inclusive processes during both planning and implementation. Excluding large parts of the population, as already argued in this book's companion volume *Defying Victimhood: Women and Post-Conflict Peacebuilding*,[1] carries the great danger of embarking on a course which might not be suitable to meet challenges and needs that can only be defined by those whose futures are expected to benefit from such transformative processes. In this concluding chapter we draw on the contributions to the book and offer a comparative discussion of the main issues and recommendations that emerge from them. We also highlight a number of priorities for future research and policy development, based on suggestions offered throughout the book.

The contributors to this volume study the roles of children and youth in dozens of post-conflict countries. They attempt to shed light on the dichotomy of the victim and the agent, and offer relevant recommendations for

Escaping victimhood: Children, youth and post-conflict peacebuilding, Schnabel and Tabyshalieva (eds), United Nations University Press, 2013, ISBN 978-92-808-1211-4

future research and policy priorities. The book examines the deficiency of child- and youth-specific peacebuilding practices by national and international players, as well as young people's struggles to escape continuing victimhood and pathways of survival criminality and instead secure better and more effective opportunities to be agents of sustainable peace. Portraying children and youth as bystanders to peacebuilding efforts might be a correct observation or a distorted view of reality in many post-conflict contexts, but accepting such a situation would surely be a misleading and highly unhealthy benchmark for building peace and reconciliation.

Not a single case offered in this book can provide a full answer as to how the complexity of child and youth participation in peacebuilding activities can be more properly understood and tackled. Yet discussing, examining and comparing the various roles children and youth do or can play in post-conflict settings – and to what extent they are safe and empowered to be active change agents – does help in capturing commonalities and differences and in understanding missed opportunities and areas for improvement. The case studies shed light on certain similarities as to how children and youth escape and move beyond victimhood to play a constructive role in conflict management and peacebuilding processes. In researching and preparing their studies, the contributors to this book benefited from interactions with numerous stakeholders and drew on analyses from other experts to form some conclusions and develop policy recommendations, which will be summarized in the remainder of this chapter.

Active agents of change: Barriers and gateways

The introductory chapter to this volume summarizes some patterns of sidelining children and youth in post-conflict recovery and reform efforts, as well as challenges in understanding the post-conflict realities of children and youth. It also examines how international and national forces responded to these challenges in order to make a positive difference. Important turning points in the international understanding of the role of children and youth in armed conflict and its aftermath were the UN Convention on the Rights of the Child (1989), Graça Machel's "Impact of Armed Conflict on Children" report (1996)[2] and UN Security Council Resolutions 1325 (2000) and 1612 (2005). Several other important resolutions and publications exposed a more coherent and systematic strategy on responses of the growing international peacebuilding community. Scholarship on post-conflict peacebuilding shows that international policymakers and donors, as well as national and local actors, increasingly recognize the importance of empowerment and socialization of children and youth during war and its aftermath (see Chapter 3).

The four main parts of this book first conceptualize child and youth roles in post-conflict peacebuilding; then discuss the impact of armed conflict on children and youth as victims and active agents of change; followed by discussions of efforts to protect and engage young people, and accounts of children and youth as peacebuilders. The authors' main concerns about lack of opportunities for the young to affect what are mostly adults' efforts to rebuild their countries and societies lie with a myriad of challenges that children and youth face in post-conflict settings.

From a one-dimensional to a multidimensional approach

The contributors object to a one-dimensional approach to the roles of children and youth in peacebuilding policy as those of victims and sinners. They criticize the approach of victims versus peacebuilders and/or angry men (troublemakers) versus constructive and positive actors. As Valeria Izzi and Chetan Kumar note, the dichotomy "youth as a threat to peace" versus "youth as a force for peace" is not a useful way to view these two roles: "The two labels are two sides of the same coin – i.e. the simplification of youth as a homogeneous category to fit the schemes and paradigms of external interveners" (Chapter 8). Similarly, Kathleen Kostelny and Michael Wessells conclude that "youth are influential as both soldiers and peacemakers" (Chapter 3). David Nosworthy observes "a tendency for children, and in particular youth, to be demonized by society – a phenomenon that can be observed around the globe" (Chapter 6).

All too often youth – primarily young males – are seen as mere troublemakers. Yet Henri Myrttinen warns that, as "young, marginalized men often do form one of the most restless sections of a post-conflict society, the phenomenon tends to be more complex than a simple equating of youth and masculinity with violence" (Chapter 4). In the post-conflict context, adolescents have often been categorized as rebellious troublemakers. This applies in particular to child soldiers, mostly young men fighting each other on all sides of a conflict as both government soldiers and rebels, generating images of child soldiers as "hardened killers and as damaged goods" (Chapter 3). As a result of this simplistic reasoning, unemployed and discontented young men might all too easily be considered as threats to security who need to be appeased with meaningful livelihood options, especially jobs. At the same time, as Izzi and Kumar claim (Chapter 8):

> There is reason to argue that the "securitization" of youth employment may have a negative impact in the long run. The fact that many youth employment programmes have been designed with the main rationale of "keeping young people busy" has meant unbalanced attention to the employability of young

people, mostly through training programmes, at the expense of the macro-economic interventions that would be necessary to make the job market work for young people in a sustainable way.

An important – and related – issue is the triangular relationship between young men, their female relatives and friends, and non-governmental and/or governmental armed forces. As Myrttinen argues, "women 'buy into' the violent enactments of masculinity, be it involuntarily or in some cases voluntarily. Mothers, sisters, wives and girlfriends provide what can be seen as logistical support for the young men: washing laundry, cooking food, caring for wounds and giving them emotional support." Yet as he observed in Dili, Timor-Leste, "At times women in communities have actively and publicly urged their young men to attack [UN peacekeepers] . . . and protected them from police searches". In fact, as he finds, "women and girls also form, wittingly or unwittingly, the 'audience' for whom many of the displays of masculinity are ultimately meant" (Chapter 4).

Demographic factors: Pros and cons

Demographic factors can be critical signposts for planning and envisioning objectives for post-conflict recovery; children and youth make up a significant share of the population in almost all conflict-affected areas. As noted by Izzi and Kumar, "Considering the sheer size of the youth population in most countries (if nothing else), it is clear that a significant change can only be achieved by a coordinated effort to address youth needs at the strategic level." At the same time, exaggeration of the significance of demographic data might be misleading in assessing multifaceted development and social issues. The youth-bulge theory in particular is disputed as an overly one-dimensional explanation of the diverse roles of young men in post-conflict developing countries (Chapter 8).

Similarly, the gender dimension is a sensitive and multilayered issue, as the concepts of masculinity and femininity are socially designed (Chapter 8). The various case studies in the book exhibit considerable variation in the levels of gender and age discrimination and segregation in war-affected areas. When examining – and responding to – the phenomenon of child soldiering, separated and unaccompanied children, and many other problems related to human security of children and youth, demographic, cultural and religious aspects need to be carefully considered.

The security-development nexus and children and youth

Izzi and Kumar conclude that many challenges in addressing young people's needs stem from "the dilemma of reconciling a development rationale with a security rationale" (Chapter 8), and possibly also the inability to understand how security issues impact on development outcomes and vice versa. Children and youth might be seen as important factors in defining development objectives, but they are not discussed with similar concern and attention in security analysis and policy planning. The scarcity of political discussion on young people in post-conflict peacebuilding can also be explained as "a reflection of the hold of political realism in security studies".[3] If security studies are dominated by realist thought, and development analysis, which pays greater attention to children and youth, fails to engage effectively with security processes, then the security needs of children and youth, as well as their significance for and contributions to a society's future security and well-being, are undervalued. As a result, both academics and policy planners "have relegated children to the margins or, even more commonly, entirely excluded children as a political actor category".[4]

The exceptions are young men, who, as mentioned above, are seen as security risks and thus often targeted first – not to reintegrate them in society or give them a viable future, let alone allow them to participate in defining that future, but to remove them as a security threat. Inadvertently, such programmes give preference to males over females (Chapter 8). As a result, as Deborah Davis observes, "donor-driven DDR programmes, with their emphasis on regional peace initiatives and the demobilization of adult combatants, have been a significant factor in stabilizing countries burdened by conflict, [but] they have done little to support local initiatives that are dedicated to rebuilding the lives of child soldiers by creating sustainable change in their communities" (Chapter 9). Interestingly, young men find in gangs what should be provided to them through meaningful post-conflict political stabilization and development: young men seek gang membership to "alleviate a social crisis linked to the need to adapt to a post-conflict settlement where the clarity of the conflict situation no longer exists; the pressure groups address personal and group grievances; and membership gives the young men a sense of purpose and, for some, economic, social and political advancement" (Chapter 4).

In this context, Nosworthy (Chapter 6) identifies a number of ill-advised approaches that are chosen to address youth violence and juvenile delinquency in post-conflict areas, such as the adoption of repressive legislation and:

> a hardening of attitudes among law enforcement and judicial officers [including through] reduction in the age of criminal responsibility; increase in the length of custodial sentences for minors (who are sometimes detained with adults – prison being acknowledged as "the school of crime"); dramatic "round-up"

actions or crackdown operations; the criminalization of vagrancy and begging; and the creation of educational detention centres (presented as alternatives to prison, but where detention conditions are often equivalent to those of prison).

A main assumption of the security-development nexus is the beneficial interrelationship of security and development.[5] An increase in security is expected to increase development, while development gains are expected to translate into greater security. As development should thus enhance post-conflict security, there is a need to promote sound economic and resource management policies that positively influence security and development, including by investing in a sustainable future for children, youth and their families and communities.

Building peace under adverse conditions

Threats to the security of children and youth take place in a variety of ways, although official statistics and studies tend not to assess the scope and magnitude of discriminatory practices against young people at the family, community and national levels. Moreover, beyond the specifics of war and post-war threat environments, many young people living in societies with precarious economic conditions and weak statehood are victimized by male and female family and community members on a daily basis, regardless of the conditions created by armed conflict. Structural violence against children and youth exists outside post-conflict conditions, yet would typically be exacerbated by them, as young people might be excluded from healthcare, education and other services. Some children and youth have a disproportionately large burden of domestic work to bear, preventing them from attending school or socializing with other children and adults. Social and cultural rites push (and confine) children into socially prescribed roles; in some cases girls are segregated in schools and public places, and adolescent girls are sexually exploited and forced into early marriage and pregnancy. Of particular concern are disabled children and youth, who might be pushed to the fringes of society and livelihoods, and out of schools or training programmes (Chapter 3). In many post-conflict societies, minority children in particular face harassment, threats and various forms of ill treatment and discrimination (Chapter 3).

Although these threats are not necessarily unique to post-conflict life, they are certainly exacerbated – and efforts to overcome them hampered – in societies that are preoccupied with rebuilding the most basic public services and community relations, and where coping mechanisms have suffered from months or years of communal violence. Moreover, conflict prevention and management – and the prevention of a resurgence of violent conflict once stopped – are critical in showing children and youth that normality is characterized by peace, not violence. As Kostelny and Wessells (Chapter 3) argue:

> Slowly the international community, including governments and bilateral donors, as well as national, regional and local communities, is realizing that war zones create powerful socialization for youth violence and soldiering. Equally powerful socialization for peacebuilding is a prerequisite for peace. The question now is whether youth will receive ongoing support as warriors or whether the international community will nourish youth as leaders in peacebuilding.

Primacy of young people's political agency

Children are often displayed "as negative agents acting as child soldiers, as positive agents contributing to post-conflict measures, as victims of violence and as focal points of various forms of international attention".[6] By perceiving children and youth as mere spectators or passive victims in a post-conflict environment, some governmental and non-governmental domestic and international actors deny or reduce their sphere of political agency, instead embracing a concept of victimhood and reinforcing existing age and gender prejudices. Children should not be characterized merely as passive or accidental beneficiaries of broader assistance and stabilization activities.

Despite their significant share in the post-conflict population, children, youth and their advocates, such as child rights defenders, lack access to decision-making and formal access to peace processes, where young people's needs could be heard and put on the (negotiating) table. However, child- and youth-centred international and local civil society organizations facilitate dialogue and information exchange among policymakers, donors, researchers and other stakeholders. For instance, to promote child and youth agency, civil society groups provide expertise and security analysis and monitor violations against child rights (Chapter 6). There are also various patterns that indicate the eagerness of children and youth to be recognized as active citizens who can respond to the numerous post-war challenges. There is evidence that young people can furthermore develop and use remarkable resilience and dynamism in adapting to harsh post-conflict conditions (Chapters 2 and 7). Azar Eskandarpour, for instance, shows that night commuting in Uganda has "developed from a spontaneous, crisis-driven survival strategy into a social institution" that helped children and their families address immediate security challenges. The practice of night commuting not only diminished violence against children but also boosted socialization and developed coping mechanisms. In fact, "The experience of night commuting shows that one must think of children as powerful and effective agents of their own development who, even during times of great adversity, consciously act upon and influence the environments in which they live" (Chapter 7).

Policy priorities and recommendations

There are a number of practical recommendations that can be developed from the discussions presented in this volume.

Strengthen the rights and opportunities of children and youth as peacebuilders

It is important to integrate young people's interests and needs in peacebuilding strategies and make the promotion of child and youth agency a significant priority in the design and implementation of peacebuilding programmes. As Vesselin Popovski puts it, they are "the most vulnerable, but simultaneously they are also among the main beneficiaries and participants in peacebuilding. Therefore any actions should be inclusive and take into account their best interests" (Chapter 5). Young people's contributions to peace and stability are gradually being acknowledged at national and international levels. However, politically and practically, such recognition has not translated into much concrete action. Their needs and interests are rarely considered in formal political and policy design processes, at least not through their direct and personal input. Children and youth should learn – and be given the opportunity – to protect themselves from being victimized, and to help define strategies that provide such protection. For them, too, "powerful socialization for peacebuilding is a prerequisite for peace" (Chapter 3). It is therefore crucial that those responsible for rebuilding a nation "make systematic efforts to support children's role as active citizens . . . [which includes] creating genuine opportunities for children to inform, influence and monitor all peace-related initiatives and actions at local, national and global levels, including formal peacebuilding processes", as Claire O'Kane, Clare Feinstein and Annette Giertsen argue (Chapter 2).

Seek and promote deeper partnerships between children, youth and adults

Children and youth should not simply be "added" to the peacebuilding community as yet another vulnerable "group at risk", but rather should be considered as multilayered dynamic populations that will inevitably play a leading role in a peaceful future. As stated so aptly by Eskandarpour, children's "vulnerability did not exclude ability" (Chapter 7). Child empowerment necessitates sufficient time and space to allow them to express their interpretations of conflict and post-conflict realities, primarily through discussions with peers and adults. The latter should respect and value their views (Chapter 2).

While adults from international and national organizations often speak on behalf of all children and youth in war-torn and post-conflict societies, which is of course laudable, it is just as important that they recognize young people's ownership of their share of the peacebuilding agenda. As noted by O'Kane, Feinstein and Giertsen, "Listening to children, taking their views seriously and recognizing the various roles and responsibilities taken on by girls and boys (within their families, communities and in broader society) require a change in the way that most adults perceive and engage with children" (Chapter 2). Yet just as the experience of war might realign gender relations in society, so it might also realign traditional relationships between young and old. Social capital is considered as a constructive factor in supporting and encouraging children and youth to respond effectively to conflict and post-conflict challenges. This does not only mean that young people need to be given their own independent voice, but also that they are taken more seriously as significant stakeholders when it comes to planning and building a common post-conflict society. Moreover, rebuilding a functioning social fabric is as important to a post-war society as rebuilding crucial infrastructure. As shown by Eskandarpour, resulting social cohesion, capital and trust are crucial building blocks in developing children's capacity for resilience (Chapter 7).

Priority should be given to children and youth who are affected by poverty and exclusion, disabled children, and ethnic and religious minorities.

Enhance mechanisms for consistent consultation with children and youth groups and child- and youth-centred civil society groups

Children and child-led groups need to be recognized and engaged as important civil society actors. They need to contribute to governance processes at local, district and national levels. Moreover, support should be provided and sustained for the development of inclusive child- and youth-led organizations, networks and partnerships, while sensitizing adults to the importance of young people's participation in peacebuilding activities (Chapters 2 and 7). Civil society groups and state institutions could identify and empower children and youth by ensuring ways and means to make them contributors to – and even leaders of – post-conflict peacebuilding activities that affect them more than any other population group.

Protect, support and empower children and young survivors of violence

It is important to strengthen the protection of children from exploitation, gender and age discrimination and abuse before, during and after war. If children and youth have been victims of structural violence before and during the war, the post-conflict environment offers opportunities to right past wrongs. In this context it is important to address key challenges such as lack of physical security, health and well-being.

Empowering survivors of gender violence, both girls and boys, to rebuild their lives and communities should be a priority in war-torn societies. This includes the establishment of child-friendly services to respond to incidents of sexual violence and child protection training for legal and health personnel. Medical and psychosocial treatment for male and female survivors of sexual violence should be provided. Both men and women should engage in a fight to end war and domestic violence against children and youth. Again, special provisions should be made for children and youth with disabilities. Programmes should offer educational and training opportunities for these groups and prepare young people with disabilities for the labour market.

This also requires the creation of special legal safeguards. O'Kane, Feinstein and Giertsen recommend that a "review of national legislation, policies and practice should be undertaken in order to build a more effective child protection system that, informed by children themselves, offers better protection of girls and boys and holds perpetrators of violence against children accountable" (Chapter 2). In many post-conflict countries, although national governments officially recognize children's rights, often the concern lies in the implementation of written law at the national and community levels. In reality, more widespread and adhered-to traditional, customary law might not be compatible with national written law and international standards, and might significantly diminish the rights of women and young people especially.

Fully incorporate a gender and age dimension at the design, implementation, monitoring and evaluation stages

Girls and boys, young women and men experience the post-conflict moment quite differently. Such differences need to be taken into account when protecting them and creating opportunities for contributions to the peacebuilding effort. For instance, Popovski observes a "lack of proper attention to girl soldiers, as gender insensitivity has in fact doubled the victimization of girl soldiers, who suffer from both age and gender discrimination" (Chapter 5), while young mean tend to be favoured over young women in the context of youth-focused peacebuilding programmes as they are considered to present a greater risk to society.

Taking proper account of young women's needs and potential contributions requires their inclusion in peacebuilding processes, "not merely by trying to get 'more girls' on board, but by gaining an understanding of the similarities and differences between the needs and priorities of young men and young women, the different ways in which they negotiate their transition to adulthood and the ways the notions of masculinity and femininity are socially constructed" (Chapter 8).

Develop child-friendly DDR

There are approximately 300,000 child soldiers around the world, and many who survive armed conflict find it difficult to establish peaceful roles and responsibilities in society. As Kostelny and Wessells note, "Socially, former child soldiers are at risk because communities may fear or reject them. Teenage former soldiers in particular may have military identities and find it difficult to re-enter civilian life." At the same time, a "key step in the prevention of youth soldiering is to engage youth in positive roles as peacebuilders" (Chapter 3). Wessells has recommended elsewhere that DDR (disarmament, demobilization and reintegration) processes should separate child soldiers from adults in order to address their particular interests, while special attention should be paid to female child soldiers.[7]

Pay more attention to educational opportunities for children and youth

One of the best investments in rebuilding a war-torn society is in educational opportunities for those whose schooling has suffered or been interrupted during times of conflict. It is thus crucial to offer ready access to quality education and vocational training, and make these available to all children and youth. Moreover, child- and youth-friendly publications and media networks should discuss basic civic education concepts. In this context it is also important to introduce programmes to improve literacy and skill in conflict resolution and peacebuilding to empower young people to play an active role in meeting post-war challenges.

Recent decades have been marked by a significant shift towards recognition of the challenges of education and socialization that children and youth face in post-conflict societies. UN programmes and institutions such as UNICEF (the UN Children's Fund), UNESCO (UN Educational, Scientific and Cultural Organization) and others have supported a number of local educational programmes related to peace education, a culture of peace[8] and conflict resolution. As Popovski notes, sustainable peacebuilding is a cross-generational exercise, which is one more reason to ensure that children and youth are included in such efforts. But if "educational programmes are primarily targeted at adults, they might ignore children's needs, discriminate against them and become problematic" (Chapter 5).

Special attention should be paid to educational curricula and practices that existed before the outbreak of armed conflict. In divided societies education might have been used a political tool and thus further contributed to ethnic and religious tension, sparking long-standing animosities. Missing out on the opportunity to reform educational programmes can reinforce and continue "the uneven distribution of education as a means of creating or preserving positions of economic, social and political privilege", introducing ideas of cultural repression and hatred, as well as manipulation of history.[9] Even if educational reforms draw international support, one has to be careful with donors' intentions and the long-term impact of their activities. In the Balkan peacebuilding context, for instance, it was observed that "ethnically-based learning centres, churches and mosques, sometimes supported by outside funding, may contribute to radicalization of adults and youth and inculcate xenophobic values and views".[10]

Without an honest look at existing educational programmes and the willingness to make far-reaching changes and reforms – and that at a fast pace, as there is little time to waste once conflict has subsided and reforms can be launched – a powerful opportunity might be missed to overcome intergroup tensions and address the sufferings and injustices of the past while offering new venues to live a peaceful future. Thus the constructive and destructive impacts of education on children and youth should be carefully assessed in conflict-ridden and/or conflict-prone societies. The development of innovative educational programmes in fundamental human rights and the empowerment of girls and boys, young women and men in post-conflict societies require plural funding, possibly through public-private partnerships, at international and national levels.

Create opportunities to enhance communication capacities among children, youth and adults

Kostelny and Wessells share the story of the Kosovar youth councils, which organized concerts, sports and recreational activities for children in refugee camps – activities that "aided the social integration of youth and children, won them the respect of the camp elders and gave youth a highly positive role in their community … This pattern continued following the return home" (Chapter 3). In this way they also contributed to rebuilding social cohesion, an important ingredient in successful and sustainable peacebuilding (Chapter 7). Izzi and Kumar highlight the significance of art-based peacebuilding, which utilizes cultural activities such as music, drama, dance and visual art as helpful instruments to reunite divided societies and restore confidence and self-respect among children and youth. Very importantly, they note that the impact of such activities should not be underestimated when compared to more high-profile peacebuilding activities: "While small in scale and low in resources, these initiatives can count on the power of peer-to-peer influence, and are therefore able to reach out to young people in a way that traditional interventions cannot" (Chapter 8).

Furthermore, media, including radio, are becoming increasingly popular in reconciliation and forgiveness. Youth groups in South Africa have produced radio shows to discuss the reconstruction of peace and social justice at the community level. In Sierra Leone youth conveyed peace messages to local listeners in a regular radio show called *Talking Drum*, supported by the non-governmental organization (NGO) Search for Common Ground (Chapter 3). Traditional and new media can serve as:

> practical and powerful ways to raise and amplify the voices of young people and help adults recognize children's capacities and potential as change agents. Increasing use of social media (Facebook, Twitter and other online and mobile phone communications) among young people also provides an important way for their voices, concerns and aspirations to be heard, and for them to share information and mobilize others to join their social cause to improve the society they live in. (Chapter 2)

Generate employment to improve livelihoods

As Izzi and Kumar observe, "The potential for youth unemployment to breed instability is seen as particularly strong in countries recently emerging from violent conflict" (Chapter 8). High levels of unemployment, particularly among male youth, have been linked to the recurrence of armed violence in societies thought to be on a successful path to peace. Myrttinen shows that "disaffected young men do not, however, act out their violence in a vacuum. They are given the social space as well as the financial and logistical support by those who are 'capitalizing on' their violent behaviour ... [including] the political and socio-economic elites who are willing to use the groups to further their own goals" (Chapter 4). He argues that peacebuilding interventions should go hand in hand with "other measures, such as an improvement of the socio-economic situation of the young men, weaning the groups off violence as a tool for addressing grievances and fostering a culture of tolerance".

Create laws and security policies that promote and strengthen child and youth rights and participation

Children and youth can be empowered by addressing their grievances in the context of transitional justice. Popovski argues that "International courts such as the International Court of Justice and International Criminal Court can play a significant role in ensuring the security of children through their adjudication" (Chapter 6). He shows that international humanitarian law (IHL) lacks

> a comprehensive child rights approach. It may be argued that whatever child-related progress is made in IHL, there will always be shortcomings, as this is a *lex specialis*, carrying the burdensome task of having to address issues of both military necessity and humanitarian aspirations. These shortages are inherent in IHL, as its origins are rooted not only in humanitarian concerns, but also in facilitating military combat.

Popovski recommends incorporating broader child rights and principles developed in human rights law (HRL) in post-conflict peacebuilding activities, particularly as IHL applies during armed conflict and international criminal law applies mainly in the immediate aftermath of armed conflict. In contrast:

> child-relevant HRL applies at all times; therefore its main principles – best interests of the child, non-discrimination and participation – are also essential in the midst of war. Peacebuilding does not need to wait until peacekeeping finishes – the two processes run in parallel.

It is furthermore extremely important to promote child and youth participation in truth commissions or traditional reconciliation forums, for instance the *gacaca* trials in Rwanda, as "Non-judicial and less-retributive mechanisms are much more child-friendly and better engage ex-child soldiers in peacebuilding instead of isolating them in prison" (Chapter 5). Nosworthy shows that past truth and reconciliation commissions have proved to be crucial ways to promote children's rights in post-war settings (Chapter 6). NGOs working on transitional justice and justice-seeking mechanisms should be supported by national and international organizations to protect human rights of marginalized (but majority!) populations, including women, children and youth. Considering a lack of public awareness about the fundamental importance of children's rights in war-torn societies, Nosworthy suggests:

> Good governance with a view to securing democratic progress implies that the state, which is at once the source and the guarantor of human rights, must strive to inform public opinion on child rights and deal with children in line with international norms and standards, including using deprivation of liberty only as a measure of last resort. (Chapter 6)

Furthermore, "Children will require special protection and assistance and robust rehabilitation, supported by adequately resourced community-based reintegration programmes." When dealing with juvenile offenders he recommends alternatives to the "institutionalization of children [which] may include care, guidance and supervision orders, counselling, probation, foster care, education or vocational training, restitution and compensation of victims. However, it is important not to overlook the fact that these alternative solutions also need to provide legal safeguards and protect the rights of the children involved." This requires the establishment of "mechanisms for dialogue with local law enforcement agencies on child protection concerns, including complaints mechanisms" (Chapter 6).

International and national actors: Overcoming constraints and building stronger partnerships

Promote the integration of child and youth perspectives in peacebuilding and reconstruction agendas

The capacities of international organizations and multilateral and bilateral contributors to peacebuilding operations need to be strengthened in responding to child- and gender-specific needs and interests. After assessing practices on the ground and at headquarters, partnerships between various organizations involved in a particular post-conflict context should pave the way to child- and youth-sensitive conflict prevention and peacebuilding. These efforts need to be supported by – and build on – an increasing visibility of children and youth on international security, development and peacebuilding agendas (Chapter 3 and other chapters). Concerted peacebuilding actions to engage children and their families should include civil society organizations, multilateral institutions, local and national governments, international and local academic communities, educators at primary, secondary and tertiary levels, faith-based groups and the business sector. Post-conflict educational and research initiatives need to pay closer attention to the interests of children and youth.

Reinforce and showcase commitments of international and national actors to promote young people's rights in the aftermath of conflict

International and national child- and youth-centred policies to address post-war challenges contribute to lowering the risk of conflict recurrence. National peacebuilding strategies should refer – and adhere – to all basic provisions of the UN Convention on the Rights of the Child and other UN documents. Successful peacebuilding interventions – and in this context particularly those directed at the needs of children and youth – need to be showcased, analysed and considered as models for creative replication in other post-conflict situations.

Embrace a "do-no-harm" approach

As in all peacebuilding activities, child- and youth-centred programmes need to consider potential negative effects of a particular project on children, youth or the broader society. For instance, the benefits of a youth programme should be weighed against the possible risk of "doing harm" by creating unreasonable expectations or reinforcing tensions among different groups of youth (Chapter 8).

Izzi and Kumar discuss potential unintentional negative consequences of efforts to meet the needs of children and youth in the context of post-conflict peacebuilding programmes. They warn of the failure by such activities to reconcile development and security rationales. If the reasoning for youth programmes in particular is driven too heavily by security considerations, and young people "are targeted not primarily in view of their particular vulnerability to unemployment, but because unemployed and disaffected young people (read: young men) are seen as a potential threat to security", this can have harmful consequences. As they point out, if otherwise beneficial employment programmes "are based on the assumption that young people 'at risk' should be targeted, the message sent to them is that presenting a threat to society 'pays off': being the 'dangerous ones' makes them eligible for priority support and help, compared to those who do not pose a risk". In addition to this undesirable message, such an approach has a further unintentional negative consequence: it "favours males over females, as the former are considered to be the troublemakers who need to be kept busy and off the streets". Instead, participation of all should be encouraged, regardless of whether participants present a potential threat to society or not. They identify an important lesson that should guide all well-intentioned interventions on behalf of children and youth: "The (understandable) urge to 'do something' for young people should not come at the expenses of careful reflection on what is best to do and how it is best to operate" (Chapter 8).

Support and engage child- and youth-centred civil society organizations

Children and youth will continue to be dependent on adult champions to promote their causes and get their needs reflected in greater peacebuilding strategies and activities. As argued by Nosworthy, despite repeated calls on national and international peacebuilding communities to support civil society groups that advocate on behalf of child and youth interests, their voices are often not strong enough or even go unheard when peacebuilding strategies and programmes are designed. Children's rights defenders should be involved in consultative processes of development and security policies, specifically when strategies are designed to foster social integration and support children and youth, as well as other disadvantaged groups (Chapter 6). Adult-run initiatives and civil society actors:

> can cooperate in identifying and providing the arrangements and conditions needed to support children and young people to speak with decision-makers at various levels. They can find ways to build and strengthen children's and young people's groups at local, subnational and national levels so that regular or permanent cross-generational dialogue forums can be established between government and groups of young people's representatives and, in turn, can create national ongoing intergenerational dialogue. (Chapter 6)

Eskandarpour also stresses that "support should be provided and sustained for the development of inclusive child- and youth-led organizations, networks and partnerships while sensitizing adults to the importance of children's participation in peacebuilding activities" (Chapter 7). In short, child and youth rights activists should engage in organized advocacy and monitoring of peacebuilding activities, as well as in giving their clientele opportunities to have their own voices heard.

Act locally: Engage conflict-affected communities

In recognition of the fact that the road to peace is always long, "the sustainability of local peacebuilding initiatives depends on the development of community-level social capital, so that conflict-affected communities can play an active role in their own healing and development" (Chapter

9). As Deborah Davis argues, if we want to avoid "further dependence on external sources of aid, donors would do well to work with national and local governments to develop mechanisms to support grassroots peacebuilding initiatives, so that communities torn apart by the abduction and destruction of their children can leave their victimhood behind and become agents of their own development" (Chapter 9). As pointed out already, in the interest of child- and youth-centred peacebuilding, better coordination between international and national players to prevent duplication and waste of scarce resources is needed. Nosworthy underlines the importance of facilitating a dynamic mix of international and local efforts in peacebuilding processes which avoids promoting "an exclusively external agenda and fail[ing] to embrace the primacy of local ownership" (Chapter 6).

Policy research

Deepen knowledge on child- and youth-centred peacebuilding

Existing empirical research suggests that child-sensitive analyses ought to be an integral part of UN, regional organizations' and national governments' designs and evaluations of peace operations and other international and national post-conflict peacebuilding interventions. Public-private partnerships should be promoted to secure the funding sources required for generating a more thorough and empirically based knowledge of child- and youth-centred peacebuilding at international and national levels.

Make sure to include – and consult – child-, youth- and gender-specific data in peacebuilding programming

The planning, implementation and evaluation of peacebuilding activities need to be routinely informed by age- and sex-disaggregated data. Characteristics such as ethnicity and social and other indicators should be considered. Moreover, more comprehensive data on child and youth populations in post-conflict societies will help eliminate knowledge gaps and improve processes of international and national decision- and policy-making as well as programme design and implementation. It is important to consider children and youth as groups with diverse development and security needs and interests. An inclusive approach to peacebuilding design and implementation can only be assured if all those who matter and hold a stake in the society's future have a say in determining the shape that their future will take.

Invest in research on the resilience and strength of children, youth and families in post-war societies

It is surprising how little has been written about the concept of resilience, social capital and cohesion – and other factors that promote resilience of children and youth in post-conflict societies. To help youth and children respond more effectively to war and post-war challenges, more studies are needed to understand their capacities to resist, avert and cope with the many structural and direct threats affecting their security and well-being (Chapter 7). In addition, youth participation remains an under-researched topic. As Valeria Izzi notes:

> There has not been any study comparing the conditions of "violent" youth with those of "resilient" youth. The focus is normally on violent youth, and then there is a list of conditions that led to violence (unemployment often being top of the list). But these same conditions are also experienced by those who do not resort to violence.[11]

Thus while "it is certainly important to understand the motivations of youth who are mobilized (or mobilize themselves) for violence, it is equally important to consider those who faced with the same challenging conditions and lack of opportunities – choose not to resort to violence" (Chapter 8). An exploration of how to learn from experiences with peaceful youth, enhance children's agency, build up young people's capabilities and increase their opportunities for contributing to peacebuilding efforts is needed.

Conclusion

As Nosworthy puts it so aptly, "children and youth, their families and their communities are all security providers in their own right, and the importance of their engagement needs to be at the heart of security policy development" (Chapter 6). In many ways, they are the grassroots equivalent of the security sector. If post-conflict peacebuilding efforts do not succeed in giving child and youth concerns the political space and attention they require, international and national peacebuilding activities are incomplete at best and will possibly fail to become sustainable. It would also be a mistake to view young people's participation in political, social and economic affairs to be merely an oddity that might be limited to the unique cases of post-conflict transformation societies. Children and youth are entitled to be active agents of change in efforts to ensure healthy and safe lives for themselves, their families and society overall. Yet in post-conflict environments, children and youth run the risk of becoming marginalized and disadvantaged if they cannot manage to escape victimhood and be given opportunities to take their future into their own hands, assisted by adults of peacebuilding agents who are sensitive to their needs and requirements.

A major key to progress towards peace and security depends on child and youth empowerment and their ownership of the peacebuilding process. We hope that this volume contributes to a better appreciation of the need to pay more attention to these issues and to generate new ideas, scholarship and practical recommendations on offering children and youth the political space they require for making themselves heard, noticed and taken more seriously.

Notes

1. Albrecht Schnabel and Anara Tabyshalieva (eds), *Defying Victimhood: Women and Post-Conflict Peacebuilding*, Tokyo: United Nations University Press, 2012.
2. UNICEF, "Impact of Armed Conflict on Children", 1996, www.unicef.org/graca/.
3. Charlotte Wagnsson, Maria Hellman and Arita Holmberg, "The Centrality of Non-traditional Groups for Security in the Globalized Era: The Case of Children", *International Political Sociology* 4(1), 2010, p. 1.
4. Ibid.
5. Albrecht Schnabel, "The Security-Development Discourse and the Role of SSR as a Development Instrument", in Albrecht Schnabel and Vanessa Farr (eds), *Back to the Roots: Security Sector Reform and Development*, Münster: LIT Verlag, 2012, pp. 29–73.
6. Wagnsson, Hellman and Holmberg, note 3 above, p. 3.
7. Michael G. Wessells, *Child Soldiers: From Violence to Protection*, Cambridge, MA: Harvard University Press, 2006, p. 179.
8. For more information see UNESCO, "Culture of Peace and Non-Violence", www.unesco.org/new/en/bureau-of-strategic-planning/themes/culture-of-peace-and-non-violence/.
9. The constructive and destructive impacts of education in conflict-prone zones on children and youth are discussed in a UNESCO report: Kenneth Bush and Diana Saltarelli (eds), "The Two Faces of Education in Ethnic Conflict: Towards a Peacebuilding Education for Children", UNICEF Innocenti Research Centre, Florence, 2000, p. 34, www.unicef-irc.org/publications/pdf/insight4.pdf.
10. Wayne Nelles, "Bosnian Education for Security and Peacebuilding?", *International Peacekeeping* 13(2), 2006, p. 237.
11. Conversation with Valeria Izzi, a contributor to this volume.

Index

J

K

United Nations University Press is the publishing arm of the United Nations University. UNU Press publishes scholarly and policy-oriented books and periodicals on the issues facing the United Nations and its peoples and member states, with particular emphasis upon international, regional and transboundary policies.

The United Nations University was established as a subsidiary organ of the United Nations by General Assembly Resolution 2951 (XXVII) of 11 December 1972. The United Nations University undertakes a wide range of activities focused on knowledge generation (basic and applied research, and foresight and policy studies), education and capacity development (developing human and organizational capabilities), and knowledge transfer and sharing (communications, dissemination and outreach). The University operates through its institutes and programmes located throughout the world, and its planning and coordinating centre in Tokyo.

Lightning Source UK Ltd.
Milton Keynes UK
UKHW04f0928220918
329346UK00001B/33/P

9 789280 812114